U0117784

故宫经典 CLASSICS OF THE FORBIDDEN CITY

明清扇面图典 FAN PAINTINGS OF MING AND QING DYNASTIES

故宫博物院编
COMPILED BY THE PALACE MUSEUM
故宫出版社
THE FORBIDDEN CITY PUBLISHING HOUSE

图书在版编目（CIP）数据

明清扇面图典 / 李湜主编 .-- 北京：故宫出版社，2016.8
（故宫经典）
ISBN 978-7-5134-0844-8

Ⅰ．①明… Ⅱ．①李… Ⅲ．①扇－中国画－作品集－中国－明清时代 Ⅳ．①J222.48

中国版本图书馆 CIP 数据核字（2016）第 027126 号

故宫经典

明清扇面图典

故宫博物院编
出 版 人：王亚民
编　　纂：李　湜
翻　　译：王　鹏
图片资料：故宫博物院资料信息部
责任编辑：江　英　王冠良
设　　计：王　梓
责任印制：马静波　常晓辉
出版发行：故宫出版社
地址：北京东城区景山前街4号　邮编：100009
电话：010-85007808　010-85007816　传真：010-65129479
网址：www.culturefc.cn
邮箱：ggcb@culturefc.cn
制版印刷：北京雅昌艺术印刷有限公司
开　　本：889×1194毫米　1/12
印　　张：26.5
版　　次：2016年8月第1版
2016年8月第1次印刷
印　　数：1～3000册
书　　号：978-7-5134-0844-8
定　　价：360.00元

经典故宫与《故宫经典》

郑欣淼

故宫文化，从一定意义上说是经典文化。从故宫的地位、作用及其内涵看，故宫文化是以皇帝、皇宫、皇权为核心的帝王文化和皇家文化，或者说是宫廷文化。皇帝是历史的产物。在漫长的中国封建社会里，皇帝是国家的象征，是专制主义中央集权的核心。同样，以皇帝为核心的宫廷是国家的中心。故宫文化不是局部的，也不是地方性的，无疑属于大传统，是上层的、主流的，属于中国传统文化中最为堂皇的部分，但是它又和民间的文化传统有着千丝万缕的关系。

故宫文化具有独特性、丰富性、整体性以及象征性的特点。从物质层面看，故宫只是一座古建筑群，但它不是一般的古建筑，而是皇宫。中国历来讲究器以载道，故宫及其皇家收藏凝聚了传统的特别是辉煌时期的中国文化，是几千年中国的器用典章、国家制度、意识形态、科学技术，以及学术、艺术等积累的结晶，既是中国传统文化精神的物质载体，也成为中国传统文化最有代表性的象征物，就像金字塔之于古埃及、雅典卫城神庙之于希腊一样。因此，从这个意义上说，故宫文化是经典文化。

经典具有权威性。故宫体现了中华文明的精华，它的地位和价值是不可替代的。经典具有不朽性。故宫属于历史遗产，它是中华五千年历史文化的沉淀，蕴含着中华民族生生不已的创造和精神，具有不竭的历史生命。经典具有传统性。传统的本质是主体活动的延承，故宫所代表的中国历史文化与当代中国是一脉相承的，中国传统文化与今天的文化建设是相连的。对于任何一个民族、一个国家来说，经典文化永远都是其生命的依托、精神的支撑和创新的源泉，都是其得以存续和赓延的筋络与血脉。

对于经典故宫的诠释与宣传，有着多种的形式。对故宫进行形象的数字化宣传，拍摄类似《故宫》纪录片等影像作品，这是大众传媒的努力；而以精美的图书展现故宫的内蕴，则是许多出版社的追求。

多年来，故宫出版社出版了不少好的图书。同时，国内外其他出版社也出版了许多故宫博物院编写的好书。这些图书经过十余年、甚至二十年的沉淀，在读者心目中树立了“故宫经典”的印象，成为品牌性图书。它们的影响并没有随着时间推移变得模糊起来，而是历久弥新，成为读者心中的故宫经典图书。

于是，现在就有了故宫出版社的《故宫经典》丛书。《国宝》、《紫禁城宫殿》、《清代宫廷生活》、《紫禁城宫殿建筑装饰——内檐装修图典》、《清代宫廷包装艺术》等享誉已久的图书，又以新的面目展示给读者。而且，故宫博物院正在出版和将要出版一系列经典图书。随着这些图书的编辑出版，将更加有助于读者对故宫的了解和对中国传统文化的认识。

《故宫经典》丛书的策划，无疑是个好的创意和思路。我希望这套丛书不断出下去，而且越出越好。经典故宫藉《故宫经典》使其丰厚蕴涵得到不断发掘，《故宫经典》则赖经典故宫而声名更为广远。

目 录

明清扇面画：一部小中见大的明清绘画史

李湜

扇，又称箑、萐，出现于上古时期，东汉许慎《说文解字》记载："萐蒲，瑞草也。尧时生于庖厨，扇暑而凉。"扇自生成后至今，具有各种样式。扇面品类从材料上分，有纸、羽、蒲、葵、蕉、麻、藤、竹、绫、绸、绢、纱扇等；从用途上分，有礼仪扇、舞蹈扇和生活用扇等；从使用方式上分，有可随意开合的折扇和不可折叠的纨扇等。

折扇，又称"撒扇"、"聚头扇"、"聚骨扇"、"便面"等，南齐时初具雏形，但工艺尚粗陋。自唐朝始，制作精美的日本、朝鲜折扇作为贡品传入中国，如宋郭若虚《图画见闻志·高丽国》记："彼使人每至中国，或用折叠扇为私觌物。"至宋朝，折扇开始受到文人们的关注，宋赵彦卫《云麓漫钞》、邓椿《画继》以及苏东坡笔记中，皆有关于折扇特性及制作等方面的论述。明初，折扇受到明皇室的喜爱，成祖朱棣见到朝鲜所贡折扇精致灵巧，特颁用其式，谕令工匠大量制造，以赐群臣。宣宗朱瞻基受祖父朱棣的影响，对折扇更是偏爱有加，他在29岁时创作了大型折扇画——《山水人物图》。在明皇室的风尚影响下，很快形成了四川、江浙等地折扇生产中心。折扇不仅成为从皇宫到庶民的日用品，而且成为文人题诗作画的载体。至清代，折扇的制扇、画扇、赏扇、藏扇进入全盛期，南、北方都涌现出职业的扇庄与商人，如北京的"齐建隆"、"戴廉增"、"和忠兴"，天津的"杨柳青"，杭州的"王星记"等，它们以经营折扇书画生意，名噪一时。

以扇面为载体写字作画，最早出现在纨扇上，汉、晋时就有班婕妤题扇诗、王羲之为卖扇老媪书扇的故实。在折扇上绘画，最迟也不晚于宋代，元郑元祐《题赵千里聚扇上写山次伯雨韵》曾形容宋赵千里绘的折扇山水画具有恢弘的气势："宋诸王孙妙磅礴，万里江山归一握。卷藏袖中舒在我，清风徐来縠衣薄。"明詹景凤《东图玄览》则记曾见过南宋马远、马麟父子画的绢本折扇面："马远竹鹤、马麟桂花二册，本是一折叠扇两面，与今折叠扇式无异，折痕尚在，皆绢素为之。"折扇绘画的蔚然成风，是从明代"吴门画派"开始的。吴门，今属苏州，是折扇制造业的发达地区之一。这里自古以来就是文人荟萃之地，书画家、文学家、收藏家等名家辈出，雅集宴饮，相互推重，从而形成崇尚书画的文化氛围。折扇开合自由并可出入怀袖，便于书画、携带和把玩，因此逐渐被赋予丰富的文化内涵，成为以沈周、文徵明、唐寅、仇英为首的吴门书画家得心应手地挥洒翰墨的载体，折扇扇面绘画也从此成为与立轴、手卷、册页等并列的绘画形制。

故宫博物院藏有明清时期的折扇画页数千件，以藏品数量大、画作品质高而居于世界各博物馆之首。本书收录的198幅图只是故宫藏品中的凤毛麟角，更是中国绘画史中的沧海一粟，然而，却涵盖了明清绘画的主要流派和画家的重要作品，既表现出每位画家的个人风格，又体现了明清时代的画坛特点，可以说它们以精致的形式"描绘"了明清绘画史。从明沈周《秋林图》、唐寅《枯木寒鸦图》、文徵明《兰竹石图》、谢时臣《选梅折枝图》、陆治《仿倪

瓒山水图》以及丁云鹏《竹石云泉图》等画作可见，明中期以沈周为首的“吴门画派”，除参学五代董源、宋人巨然诸家的画法外，更多的是向元代的文人画家们学习，如他们承袭了赵孟頫“以书入画”及“画贵有古意”的创作宗旨，师法了黄公望的水墨浅绛法，摹学了倪瓒萧散高逸的风韵，效仿了王蒙、吴镇于缜密谨严的法度中，不失清婉的意境等。他们像元人那样注重笔墨的表现力，强调画面的感情色彩和幽淡的意境，借绘画表达自己对社会的看法或者自己的某一种心境，追求人品与画品的统一以及恬静平和的文人书卷气。从董其昌《仿倪瓒山水图》、赵左《山水图》、沈士充《危楼秋雁图》、程嘉燧《秋游赏月图》、蓝瑛《青山红树图》、项圣谟《天寒有鹤守梅花图》、邵弥《松岩高士图》等折扇画可见，明末以董其昌为首的“华亭派”、赵左为代表的“苏松派”、沈士充统领的“云间派”、程嘉燧为前导的“新安派”、蓝瑛为首领的“武林派”和“画中九友”之一的邵弥等人，在董其昌秀逸而空泛的画风和“崇南贬北”的画学理论影响下，注重表现自己的胸中丘壑，强调的是皴、擦、点、染的技法运用，追求的是笔墨的自身变化和趣味以及“南宗”绘画古雅秀润的格调。

在明代晚期的折扇画创作上，陈洪绶以独树一帜的画风最值得一提，从本图录所收录的其《人物图》、《秋江泛艇图》、《水仙竹石图》、《花石蝴蝶图》、《梅石图》中可见，其表现题材广泛，山水、花鸟、人物画各具神采；创作方式多样，工笔、写意、重彩、水墨等各擅胜场。最为重要的是，他的画作尤其是人物、花鸟画没有受到明末崇古思潮的影响，而是另辟蹊径，其人物画糅合传统艺术与民间版画之长，利用夸大人物个性特征和衬托对比的手法，增强主体人物的表现力，追求高古格调和画面的装饰效果。同时，他还将这种装饰意趣巧妙地运用到其花鸟画的创作中。陈洪绶的这种画风对清末的画坛影响很大，“海派”任熊、任颐等人都继承了他的传统。

从清王鉴《花溪渔隐图》、王翚《山川浑厚图》、弘仁《松竹幽亭图》、原济《奇峰图》、龚贤《山水图》、查士标《策杖寻幽图》、高翔《山水图》等折扇画可见，清代画坛虽然同样是画派林立，但自清初始，它就明显地分为守旧与创新两大流派：以王时敏、王鉴、王翚、王原祁“四王”为代表的守旧派，推崇“董巨”及“元四家”，尊奉董其昌的文人画理念，以笔笔有古意为创作的宗旨，即如王翚《清晖画跋》所言：“以元人笔墨，运宋人丘壑，而泽以唐人气韵，乃为大成。”他们强调画作的儒雅平和“书卷气”，与清朝统治者基于程朱理学所倡导的“清真雅正”的衡文标准相一致，而成为山水画坛正宗，其影响力直至清末；活动于江南地区的“四僧”（朱耷、原济、髡残、弘仁）、“金陵八家”（龚贤、樊圻、高岑、邹喆、吴宏、叶欣、胡慥、谢荪等）、“新安画派”（查士标、孙逸、汪之瑞、程邃等）、“扬州画派”（金农、高翔、郑燮等）以及清后期活动于上海地区的以任熊、任颐为代表的“海派”属于创新派。他们在艺术上也承袭古人的传统，但是同时又反对泥古不化，反对把山水画艺术降低为单纯的皴擦点染的笔墨技术。主张在师法传统的基础上，师法自然造化，以“我用我法”“物

我合一”的方式表现“天地之万物”,注重的是性灵的抒发、个性的张扬。

在故宫博物院现藏的折扇画中，还有百余幅清代宫廷画家的作品。自明代始兴的折扇画艺术同样受到清皇室的喜欢，而曾六下江南、能书擅画的清高宗弘历对折扇画更是青睐有加。他不仅亲自创作《白莲图》《墨荷图》等，而且还广泛搜罗流散于民间的名家、名扇，大量折扇画作由此汇入宫中。1743年，特命词臣画家张若霭把宫中所藏的名扇两箧共300把编目、列序，题名为《烟云宝笈》，以示珍爱。在高宗皇帝的积极参与和支持下，清宫内涌现出来自不同阶层的画家群,有以张宗苍、方琮、丁观鹏为首的专门在内廷画院机构“如意馆”等处供职的职业画家；有以弘旿、弘昕、永瑢为代表的积极学习汉文化，在理政之暇把游戏翰墨作为一种消遣的皇族宗室书画家；有以董邦达、钱维城、邹一桂为代表的兼任官职的词臣画家等。由于参与折扇画创作的人数众多，清朝成为画坛上留存宫廷折扇画最多的一朝。

因为画面形状的限定，折扇画具有独特的构图样式。如在外形上，它上下边呈半圆弧状，左右边向下内收，这就有别于画幅周正的卷轴册。在上宽下窄的扇面里，必须把握所画物象的重心，以避免人物、山石、房舍、树木等因随扇形而倾斜。从蒋嵩《旭日东升图》、王铎《山水图》、吴宏《秋林读书图》、邹喆《山水图》、华嵒《晴霞飞鸟图》、刘度《雪山行旅图》、恽寿平《罂粟花图》、王概《东园万竹图》及任薰《停琴待月图》等画作可见，画家们突破传统的构图模式，采用了随扇面底边设景布势的方式，这种方式是扇面画构图中最常使用的方式，不仅能突显作者奇思妙想的才智，而且更易形成妙趣横生的画境，在有限的篇幅内，最大可能地展现出折扇画“化有限为无限”、“小中见大”、“精致而微”的美学魅力。如蒋嵩《旭日东升图》扇中，展示了大海汹涌澎湃的强大气势；邹喆《山水图》扇中，表现出南京地区万木争荣的壮观景象。

折扇画的画面材质除采用卷轴册使用的熟宣和绢本外，还选用在熟宣上泥金的金笺，或者是洒金的洒金笺。金笺质地坚韧凝滑，不吸墨、色，所绘物象易流滑板滞，因此它也更能体现画家高超的笔墨技巧，如，文徵明《兰花图》和马守真《兰竹石图》中的每片兰叶，都是一挥而就所成，不受束缚的笔墨使得线条飘逸、叶片洒脱舒展，由此展示了他们娴熟的笔墨功力。金笺尤其是在泥金扇面上设色，要处理好颜料与金地间的关系，蓝瑛《青山红树图》和陈洪绶《花石蝴蝶图》做出了极佳的典范，他们所绘山石及树木或花卉与蛱蝶，不仅彼此间的冷暖色调和谐，而且它们与金色的扇底交相映衬，给人炫目堂皇的审美感受。

折扇画幅通常纵长18厘米、展幅阔55厘米左右，其画幅尺寸相对有限。而历代中国画家正是在这相对有限的画面中，经营意匠，展现自身的笔格墨韵。折扇画面虽小，却既可涵泳天地自然，亦可承载中国艺术精神，它以“小中见大”的形式，为中国绘画史书写出一种精致之美，其独特的神韵毫不逊于鸿篇巨制。

Paintings on Folding Fans :
A Miniature History of Painting Art in the Ming and Qing Dynasties

I

The history of Chinese folding fan painting can be traced back to the North Song Dynasty (960~1127). At that time, renowned scholars including Su Dongpo, Zhao Yanwei, and Deng Chun loved folding fans. Gradually, as instruments used to induce airflow for the purpose of cooling, folding fans became carriers of calligraphy and painting. Zheng Yuanyou, a scholar of the Yuan Dynasty (1271~1368), praised the landscape painting that Zhao Qianli, an artist of the Song Dynasty, painted on a folding fan in a poem for its magnificent ambience. Zhan Jingfeng, a calligrapher and painter of the Ming Dynasty (1368~1644), described the silk folding fan paintings by Ma Yuan and his son, Ma Lin, in his *Review of Eastern Paintings*: "The bamboo and crane painting by Ma Yuan and the sweet osmanthus painting by Ma Lin were originally painted on the two sides of a folding fan. Both of the two folding fan paintings were painted on silk, with obvious lines made of folding."

Early in the Ming Dynasty, folding fans became popular among members of the royal family. Inspired by the exquisite folding fans sent by Korea as tributes, Zhu Di, or Emperor Chengzu (r.1402~1424), ordered artisans to produce a large quantity of similar folding fans, with which the emperor rewarded his officials. Zhu Zhanji, or Emperor Xuanzong (r.1425~1435), showed even greater favor of folding fans than his grandfather Zhu Di. In 1427, the second year after he ascended the throne, Zhu Zhanji, who was expert in painting, painted a hermit reading under a pine tree together with his boy attendant and another hermit picking chrysanthemum flowers respectively on the front and reverse sides of a huge folding fan that measured 59.5 centimeters long and 152 centimeters wide. In this way, the emperor expressed his yearning for an easygoing life in wilderness. Soon, folding fans spread from the royal family to people from all walks of life, and Sichuan, Jiangsu and Zhejiang provinces became major producers of folding fans at that time. Moreover, it became increasingly popular for calligraphers and painters to write or paint on folding fans.

The production, appreciation and collection of folding fans reached the zenith in the Qing Dynasty (1644~1911). Shops and merchants specializing in hand fans business mushroomed throughout the country. Of them, the most famous were Qijianlong, Dailianzeng and Hezhongxing in Beijing, Yangliuqing in Tianjin, and Wangxingji in Hangzhou. The number of artists engaged in folding fan painting in the Qing Dynasty was obviously more than that of the Ming Dynasty, so was the quantity of folding fan paintings that remain today.

Despite the fact that Ming and Qing paintings primary exist in forms of scrolls and albums, folding fan paintings reflect the history of painting in the Ming and Qing dynasties in a microcosmic manner.

II

Apart from court painters, Jiangsu and Zhejiang painters, who were collectively known as the "Zhe School," dominated the art circles of the early Ming Dynasty. A number of excellent artists

emerged during the period, including Bian Jingzhao, Zhao Lian, Jiang Zicheng, Guo Chun, Xie Huan, Dai Jin, Li Zai, Shi Rui, Zhou Wenjing, Shang Xi, Ni Duan, Lin Liang, Liu Jun, Wang E, Lu Ji, Zhu Duan, and Wu Wei. By that time, as a newly born art genre, folding fan painting had yet to be widely accepted by court painters and Zhe School painters. Only a few artists attempted to paint folding fans, of whom the most famous was Wu Wei (1459~1508), a court painter and a representative of the Jiangxia School of painting. A fan bearing his painting Ladies is now collected in Shanghai Museum. Wu's figure paintings are very special. His Spring of Wuling and Singing and Dancing feature delicate brushwork, which modeled after the style of Li Gonglin, a renowned painter of the Northern Song Dynasty. On the contrary, his Reading under the Tree and Tai Chi feature bold and vigorous lines, which modeled after the style of Tang-Dynasty (618~907) painter Wu Daozi. Despite their varied styles, all of his paintings depicted figures vividly and accurately and demonstrated Wu's great accomplishment in painting. Following Wu Wei and Dai Jin, many other artists of the Zhe School began to draw figures and landscapes on fans. Those folding fan paintings, including Watching Waterfall by Zhang Lu, Sun Rising by Jiang Song and Snow Landscapes by Li Zhu (both collected in the Palace Museum in Beijing) and Reading in Riverside Pavilion by Li Zhu (collected in Shanghai Museum), on the one hand, demonstrated that those artists learned from the court painting of the Southern Song Dynasty (1127~1279) and formed a simple but bold painting style, and on the other hand, they evidenced that those artists had got accustomed of the unique formats of fan paintings and mastered fan painting skills.

By the mid-Ming Dynasty, along with the rise of the Wumen School of painting, folding fan painting had gained popularity. Many artists entered the realm of folding fan painting, and they created countless masterpieces, such as Shen Zhou's fan painting Small Pavilion in Woods, Wen Zhengming's Excellent Scholar with Pines and Rocks, and Chen Daofu's Red Plum and Daffodil that are housed in Shanghai Museum, Xie Shichen's fan painting Landscapes that is collected in Tianjin Museum, and Wen Jia's fan painting Mountain Pavilion and Double Trees and Wang Guxiang's Plum Blossoms and Daffodil that are housed in Nanjing Museum. Painters from the Wumen School, represented by Shen Zhou (1427~1509), inherited the painting styles of Dong Yuan of the Five Dynasties (907~960) and Ju Ran of the Song Dynasty. At the same time, they learned more from painting maters of the Yuan Dynasty. For instance, they inherited Zhao Mengfu's art philosophy that advocated "combination of calligraphy and painting" and "old sense of painting." They also learned the light ink-and-wash brushwork from Huang Gongwang and the ingenious poetic style from Ni Zan, and modeled after Wang Meng and Wu Zhen's meticulous but elegant painting style. Like Yuan-Dynasty painters, they paid great attention to the expressiveness of every stroke, so as to depict emotions behind images and create an elegant atmosphere. With their paintings, they expressed their certain moods or their views of the world and tried to pursue the compatibility between art and morality and an easygoing, scholarly style.

The rise of the Wumen School of painting not only rejuvenated the scholarly painting of the Yuan Dynasty and enhanced the cultural connotations of their painting, but also pushed forward the development of art in the Ming Dynasty. Many artists from the Wumen School, such as Lu Zhi, Qian Gu, Chen Chun, and Zhou Zhimian, realized great achievements in their respective realms. Their unique styles were illustrated on their fan paintings. For instance, Chen Chun's fan paintings Peony (collected in the Palace Museum) and Flowers (collected in Guizhou Museum) demonstrate the charm of the freehand ink-and-wash flower-and-bird painting. Zhou Zhimian's fan paintings Flowers (collected in Tianjin Museum), Plum Blossoms and Birds (collected in Guangzhou Art Museum), and Two Swallows and Pear Blossoms (collected in Shanghai Museum) combine realistic and freehand styles.

In the late Ming Dynasty, various schools of painting emerged, including those named after their places of origin such as the Huating School, Songjiang School, Yunjian School, Xin'an School, Wulin School, and Jiaxing School. By the time, it had become a popular trend for artists to paint hand fans. Fan paintings by artists from every school of painting can be found today. Among them are The Landscape Painting after Ni Zan's Style (collected in the Palace Museum), The Picture of Landscapes (collected in Shanghai Museum) and Hazy Islet and Rolling Hills (collected in Anhui Museum) by Dong Qichang (1555~1636), a leader of the Huating School; The Picture of Landscapes (collected in the Palace Museum) and Mountain Residence (collected in Anhui Museum) by Zhao Zuo (fl. early 17th cent.), a representative of the Songjiang School; High Tower and Wild Geese in Autumn (collected in the Palace Museum) and Mountain in Clouds (collected in Hubei Museum) by Shen Shichong (fl. early 17th cent.), head of the Yunjian School; Enjoying the Moon on an Autumn Trip (collected in the Palace Museum), Distant Mountain in the Sun (collected in Anhui Museum) and Pines and Hawks (collected in Tianjin Museum) by Cheng Jiasui (1565~1643), a pioneer of the Xin'an school; Water Pavilion in Autumn Forest (collected in Nanjing Museum), River and Mountain in Flying Snow (collected in Sichuan Museum), Listening to Spring in Water Pavilion and Plum Blossoms and Birds (collected in Guangzhou Art Museum) by Lan Ying (1585~1666?), a founder of the Wulin School; and Cranes Guarding Plum Blossoms in Chilly Winter (collected in the Palace Museum) and Plum Blossoms (collected in Anhui Museum) by Xiang Shengmo (1597~1658), a leader of the Jiaxing School.

Dong Qichang, who ever served as the Minister of Rites, was the most influential painter in the late Ming Dynasty. He took an active part into art practice. In addition to folding fan paintings, he also created many landscape paintings in forms of scrolls and albums. Moreover, based on the theory of the Zen Buddhism that was divided into the north and south sects, he defined scholarly painters who focused on ink-and-wash painting as the "South School" and artists who excelled at color paintings as the "North School." Dong declared himself as an orthodox representative of the "South School" and listed Zhao Mengfu of the Yuan Dynasty and Shen Zhou from the Wumen School into the "South School." Influenced by Dong's elegant and freehand painting style and his art theory that advocated the "South School" was superior to the "North School," painters at that time preferred to copy ancient paintings and indulge themselves in seeking the fun of brushwork. They attempted to depict their intricate thoughts through the use of various techniques such as wrinkling, brushing, spotting, and rendering. Moreover, they pursued the variation and fun of brushwork, as well as the classic, elegant style that the "South School" advocated.

Chen Hongshou (1597~1652), a painter of the late Ming Dynasty, was also worth mentioning. Immune from the trend of modeling after ancient paintings, his figure and flower-and-bird paintings demonstrated a unique style. In his fan paintings such as Picture of Figures, Daffodil, Bamboo and Rock, Flowers, Rocks and Butterflies (all collected in the Palace Museum), and Picture of Figures and

Their Tales (collected in Shanghai Museum), Chen incorporated the techniques of folk block print into his figure painting. He excelled at enhance the expressiveness of the main subjects through exaggerating the features of the figures and contracting them with background characters. In terms of painting style, he pursued classic beauty and stressed decorative effect. He also skillfully created such decorative effect in his flower-and-bird paintings. Chen's painting style cast a far-reaching influence on painters in the late Qing Dynasty, including the Four Rens of the Shanghai Painting School (namely, Ren Xiong, Ren Xun, Ren Yi, and Ren Yu).

III

In its early years, the Qing Dynasty implemented a series of political policies to reinforce its reign and eliminate the capitalism sprouting in the Ming Dynasty. It also took iron-handed measures to prohibit thoughts that called for innovation and fought against feudal etiquette. In this circumstance, the literature, art and philosophy circles began to be dominated by conservatism, instead of innovation.

At that time, conservative painters represented by the "Four Wangs" – namely, Wang Shimin (1592~1680), Wang Jian (1598~1677), Wang Hui (1632~1717), and Wang Yuanqi (1642~1715) – became the mainstream in the art circles. They worshiped Dong Yuan and Ju Ran of the Five Dynasties Period and Huang Gongwang, Ni Zan, Wu Zhen, and Wang Meng of the Yuan Dynasty. They also advocated the scholarly painting theory of Dong Qichang, and attempted to model after ancient paintings in every stroke. Just as Wang Hui said in his Qinghui Painting Postscripts, "an accomplished painter should model after the brushwork of Yuan-dynasty painters, the intricate thoughts of Song-dynasty painters while learning the style of Tang-dynasty painters."

Of course, the Four Wangs did not merely copy from ancient artists, but incorporate their innovative understandings of art. While learning the dynamic, elegant style of Yuan painters, they abandoned the carelessness illustrated in paintings of the Yuan Dynasty. This was evidenced by Wang Shimin's Picture of Landscapes (collected in Tianjin Museum) and another fan painting of the same name collected in Shanghai Museum, Wang Jian's fan paintings Fishing Hermit on Flower Stream (collected in the Palace Museum) and Fishing Hermit on Clear Stream (collected in Shanghai Museum), Wang Hui's Magnificent Landscapes (collected in the Palace Museum) and River Town in Early Summer (collected in Jilin Museum), and Wang Yuanqi's Picture of Landscapes (collected in Liaoning Museum) and A Copy of Yi Feng's Landscape Painting (collected in Jilin Museum). They added vitality and dynamics to the painting style of the Yuan Dynasty. For instance, they maintained aesthetic appeal of Huang Gongwang's landscape paintings that typically featured "magnificent mountains and lush plants," but rejected the lonesome, desolate ambience that met the Taoist and Buddhist aesthetics in the paintings of the Yuan Dynasty. Eventually, they formed a mild, conventional style that combined tradition and innovation. This painting style conformed to the Qing rulers' advocacy of peace, elegance, and fairness based on the Neo-Confucianism, thus winning their favor and support. For this reason, it was deemed as the orthodox school of the landscape painting throughout the Qing Dynasty. At that time, painters who followed the style of Wang Hui were called the "Yushan School," including Yang Jin, Hu Jie, Xu Rong, Li Shizhuo, and Monk Shangrui. Followers of Wang Yuanqi, including Tang Dai, Wang Jingming, Huang Ding, Wen Yi, and Wang Yu, were called the "Loudong School."

In the early Qing Dynasty, there were another two painters famous for fan painting: Wu Li (1632~1718), who excelled at landscape painting, and Yun Shouping (1633~1690), who was skilled in both landscape and flower-and-bird paintings. The two and the "Four Wangs" were together known as the "Six Famous Painters of the Early Qing Dynasty." When he was young, Wu Li

learned from Wang Shimin and Wang Jian. For this reason, Wu also adored the painting style of Huang Gongwang and Wang Meng of the Yuan Dynasty and Tang Yin of the Ming Dynasty. Wu converted to Catholicism in his middle age. His trip to Macao, then a Portuguese colony, enabled him to have a close contact with Western painting, which broadened his artistic vision. Through absorbing the advantages of various painting styles, Wu formed his own style that featured depiction of real scenery. His fan paintings, such as Poetic Meditation of Forest Lake (collected in the Palace Museum), Spring Wild Geese in South China (collected in Shanghai Museum), and Picture of Landscapes (collected in Tianjin Museum), demonstrate that his landscape paintings boast novel composition and powerful strokes, quietly different from the painting style of the Four Wangs. Yun Shouping focused on landscape painting in his early years and then shifted to flower-and-bird painting. He realized remarkable achievements in this genre of painting. Based on the styles of Ming-dynasty painters Shen Zhou and Sun Long and the boneless flower-and-bird painting techniques of Xu Chongsi of the Northern Song Dynasty, Yun invented a new flower painting style that used no lines but directly applied color pigments on paper. The style was known as "Orthodox Sketch School." Yun created a number of fan paintings depicting flowers in this style, such as Poppy Flower collected in the Palace Museum, Orchid and Rock collected in Liaoning Museum, Chrysanthemum and Colored Rock and Autumn Flower collected in Shanghai Museum, and Peonies in Spring collected in Jilin Museum.

As conservative painters represented by the Four Wangs dominated the art circle, the Four Monks (namely, Zhu Da 1624~1705, Yuan Ji 1642~1707, Kun Can 1612~1673, and Hong Ren 1610~1663), the Eight Masters of Nanjing, and painters from the Xin'an Painting School began to call for art innovation. Of them, the Four Monks made were the most famous and influential. Despite the fact that they also inherited traditional styles of ancient artists, they refused to stubbornly follow old rules and downgrade the landscape painting art into a display of painting techniques such as wrinkling, brushing, dotting, and rendering. They persisted that while inheriting traditions, artists should draw from nature and depict "everything in the world" in a way that combined objects and subjects. Such an idea was illustrated on their folding fan paintings. For instance, Yuan Ji trekked hundreds of miles to Lushan Mountain and Yellow Mountain to draw inspiration from nature. He advocated that a landscape painter should "travel all peaks before he drafted his painting." Moreover, he created many excellent landscape paintings that featured powerful brushwork and ingenious composition. For example, his fan painting Marvelous Peak (collected in the Palace Museum) illustrates the magnificent Lotus Peak and Wenshu Temple with the technique of "creating something from nothing." In the painting, floating clouds bring out magnificent mountains. Such an illustrating method was unprecedented. No artists could create such an excellent painting without personally being there.

Most of the Eight Masters of Nanjing and the Xin'an Painting School lived the life as a hermit. They indulged themselves in poetry and painting. Despite their varied styles, they shared similar art appeal, and their works were all with distinctive individuality that could impress their viewers. The Eight Masters of Nanjing include Gong Xian, Fan Qi, Gao Cen, Zou Zhe, Wu Hong, Ye Xin, Hu Zao, and Xie Sun. Of them Gong Xian (1618~1689) was the most famous and had the greatest achievement. Based on the painting styles of Dong Yuan and Ju Ran of the Five Dynasties Period, he absorbed the essence of the northern painting school of the early Song Dynasty and learned from the painting styles of Mi Fu and his son, as well as Wu Zhen and Shen Zhou, forming his unique "accumulated-ink" technique. With this technique, Gong created a number of excellent fan paintings, such as Ink Landscapes collected in the Palace Museum, Landscape Painting for Mizhi collected in the Museum of Guangxi Zhuang Autonomous Region, and Picture of Landscapes collected in Sichuan Museum.

The Xin'an Painting School, headed by Hong Ren, included Zha Shibiao, Sun Yi, Wang Zhirui, and Cheng Sui, who mainly lived in Xin'an (today's Anhui Province). They inherited the painting style of the Yuan Dynasty and often depicted the sea of clouds, pine trees, and grotesque rocks of the Yellow Mountain. Their painting style was similar to that of the Yellow Mountain Painting School represented by Mei Qing. They focused on expressing their feelings and showcasing their individuality via their fan paintings, evidenced by Hong Ren's Tranquil Pavilion with Pine and Bamboo Trees and Elegant Charm of Nangang and Zha Shibiao's Old Man Seeking Tranquility, all collected in the Palace Museum, as well as folding fan paintings housed in Shanghai Museum, Liaoning Museum, and Tianjin Museum.

In its heydays, the Qing Dynasty boasted united territory, stable society, and prosperous economy, as well as a boom in art creation. Two major painting schools, with Beijing and Yangzhou as the center, respectively, were formed. While court paintings gained popularity in Beijing, the emerging Yangzhou School also drew much attention. Painters from both painting schools left countless folding fan paintings.

With the support of Emperor Qianlong (r. 1735~1795), various groups of painters emerged in the Qing court. There were professional painters working with the imperial painting academy named Office of Fulfilled Wishes (Ruyi guan), represented by Zhang Zongcang, Fang Cong, and Ding Guanpeng. There were also painters and calligraphers from the royal family such as Yun Xi, Hong Wu, Hong Xin, Yong Rong, who made calligraphy and painting as their hobbies, as well as painters who were also scholarly officials represented by Dong Bangda, Qian Weicheng, and Zou Yigui. Some of them painted folding fans upon the decrees of the emperor, some painted for their friends, and others just painted for themselves. For this reason, the Qing Dynasty left court fan paintings more than any other dynasties of ancient China.

Emperor Qianlong, who was good at both calligraphy and painting and traveled southern China six times, was in favor of folding fan paintings. He not only personally created those fan paintings such as Ink Pine, Ink Orchid, White Lotus, and Ink Lotus (all collected in the Palace Museum), but also collected countless folding fan paintings by famous painters. In 1743, the emperor ordered Zhang Ruoai, a court painter, to catalog 300 folding fans housed in the Imperial Palace and made them into an album named *Treasure Box of Mist and Cloud*.

The Yangzhou Painting School (also known as "Eight Eccentrics of Yangzhou") with Jin Nong (1687~1763/4) as the head contrasted with court painters. During the reign of Emperor Qianlong, Yangzhou was a metropolis on the southeast coast that boasted convenient transportation, flourish commerce, and splendid culture. It gathered artists from around the country, and the Eight Eccentrics of Yangzhou were the most famous. The representatives of the Yangzhou painting school included Jin Nong, Li Zhi, Huang Shen, Wang Shishen, Zheng Xie, Li Fangying, Gao Xiang, Luo Pin, Hua Yan, and Gao Fenghan. All of these painters ever painted fans, such as Jin Nong's Plum Blossoms (collected in Anhui Museum), Huang Shen's Girls with Flowers (collected in Tianjin Cultural Heritage Company), Hua Yan's Morning Glows and Flying Birds (collected in the Palace Museum), and Luo Pin's Picture of Landscapes (collected in Shenyang Palace Museum). Despite the fact that they were not all natives of Yangzhou, they shared similar social experience when they spent most of their lives there. They had insight into official corruption, fickleness of the world, and sufferings of ordinary people. They inherited the freehand wash-and-ink painting style of Chen Chun, Xu Wei, Yuan Ji, and Zhu Da, but refused to stick to any conventional rules in the path toward free expression. They further developed the splash-ink technique and formed their distinctive style. They sought innovation and change in art creation, which was quite different from the trend of modeling after ancient orthodox painting style that prevailed at that time. To some extent, they even abandoned the "scholarly appeal" that

advocated elegance and peace, but developed a freehand painting style that focused on expressing individual emotions and met commercial demand. For this reason, they were considered "weird" at that time, hence their nickname "Eight Eccentrics." The Yangzhou painting School cast a far-reaching influence, and even contemporary artists Zhao Zhiqian, Wu Changshuo, and Ren Boren learned its style and techniques in their flower paintings.

In its late years, the Qing Dynasty became increasingly corrupted and suffered from repeated uprisings and foreign invasions. China gradually turned into a semi-colonial and semi-feudal country. Upon the request of foreign invaders, the Qing court opened Shanghai and Guangzhou as trading ports. The two cities then became important commercial hubs and newly-rising art centers, fostering the emergence of the Shanghai and Lingnan painting schools.

The early representatives of the Shanghai Painting School were Zhang Xiong (1803~1886), Zhu Xiong (1801~1846), and Ren Xiong (1823~1857), collectively known as "Three Xiongs." Ren Xiong, Ren Xun (1835~1893), Ren Yi (1840~1896), and Ren Yu (1853~1901) were collectively known as "Four Rens." In its late period, the Shanghai School had Wu Changshuo as its major representative. Although they never settled in Shanghai, famous painters Zhao Zhiqian (1829~1884) and Xu Gu (1824~1896) were also deemed as representatives of the Shanghai School. Painters from the painting school also created many folding fan paintings, including Zhang Xiong's Garden Balsams (collected in the Palace Museum) and Crabapples and Birds in Spring (collected in Anhui Museum), Xu Gu's Chrysanthemum (collected in the Palace Museum) and Golden Fish (collected in Anhui Museum), Ren Xiong's Peony (collected in the Palace Museum), Ren Xun's Hardy Banana in Snow (collected in Anhui Museum) and Picture of Flowers and Birds (collected in Zhejiang Museum), Ren Yi's Birds and Bamboos in Winter (collected in Guangzhou Art Museum), Picture of Orchid, Bamboo and Chicken (collected in Zhejiang Museum) and Magnolia and Mynah (collected in Duoyunxuan Gallery), and Zhao Zhiqian's Hydrangea with Red Leaves (collected in Tianjin People's Art Press), Day Lily (collected in Duoyunxuan Gallery) and Fragrant Chrysanthemum (collected in Zhejiang Museum). These paintings demonstrated that as commercialized scholar-artists, painters of the Shanghai School sought an aesthetic style suiting both refined and popular taste to meet the need of the burgers class. Therefore, while inheriting the style of traditional scholarly painting, their paintings also drew inspiration from folk art, absorbed techniques of Western painting, and even learned from seal cutting. Those artists incorporated expression forms of calligraphy and seal cutting into their paintings, ushering in a new era of scholarly flower-and-bird painting. They made vegetables and fruits that were common in daily life as the subjects of their works, thus expanding the expression spectrum of traditional flower-and-bird painting. With bold and unconstrained brushwork, bright colors, powerful strokes and the absorption of calligraphy and seal cutting, they gave those common subjects like flowers, vegetables, fruits, birds, and fish magnificent and unrestrained artistic appeal.

Guangzhou is located south of the Wuling Mountains, so painters in the area were called the Lingnan (literally, "south of Wuling") School. Of them were Su Liupeng who learned from the styles of Song and Yuan artists and was expert in painting ordinary people and folk tales, Su Changchun who was good at portraying deities and Buddhist figures with ordinary people in southern China as prototypes, Ju Lian who modeled after Yun Shouping's flower-and-bird painting that featured light colors and elegant style, and Ju Chao who excelled at depicting flowers and birds with boneless techniques. In the early 20th century, Gao Jianfu, Gao Qifeng, and Chen Shuren pushed the Lingnan School to its zenith. The folding fan paintings created by Ju Lian outnumbered that by any other painter from the Lingnan School. Ju Lian liked raising flowers and birds. When he was young, Ju Lian learned painting from his brother Ju Chao, as well as famous painters Song Guangbao and Meng Litang. He absorbed the essences of various painting schools and formed his own style. Ju Lian was skilled

in depicting flowers, birds, insects, and figures, and such subjects were particularly suited to be painted on folding fans. His fan paintings Picture of Bamboo, Rock and Daffodil, Picture of Two Chickens, Picture of Grass and Insects, Picture of Flowers, Picture of Vegetables and Fruits, and Picture of Flowers and Insects are now collected in the Palace Museum. All of them are in realistic style and feature bright colors and lifeless brushwork.

In the late Qing Dynasty, conservative painters, who inherited the painting style of the Four Wangs, confined themselves to copying their ancient predecessors and refused to make innovation, thus gradually fading away from the public's sight. Without the support from the royal family, the court painting also declined. Fortunately, painters from the Shanghai and Lingnan painting schools injected vigor into the art circles with their innovative spirit.

Ⅳ

The folding fan paintings of the Ming and Qing dynasties represented all major painting genres and their respective styles of the historical period. A thorough research of them can reveal the complete history of the painting art of the Ming and Qing dynasties.

Folding fans are different from other forms of painting carriers like vertical scrolls and handscrolls in terms of shape and material. This creates the unique expression and aesthetics of Chinese folding fan painting.

Due to restriction on format, Chinese folding fan painting had formed its unique way of composition. Unlike rectangular scroll paintings, folding fan painting requires its painter to pay particular attention, so as to prevent the subjects such as figures, mountains, buildings, and trees from looking oblique on the fan. Some ancient artists broke the traditional methods of composition and skillfully composed their paintings along the bottom line of the folding fans on which they painted, evidenced by Watching Waterfall by Zhang Lu, Sun Rising by Jiang Song, Poetic Meditation by Lake in Forest by Wu Li, Poppy Flowers by Yun Shouping, and Flying Birds and Morning Glow by Hua Yan. This later became the most-used composition method in folding fan painting. By this method, artists could not only give full play to their wits and skills and create an interesting ambience in their paintings, but also maximally demonstrate the aesthetic charm of folding fan paintings by "creating infiniteness from limitedness, giving the big picture with small details, and drawing something delicate and exquisite."

Initially, the paper used for folding fan painting was usually coated or splashed with gold mud. It was until the Qing Dynasty that folding fan painters began to paint on treated Xuan paper and silk. Even so, golden paper remained the primary material of folding fan painting. Golden paper is rigid, slippery and non-porous, which requires artists to have superb skills when drawing on such paper. Otherwise, what they paint will appear stiff and lifeless. Moreover, it is difficult to apply colors on golden paper, especially gold-coated paper. This requires that an artist must have a strong sensitivity towards hues and are capable to skillfully incorporate the background color into the folding fan painting. Lan Ying and Chen Hongshou, both painters of the later Ming Dynasty, were masters in this regard. Lan's folding fan painting Green Mountains and Red Trees and Chen's Flowers, Rocks, and Butterflies, both collected in the Palace Museum, feature rich colors. The mountains, rocks, trees, flowers, and butterflies they depicted are in harmony with each other and set off with the golden background, creating impressive visual effects.

Typically, a folding fan painting is 18 centimeters long and 55 centimeters wide. Despite its limited size, artists of the Ming and Qing dynasties displayed infinite emotions with their creativity. Such a small painting could not only showcase the limitlessness of nature, but also bear the spirit of Chinese art. In fact, this genre of painting demonstrated both artists' personal styles and the universal characteristics of Ming and Qing paintings. They subtly depicted the history of painting art in the Ming and Qing dynasties.

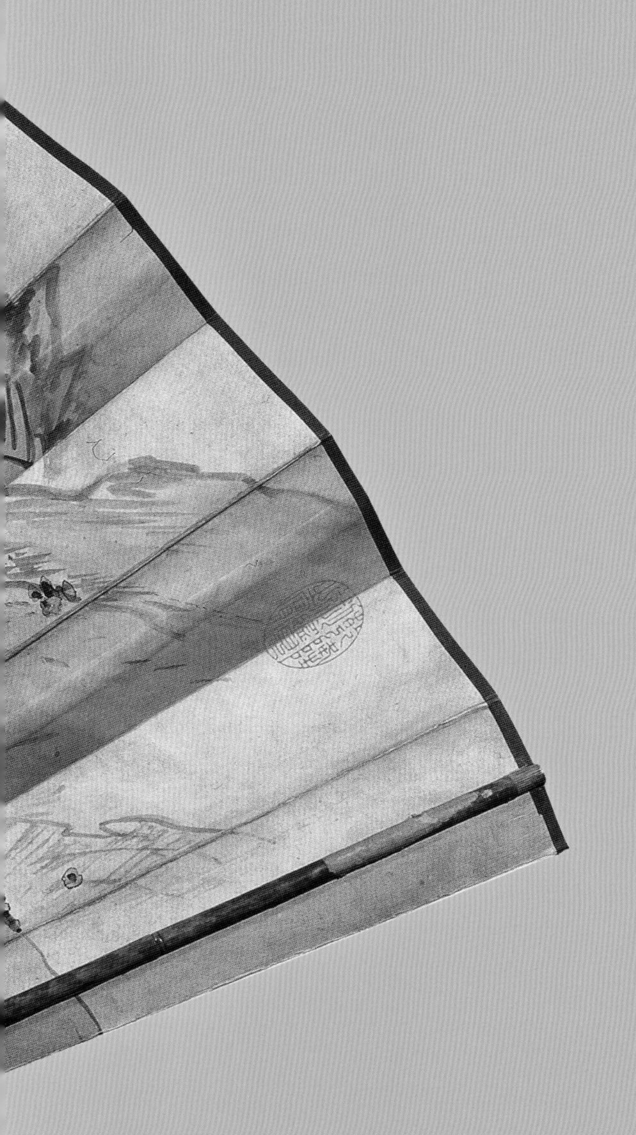

明清扇面精品

Fan Paintings of Ming and Qing Dynasties

1. 山水人物图扇

朱瞻基绘 纸本 设色

纵 59.5 厘米 横 152 厘米

扇面有自题：“宣德二年春日，武英殿御笔。”钤“武英殿宝”朱文印。“宣德二年”是 1427 年，朱瞻基时年 29 岁。

朱瞻基（1399～1435 年），明仁宗朱高炽长子。《大明实录》记他于“己卯（1399 年）二月九日生”，永乐九年（1411 年）立为皇太孙，洪熙元年（1425 年）即位，明朝第五位皇帝，年号宣德，庙号宣宗。他执政期间，能够任人唯贤，纲纪修明。他雅尚翰墨，在书画方面有着较高的造诣，所绘山水、人物、走兽、花鸟、草虫等，宗法宋人，笔墨写实生动，富有感染力。

该扇两面绘画，一面绘高士携童子松下展卷，另一面绘高士采菊赏花。高士身着明黄色衣袍，暗示出其尊贵的皇族身份。朱瞻基自年少时起，便多次随祖父朱棣巡幸征讨各地，历经烽烟战火。他登极做皇帝的第一年，三月派兵进击交阯（今越南）征剿叛寇，八月亲自率兵平汉王朱高煦的反叛。此图是他称帝的第二年春所绘，面对新年伊始，面对曾经有过的频繁战事，他极其渴望过一种平和享乐的生活。故宫博物院收藏的《朱瞻基斗鹌鹑图》轴、《朱瞻基行乐图》卷也印证了他称帝期间的确过着一种安乐的生活。此扇页是目前所知传世最早的大幅折扇画，它已经失去了纳凉祛暑的实用功能。图中人物造型生动准确，山石、树木笔法尖峭，皴法松秀，既有元人遗韵又得宋人笔墨之工，表达了朱瞻基作为皇帝怡志林泉的闲雅情趣。

2. 山水人物图扇页

周臣绘　金笺 墨笔

纵 20 厘米　横 54 厘米

扇页有自题:“东村周臣。”钤“周氏舜卿”白文印。

周臣（生卒年不详，活动于 15 世纪末），字舜卿，号东村，吴县（今江苏苏州）人，寿八十余。擅画山水、人物、花鸟，画法主宗南宋李唐、马远等院体画风，并受文人画的一定影响，具有较为深厚的功力。“明四家”中的唐寅、仇英是其弟子。

图绘远景峰峦石壁，近景高士草堂闲坐。画风承袭了宋代的“院体”传统。山石轮廓以劲爽粗健的线条勾勒，石面以浓淡墨渍染。人物虽小如寸豆，但是真实具体，各尽其态，给清幽静寂的山野增添了高古的格调。

3. 明皇游月宫图扇页

周臣绘　金笺 设色

纵 18.6 厘米　横 50 厘米

扇页有自题:“东村周臣写明皇游月宫图。”钤“舜卿”白文方印。

这是一幅带有作者美好想象的画作。表现的是《唐人小说》中“明皇李隆基曾偕方士梦游月中宫殿的情景”。全图笔法工细，继承了南宋笔墨精妙的传统，注重人物个性的展示、人物与环境的配合，以及不同社会阶层人物神态、服饰的刻画。图中展现了唐明皇高贵典雅的形貌、侍从恭敬谦卑的表情和侍女们端庄优雅的气质等，由此可见周臣具有以形写神的较强功底。

4. 桃鹤图扇页

周臣绘　金笺 设色

纵 14.5 厘米　横 42.2 厘米

扇页有自题:"东村周臣。"钤印模糊不辨。

图绘笑醉春风的桃花和高空盘旋的仙鹤。作者在构图上颇具机巧，扇面的远景是烟雾迷蒙的连绵山峦，它轻描淡染，若隐若现，成为"虚"景。扇面的近景是笔笔刻画写实的山石、桃树及仙鹤。远景的"虚"与近景的"实"相互呼应，成功地扩展了画作的进深空间。图中右侧的山石以笔墨勾勒定型并且加以皴擦，从视觉上它比左侧的仙鹤更加引人注目。作者为了平衡左右画面，巧妙地在山石上绘一桃树，稀疏劲瘦的桃枝从右向左伸探，它成为联结左右画面的桥梁，同时引导人们关注体态娇小的仙鹤。

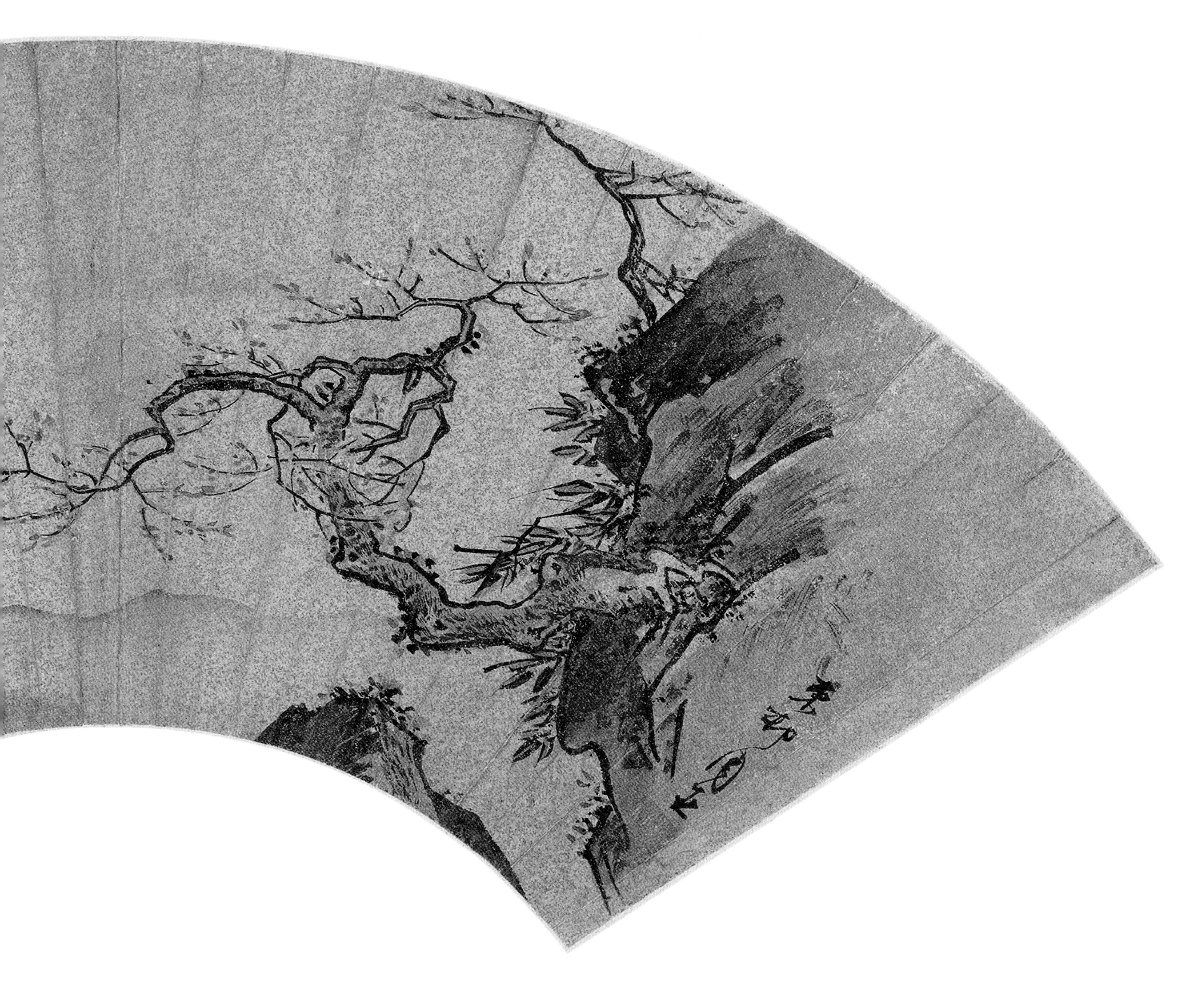

5. 秋林图扇页

沈周绘　金笺 墨笔

纵 16.2 厘米　横 45.5 厘米

扇页有自题：“兀兀小桥外，独行人不知。秋风将落叶，故向鬓边吹。沈周。”钤“沈氏启南”朱文印。

沈周（1427～1509 年），字启南，号石田、白石翁等，长洲（今江苏苏州）人。出身于书画世家，自幼能书善画，淡于功名。其山水、花鸟，博采宋元诸家，自成一格。善用重墨浅色，饶有韵致。与文徵明、仇英、唐寅合称“明四家”，是文人画承上启下的代表人物。著《石田诗钞》。

图绘树叶飘零的深秋时节，高士策杖独行的情景。纵观沈周作品，有粗细两种画风，细笔略似王蒙，粗笔近似吴镇。此图属于沈周晚年的粗笔一格。在创作上，他以擅长的中锋、润墨点染物象，具有苍润挺健的视觉效果，令画面不因构图的简约而显得单薄，同时也通过该小品表现出其笔墨浑厚的特点。

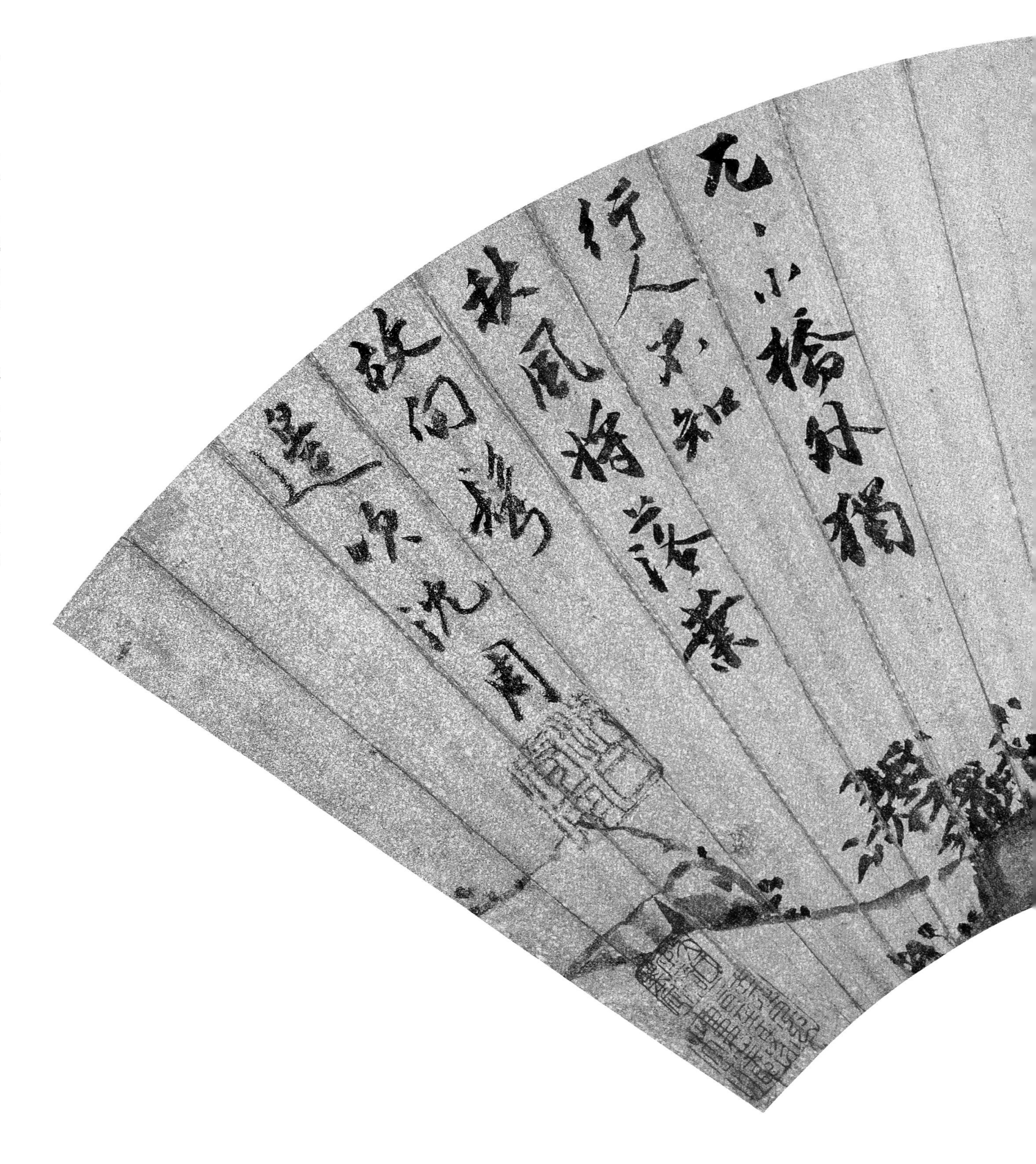

6. 江亭避暑图扇页

沈周绘　金笺 设色

纵 18 厘米　横 46 厘米

扇页有自题：“池上一亭好，夕阳松影中。正无避暑地，认是水晶宫。沈周。”钤“启南”朱文印。

此图是幅笔笔紧贴诗意的画作。图绘夕阳下，高士策杖至江亭避暑的小景。扇面构图为左右开合式，设色以绿色为主，其青翠明洁的色调与简约的景致相呼应。清爽、平淡的审美意趣与消除烦躁求得清凉的避暑主题相契合，标示出远离世俗寻幽独行的高士其平和雅淡的心境。

7. 旭日东升图扇页

蒋嵩绘　金笺 墨笔

纵 17.4 厘米　横 48.4 厘米

扇页有自题:“三松。”钤“三松”朱文印。

蒋嵩(生卒年不详,活动于 15 世纪),字三松,号徂来山人等,江宁(今江苏南京)人。擅画山水、人物。山水初学元代吴镇之法,后宗吴伟,与郑文林、张路等同为浙派后期重要画家。他们的笔墨豪放恣纵,不注重细节的刻画,被讥讽为“狂态邪学”。

在中国古代绘画中,单纯表现海上日出的画作极少。此图以平实的章法表现了最令人心动的海上景观。全幅构思独特,以近景飞溅的浪花和中景汹涌的波涛,烘托出远景冉冉升起的旭日。旭日的四周以淡墨晕染云雾和水汽,将旭日映衬得光华四射,充满无限的魅力。

8. 山水图扇页

蒋嵩绘　金笺 墨笔

纵 17 厘米　横 51.2 厘米

扇页有自题："三松为西园作。"钤"三松印"白文印。

此图是一幅绘其意不绘其形的画作。远景的峰峦岭岫没有被具体地刻画，仅用淡墨晕染山头，勾勒出大体的形貌。中景的平湖静水则不着一笔，完全靠远景的山与近景河岸的夹衬暗示出来。近景枯荣相伴的杂木，以浓淡墨直接点染叶片，运笔洒脱，墨气淋漓。平坡处相向交谈的高士不见眉目的刻画，仅略具形态。简约的构图和概括的表现技法，没有令画作失去画意。蒋嵩巧妙地运用虚实映照、黑白相衬和以简胜繁的艺术手法，吟唱出一曲烟云浩渺、意境空旷而不荒凉的山水清音。

9. 山水图扇页

蒋嵩绘　金笺 墨笔

纵 18.2 厘米　横 50 厘米

无款、题，钤“三松”朱文印。

此图显示出作者具有较强的把控水与墨干湿、浓淡的能力。山石、树木没有线条勾勒的束缚，全以深浅不同的墨晕染。流动的墨气展示出了江南山水迷蒙、草木华滋的地域特征，同时令画面于气象万千中气韵生动，具有“江上愁心千叠山，浮空积翠如云烟”的诗意。画风受宋“米氏云山”的影响而又有所变化，是明代文人画中难得的大写意墨笔山水。

10. 观瀑图扇页

张路绘　金笺 墨笔

纵 18 厘米　横 50.4 厘米

扇页有自题："平山。" 钤 "张路" 朱文印。

张路（生卒年不详，活动于 15 世纪），字天驰，号平山，祥符（今河南开封）人。以庠生游太学，不仕。画风受戴进、吴伟影响颇多，行笔洒脱迅捷，遒劲可观。与朱端、蒋嵩、汪肇等同为浙派名家。

图绘二人登山观瀑的情景。画中的山石杂木以饱含水分的润墨表现，用笔奔放豪爽，线条方折顿挫，富于缓疾、浓淡的变化，显然受到宋元时期粗笔水墨一派及吴伟等人水墨写意画风的影响。此作是张路不可多得的小而精之作。

11. 秋葵图扇页

唐寅绘　金笺 墨笔

纵 18.1 厘米　横 51.3 厘米

扇页有自题："叶裁绿玉蕊舒金，微贱无媒到上林。岁晚冰霜共摇落，此中不改向阳心。唐寅。"钤"唐寅"、"南京解元"朱文印二方。

唐寅（1470～1523 年），字伯虎，一字子畏，号六如居士等，吴县（今江苏苏州）人。才华横溢，文采出众，自诩为"江南第一风流才子"。其花卉喜用水墨小写意法，行笔挺秀，富有情趣。其山水多取法宋元人笔墨，行笔秀润缜密而有韵致。其人物画注重形神兼备，水墨、设色均佳。与沈周、文徵明、仇英合称"明四家"。著有《六如居士全集》。

唐寅在扇页上重点刻画了三株茁壮的秋葵，并且通过诗文赞美了秋葵在寒霜气候及与杂草丛生、荆棘相伴的恶劣环境下，仍然"此中不改向阳心"的品质。从其咏物感怀的文辞中，流露出他对人生的感悟和惆怅之情。图中以写意法刻画的秋葵，既不同于工细的宋人院体画，又与沈周的沉雄浑厚、文徵明的儒雅娟秀有别，它于灵动的勾描、晕染间自得疏散通脱的逸趣，从中可见唐寅在探索花卉写意画技法上求新求变的绘画个性。

扇页左右两边有唐寅友人孙益和、张衮的依韵和诗。整件作品图诗并茂，画作充满浓郁的文人书卷气。

12. 枯木寒鸦图扇页

唐寅绘　金笺 墨笔

纵 17 厘米　横 49 厘米

扇页有自题："风卷杨花逐马蹄，送君此去听朝鸡。谁知后夜相思处，一树寒鸦未定栖。唐寅赠懋化发解。"钤"唐伯虎诗画印"朱文印。

此图是唐寅赠友人的离别之作，画作上没有祝福之意，而是充满忧患的情绪。图绘突兀的山石后是株枝叶飘零的枯木，它与方硬的山石构筑出一个凄凉荒寒的意境。寒鸦或栖于枝头，或振翅飞临，它们的躁动没有给画作带来一丝生机，反而更增添悲苦萧瑟之感。此图虽然没有落创作的年款，但是从作者题诗的书体、精练准确的用笔、酣畅淋漓的施墨及生动传神的物象造型推断，此作应是唐寅晚年所绘，画作流露出的是他怀才不遇、孤独寂寞的情怀和对友人及自己在当下恶劣的社会环境中，难以寻求发展及惬意生存的担忧。

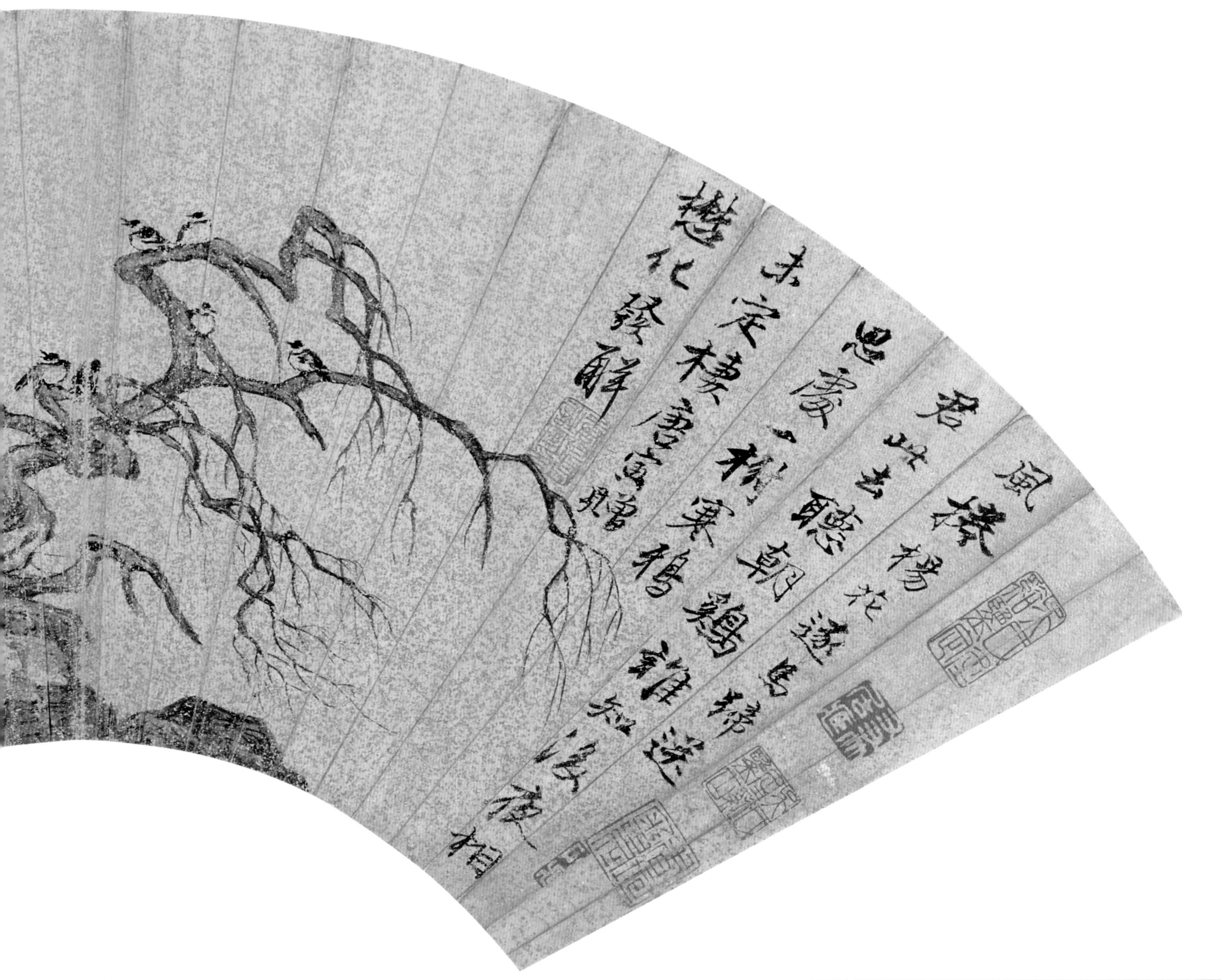

13. 兰竹石图扇页

文徵明绘　金笺 墨笔

纵 18 厘米　横 50.7 厘米

扇页有自题："徵明。"钤"文徵明印"白文印。

文徵明（1470～1559 年），原名壁，字徵明，后以字行，因祖籍湖南衡山，又号衡山居士。曾授翰林待诏，故称"文待诏"。长洲（今江苏苏州）人，出身于世代官宦家庭。书画造诣全面，山水融合赵孟頫、王蒙、吴镇、沈周画法，有粗、细两种面貌，各得其妙。兰竹学法赵子固秀雅中见洒脱。其人物画用笔细腻，富有韵致。与沈周、唐寅、仇英并称"吴门四家"（"明四家"），又与祝允明、唐寅、徐祯卿合称"吴中四才子"。著有《甫田集》。

图绘拳石与竹、兰相佐的画面。作者依元赵孟頫《秀石疏林图》中所提倡的"石如飞白木如籀，写竹还应八法通"的笔法绘竹石，追求以书入画的艺术效果。他以挥洒豪放的行草笔墨，表现出兰叶摇曳之美；以迟缓的中锋运笔，表现出竹、石的清朗与坚实。在一件作品中将不同的物象施以迥异的笔法，由此可见文氏具有高超的绘画水平。

14. 兰花图扇页

文徵明绘　金笺 墨笔

纵 16.8 厘米　横 50.9 厘米

扇页有自题:“离离水苍珮,居然在空谷。虽多荆棘枝,春风自芬馥。徵明。”钤“徵明”白文印。

此图绘兰花与荆棘相伴而生的田野风光。文氏以行草书的章法绘兰叶，笔墨迅疾，表现出一种动势之美，增添了兰随风起舞的飘逸之态，显现出较强的笔墨线条功底。其墨兰画法在明代花卉画中自成一格，颇受推崇，清范玑在《过云庐画论》中赞:“写兰以文门之法为正宗。”

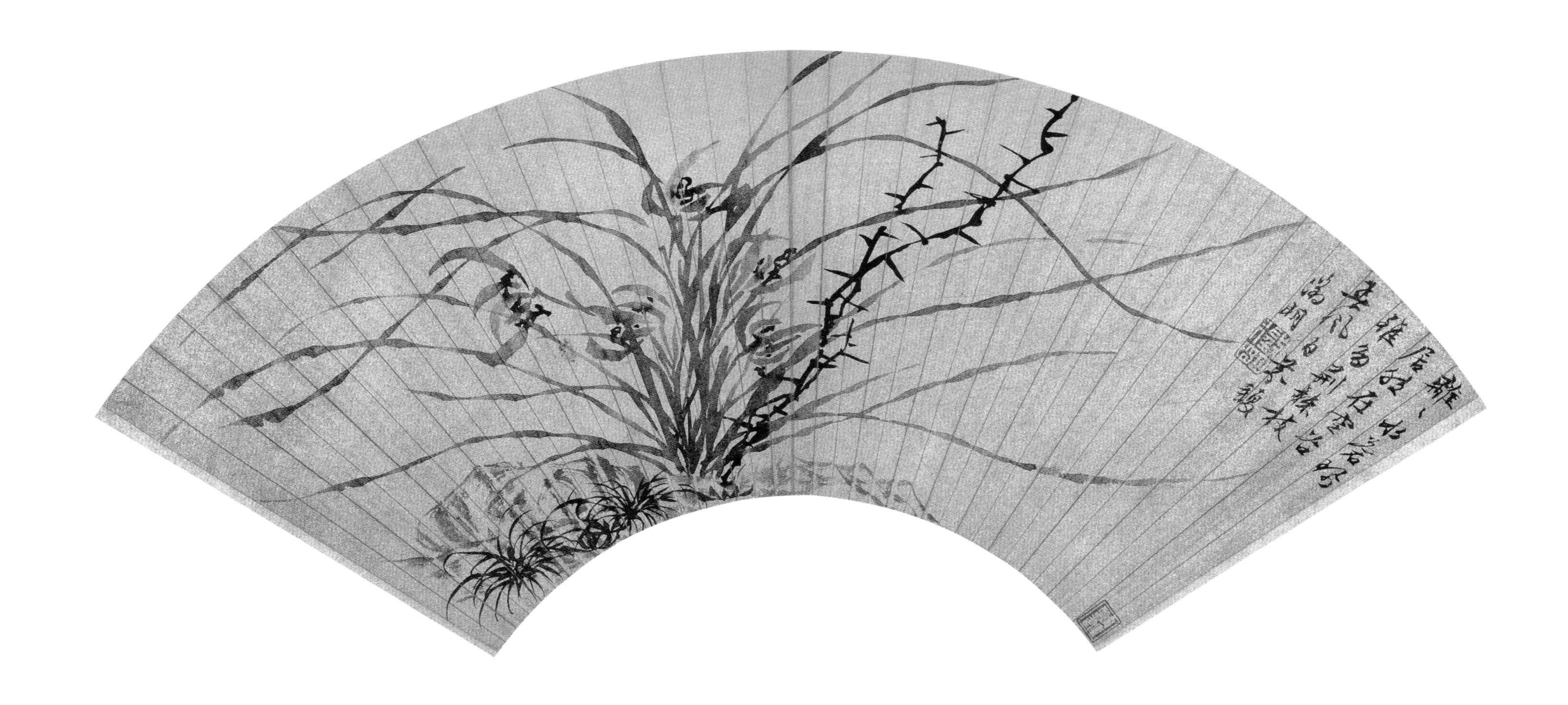

15. 红杏湖石图扇页

文徵明绘　金笺 墨笔

纵 18.5 厘米　横 51.5 厘米

扇页有自题：“三月融融晓雨干，十分春色在长安。香尘属路红云暖，总待仙郎马上看。小诗拙画奉赠补之翰学，丁酉腊月既望。徵明。”钤“徵明”白文印。“丁酉”是嘉靖十六年（1537 年），文徵明时年 68 岁。扇面左侧王守题七言诗一首。

这是一幅文徵明送给做官友人的画作。图绘有着皱、漏、透、瘦之美的太湖石与体态婆娑的杏树相依相随的小景。文徵明以工绘山水画著称，以杏树为主题的扇面画，非常难得。此图布局巧妙，石与树一左一右，呈揖对势，石以其坚实的质感衬托出树木的秀挺，增添了画作的刚柔之美。全画于苍润纯熟的笔墨间流露出的仍然是文人画的娟雅之气。

16. 天香图扇页

陈淳绘　金笺 墨笔

纵 18 厘米　横 49.7 厘米

扇页有自题："天香飘远近，国色逞风流。道復。"钤"白阳山人"、"復父氏"白文印二方。

陈淳（1483～1544 年，一作 1482～1530 年），字道復，号白阳山人，长洲（今江苏苏州）人，文徵明的弟子。他天资聪颖，通古文、诗词，善书法、绘画。其写意花卉笔墨奔放纵逸，格调清隽疏爽，是继林良、沈周之后写意花卉的重要人物，对明清的花鸟画有较大影响，与徐渭（号青藤）合称"青藤白阳"。

牡丹有"国色天香"的美誉，是中国花鸟画中最常见的花卉题材，也是陈淳最喜欢表现的题材。此图牡丹是以"勾花点叶"法表现。花瓣以白描线条勾出，叶片以水墨点染。虽然全幅为墨笔画，但是作者运墨如色，通过墨分五彩的方式，表现出了牡丹"百般颜色百般香"的韵致。

17. 牡丹图扇页

陈淳绘　纸本 设色

纵 17.2 厘米　横 50.8 厘米

扇页有自题：“道復。”钤“復父氏”白文印、“白阳山人”朱文印。

图绘一折枝牡丹的特写。粉红色的花儿作为画作的主体，醒目地居于扇面的中心，嫩绿的枝叶在花儿的两侧伸枝布叶。构图平稳，冷暖色调呼应，表现出牡丹作为花中之王雍容华贵的气质以及“绿艳闲且静，红衣浅复深”的诗意。此图的表现技法与陈淳《天香图》的不同，它是以“没骨”法绘制的，即不用墨笔勾线，通过颜料与水的交融，直接点染物象，这种技法源于北宋，苏辙记：“徐熙画花落笔纵横，其子崇嗣变格，以五色染就，不见笔迹，谓之‘没骨’。”陈淳作为花鸟大家，对此种技法熟识，并且能够娴熟地加以运用。本扇面中有文徵明的题，可见文氏与陈淳间亦师亦友的深厚友谊和他们在诗、画学上的密切交往。

18. 云山图扇页

陈淳绘　金笺 设色

纵 17.4 厘米　横 51 厘米

扇页有自题："道復。"钤"白阳山人"朱文印。

图绘烟岚起伏、云雾环山的江南景致。山石、树木全用浓淡相参的墨色点染而成，笔墨苍润浑厚，充分表现出江南湿润的气象和山光水色的情趣。图中大面积的以寥寥数笔勾染的云雾，不仅表现出弥漫蒸腾的效果，而且有效地将近景的平湖、树木与远景的山峦相连接，使得画作既饱满又富于变化，既具有舒朗的透气感又有由近至远的空间感，颇得宋米芾、米友仁山水精髓。陈淳的山水画直接师承于文徵明和沈周，但是，他更钟情于米氏云山，创作了大量仿米家山水的画作，除此扇外，还有《仿小米云山图》卷（美国弗利尔美术馆藏）、《仿米山水图》卷（故宫博物院藏）、《罨画山图》卷（天津博物馆藏）等等。

19. 选梅折枝图扇页

谢时臣绘　金笺 设色

纵 18.9 厘米　横 50 厘米

扇页有自题："林逋自是神仙客，冰玉丰姿锦绣胸。吟出横斜清浅句，暗香疏景有无中。谢时臣诗画为碧湖先生作。"钤"思忠"朱文印、"樗仙"白文印。

谢时臣（1487～1567 年后），字思忠，号樗仙，吴县（今江苏苏州）人，擅绘山水、人物，由学法沈周上溯元王蒙，形成工细兼备游艺于吴派、浙派之间的画风。

宋代名士林逋隐居杭州孤山时，清高自居，以植梅养鹤为乐。人谓他以梅为妻，以鹤为子，他也由此成为文人仰慕的隐士典范。图绘林逋正身倚梅干，目视家僮修整梅枝的情景。谢时臣以此图扇赠"碧湖先生"，有赞誉友人像林逋一样具有高逸人品的寓意。同时，也表达了他自己对林逋的敬仰之情。图中人物及树木用笔工整，线条略显方硬。山石苔点的笔法灵动，受到了沈周写意画风的影响。

20. 暮云诗意图扇页

谢时臣绘　金笺 墨笔

纵 18.5 厘米　横 50.7 厘米

扇页有自题：“百花潭上锁春云，雾磴烟岚带夕曛。渭北江东意如许，高天回首更思君。甲辰冬暮谢时臣写暮云景并赋诗。”钤“思忠”朱文方印、“樗全子”白文方印。“甲辰”是嘉靖二十三年（1544 年），谢时臣时年 58 岁。

图绘暮色笼罩下的百花潭烟云缭绕的景致。此图为水墨写意画，运笔娴熟自如，气贯笔锋，刚健洒脱。用墨富于变化，浓淡相衬。构图虚实相应，物象间层次清晰，又浑然一体。从右向左横贯画扇中部的云雾以其空灵、多变既增加了画面的高远感，又盘活了整个画面，使之具有行云流水般的气韵。

21. 云岩秋霁图扇页

陆治绘　金笺 设色

纵 15 厘米　横 46.7 厘米

扇页有自题："辛丑八月陆治写云岩秋霁。"钤"包山子"白文印。"辛丑"是嘉靖二十年（1541 年），陆治时年 46 岁。

陆治（1496～1576 年），字叔平，号包山子，吴县（今江苏苏州）人。诗、文、书、画皆工，其花鸟，无论工笔还是写意皆具意趣。其山水画，在受宋、元画家和文徵明影响的基础上，形成风骨峻峭之风，独具特色。

陆治是文徵明的画学弟子，他既能师承文氏的书卷气，又能在物象造型上有所创新。此图是他带有自家笔墨风格的典型画作。构图以奇险取势，远、近景的山石嶙峋叠嶂，其轮廓用笔已不是文氏惯用的圆劲精细笔法，而是独创地以短线条根据山形的高低、转向勾勒，通过表现山石的多棱多角，显现出山石坚硬的质感。图中点景的树木以小写意绘成，略显细弱的树貌与山石形成强烈的刚柔对比，更增强了山石奇峭的体势。

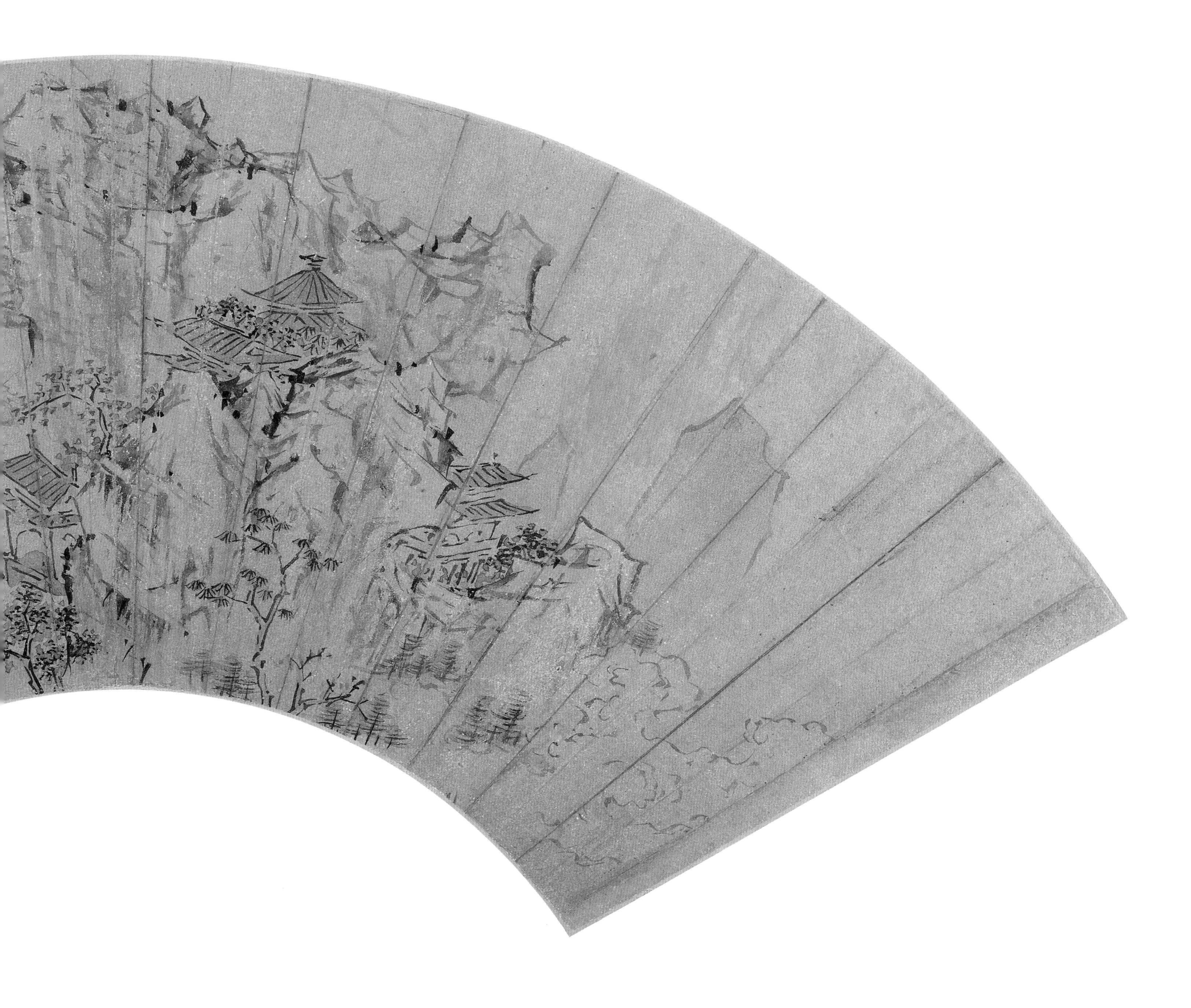

22. 仿倪瓒山水图扇页

陆治绘　金笺 设色

纵 17 厘米　横 49.2 厘米

扇页有自题："霜落平川漾浅沙，丹枫虚映荻芦花。中天已彻三更月，江上偏宜八月槎。庚戌冬日陆治为思愚画并题。"钤"叔"、"平"朱文联珠印。"庚戌"是明嘉靖二十九年（1550 年），陆治时年 55 岁。

此图一河两岸式的构图仿自元人倪瓒。山石、树木的画法则完全是陆治艺术成熟期的风貌，其山石用笔秀挺，以花青、赭石平抹涂染为主，较少皴擦；树叶以红、绿色点染，笔法灵动，显现出树木生机勃勃的朝气。

23. 蔷薇图扇页

陆治绘　金笺 设色

纵 15.9 厘米　横 49 厘米

扇页有自题：“小妹融春酒，颜如赬玉盘。薄罗初试服，含笑倚栏干。陆治作于西山斋。”钤“洞庭陆治”、“陆氏叔平”白文印二。

图绘一枝盛开的蔷薇花。构图简单，花枝布局虬曲婉转，笔墨淡雅，表现出蔷薇花于微雨或朝露后，花瓣红晕湿透的娇柔与清丽，是陆治扇面花卉画的精品。

24. 兰亭图扇页

仇英绘　金笺 设色

纵 21.5 厘米　横 31.2 厘米

本幅无作者款印，根据画风，定为仇英作。

仇英（约 1498～1552 年），字实父，号十洲，江苏太仓人，寓居苏州。初为漆工，后拜周臣为师学习绘画，曾在昆山鉴藏家周凤来、嘉兴大收藏家项元汴家观摩和临摹历代名迹，画艺遂大进，尤其在继承唐宋传统的工笔人物和青绿山水方面，取得了突出成就。其声誉与沈周、文徵明、唐寅相埒，有“吴门四家”之称。

图绘晋代著名书法家王羲之在水榭上观鹅、赏鹤的情景。全图布局清旷疏朗，湖石、绿柳沿溪布列，景色奇幻优美。人物刻画得生动而有神采。山石、溪流、白云及水榭等色泽华美而不媚俗，笔法工中带写，即师承了南宋赵伯驹、刘松年细笔一路的画风，又有所变格，不失为仇英小青绿山水画的代表作。此图扇的背面有明代书法家丰坊于明嘉靖甲子（1564 年）为项元汴写的《临王羲之帖》二则。

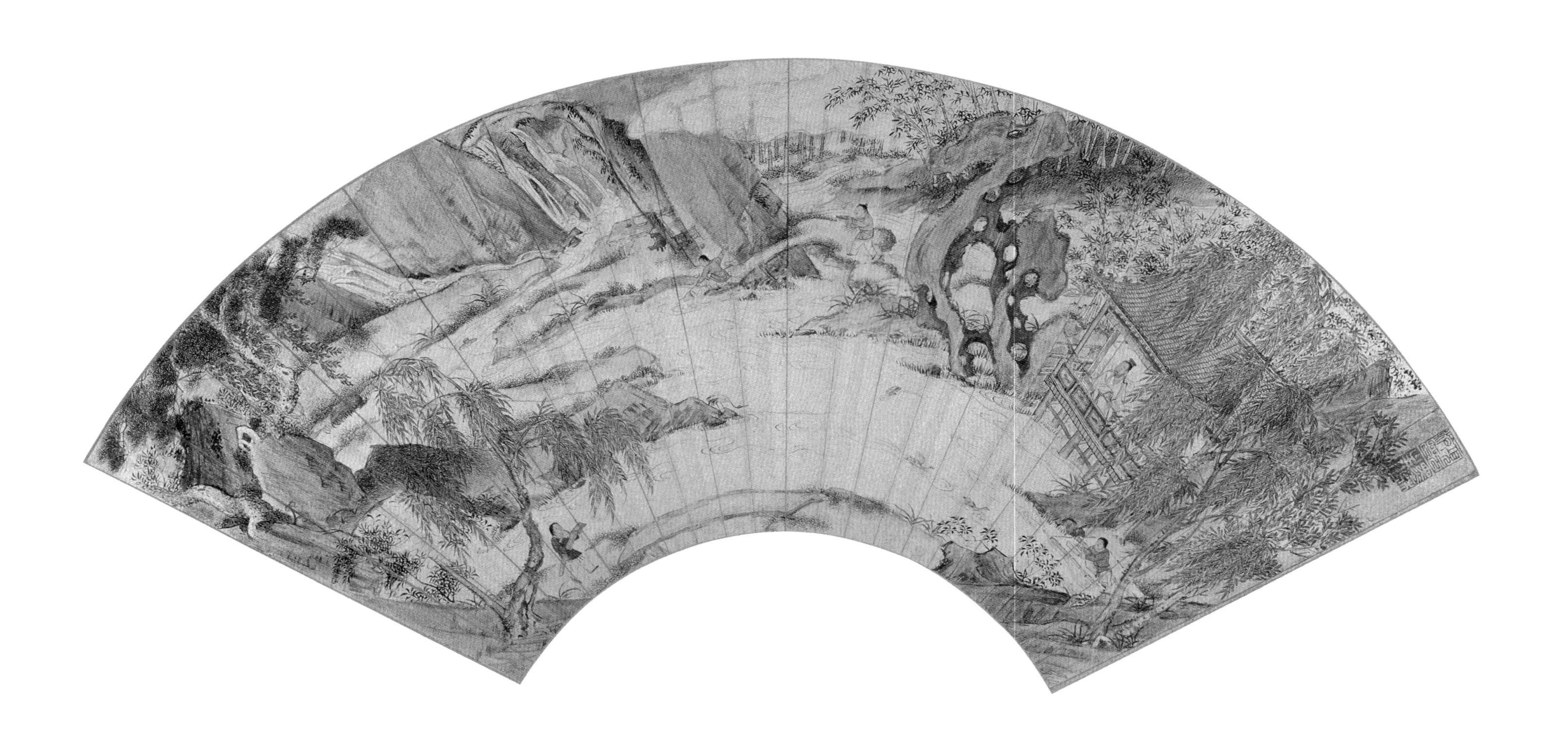

25. 花鸟图扇页

鲁治绘　金笺 墨笔

纵 18.2 厘米　横 51 厘米

扇页有自题："岐云山人鲁治。"钤"鲁治印"白文印。

鲁治（生卒年不详，活动于 17 世纪初），号岐云，吴县（今江苏苏州）人。善画花卉、翎毛，富有生趣。设色、墨笔皆爽健洒脱，李鱓、赵之谦均受其影响。画作存世不多。

图绘一禽在梅树枝头高声鸣叫的情景。扇面左右侧的花卉以不同的笔法表现，左侧的茶花以浓淡墨直接点染，表现出叶片的肥厚和汁液的充沛。右侧的梅树和水仙，以白描双勾刻画，飘逸的线条表现出它们洗尽铅华的脱俗之美。画幅不大，但是别有生趣，是作者精心之作。

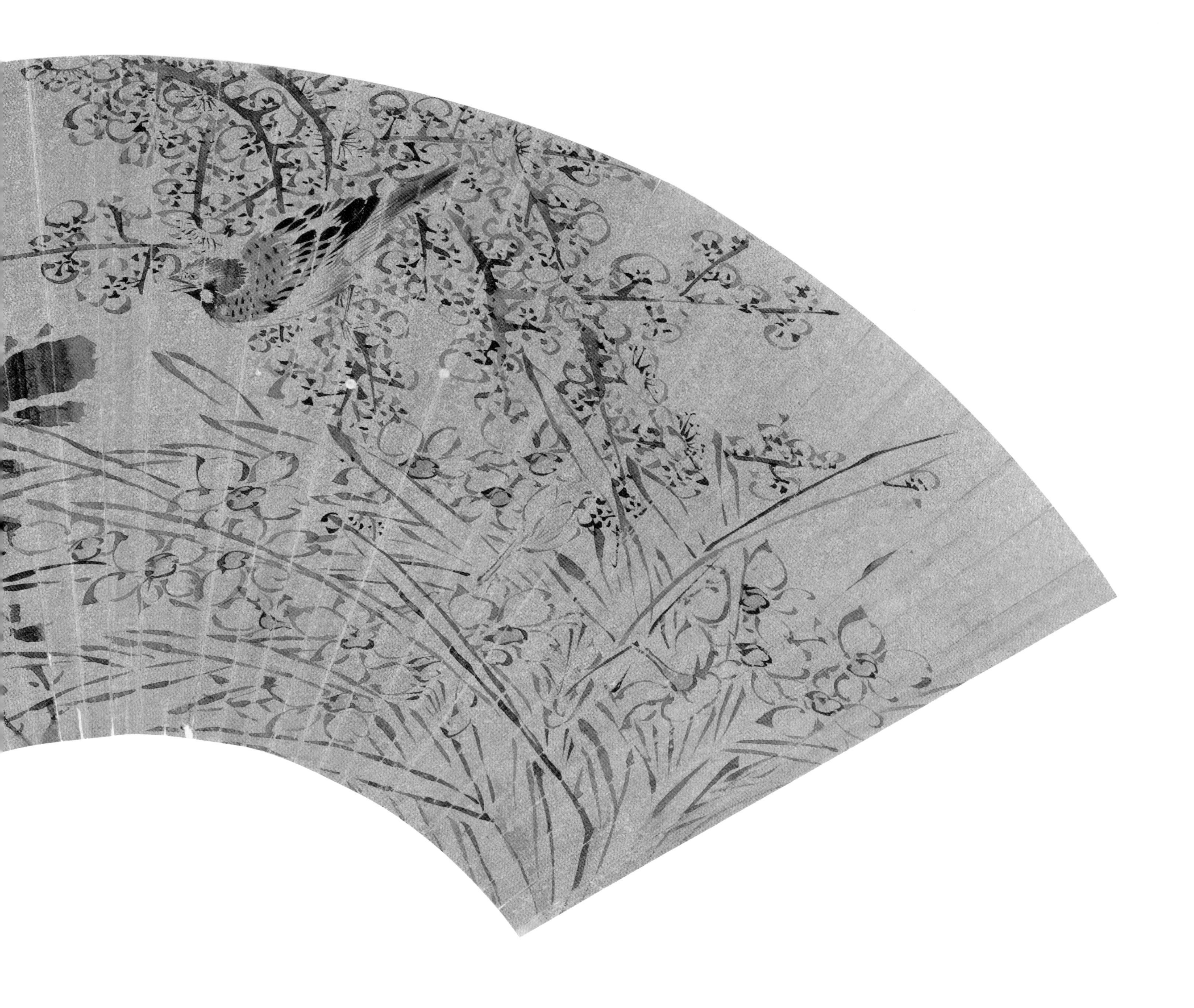

26. 荷花野凫图扇页

朱多炡绘　金笺 设色

纵 16.3 厘米　横 49.1 厘米

扇页有自题："岁丁卯七夕为嗣宗长侄写。多炡。"钤联珠朱文印"多"、"炡"。"丁卯"是明隆庆元年（1567 年）。

朱多炡（生卒年不详，活动于 16 世纪），字真吉，号瀑泉，明太祖朱元璋的儿子宁王朱权的第七代孙、"清初四僧"八大山人（朱耷）的祖父，封奉国将军，占籍南昌。他好游历，能诗文，工书画，山水宗法宋米芾、米友仁父子，喜作云烟缥缈的"米氏云山"。花鸟妙于写生，笔墨传神。

此图为野凫嬉戏小景图。荷花笔墨虚虚实实，以没骨法设色，注重水与色之间的交融，表现出荷塘为水汽所笼罩，若隐若现的含蓄之美。野凫以小写意刻画，姿态各异，造型生动，表现出作者细致的观察力和对景写生的能力。作者在七夕这个亲人相聚的特殊日子里，将此画送给长侄朱统鍒（号嗣宗），浓厚的亲情溢于画外。

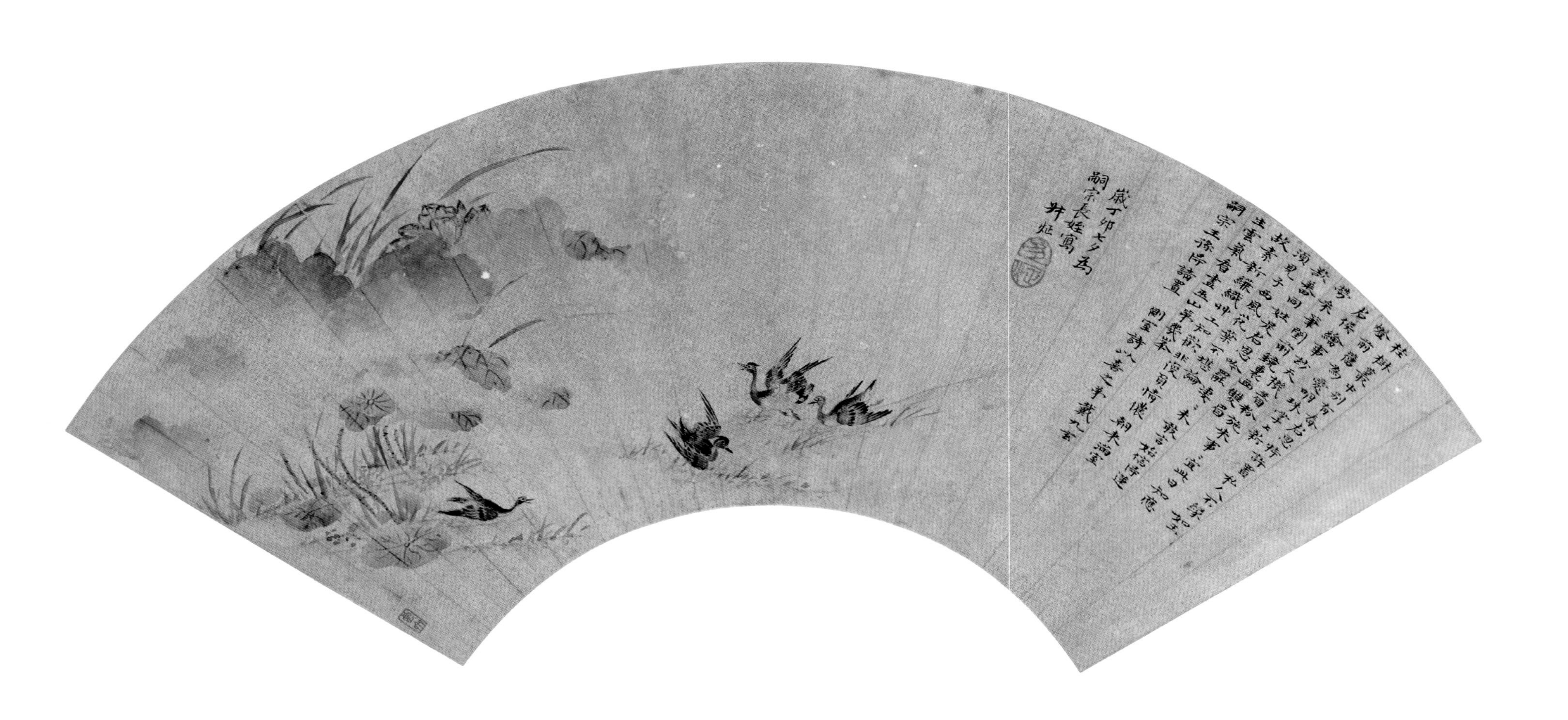

27. 山水图扇页

文嘉绘　金笺 墨笔

纵 19.8 厘米　横 54.5 厘米

扇页有自题：“高天爽气澄，落日横烟冷。寂寞草玄亭，孤云望山影。文嘉。”钤“休承”朱文印。

文嘉（1501～1583 年），字休承，号文水，长洲（今江苏苏州）人，文徵明次子。官和州学政。精鉴古，善诗文、书法，工绘山水，画承家学，明王世贞评：“其书不能如兄（文彭），而画得待诏（文徵明）一体。”他的画作设色幽淡清雅，有文徵明疏秀幽寂之风。

本图中的林木、山石笔法学文徵明的“细文”一路，用清淡而湿润的墨笔皴擦，线条工整细致，气韵苍茫澹然，意境清远高逸，表现出吴门文士怡然自得的生活趣味。

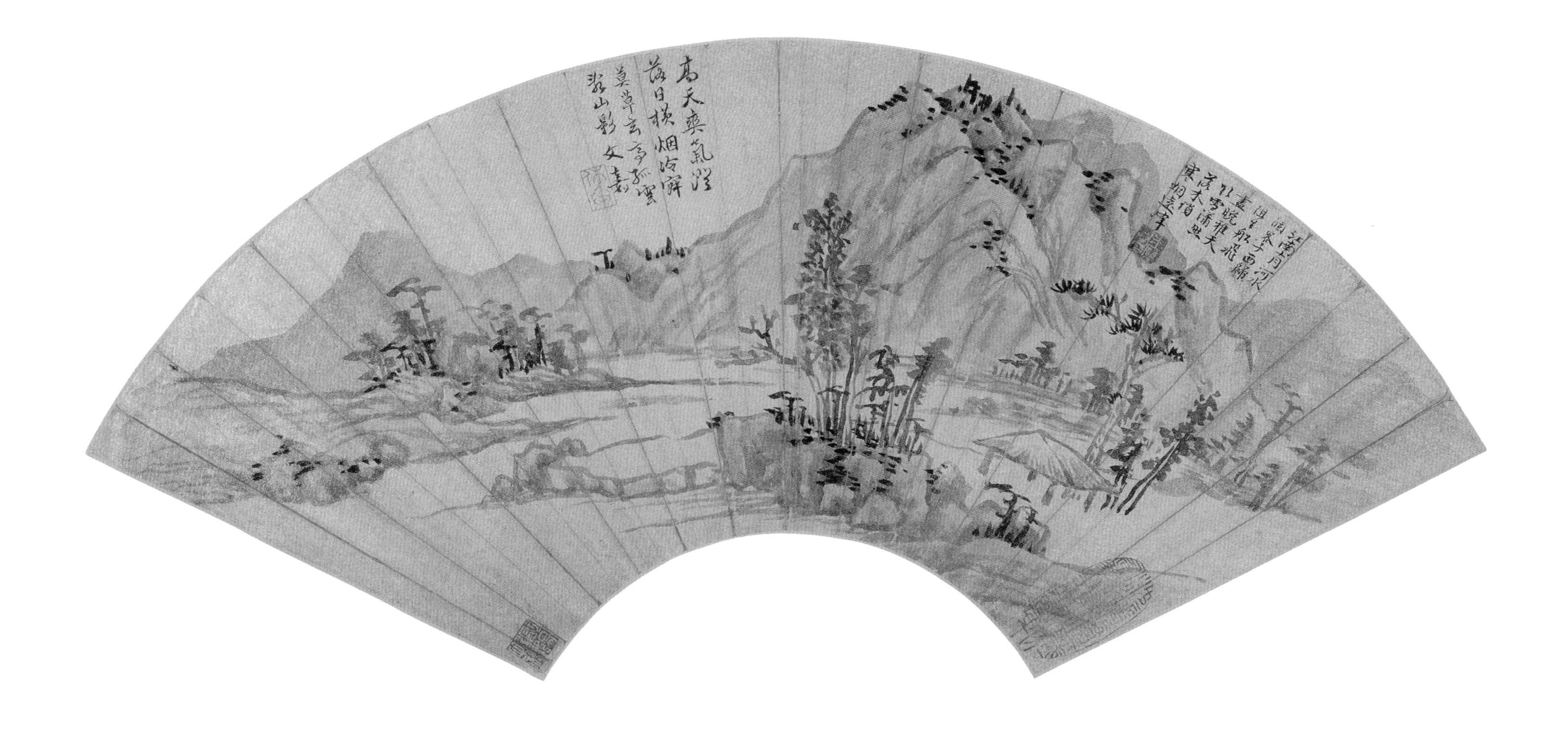

28. 山水图扇页

徐渭绘　金笺 墨笔

纵 15.8 厘米　横 47.4 厘米

扇页有自题："横江独钓为钱伯兰作，渭。"钤印模糊不辨。

徐渭（1521～1593 年），初字文清，改字文长，号天池山人、青藤道士等，山阴（今浙江绍兴）人。他自幼博学多才，书画、诗文、戏剧无所不能。其绘画，在仿南宋梁楷、明林良等人粗放笔墨的基础上，不拘成法，注重以书法笔意入画，强调画作与题诗在形式及内容上的协调统一。他运笔豪放，施墨淋漓的写意画，丰富了中国水墨画的表现技法，并对清朱耷、原济以及"扬州八怪"诸家产生了极大的影响。其书法，将宋苏轼的朴拙、米芾的洒脱融为一体，行笔于奔放迅急中内具章法，自成一格。此外，其《四声猿》杂剧，打破了元人杂剧的框格体例，新颖别致。其《南词叙录》是明代最早研究南戏的著作。

此图近景绘山石坡陀，其上植杂木数株，有的叶已凋零，表明时值寒冬。中景是空荡荡的水域，一人驾舟独钓的情形，其孤独的身影，又为画作增添了几分荒寒之意。徐渭才华横溢，但是，他生活在明王朝走向衰败，严嵩等奸臣当道，朋党之争异常激烈的时期，使得其才情难以施展，他曾在《墨葡萄》（故宫博物院藏）自题："半生落魄已成翁，独立书斋啸晚风，笔底明珠无处卖，闲抛闲掷野藤中。"比喻自己像野葡萄一样被抛在野藤里，无人问津。此图表现出的寒意、孤独正是其人生失意，抱负难酬的写照。全图用笔简练灵活，施墨华润蕴藉，造型不求形似唯求表达内心不平之气，属于徐渭典型的山水画风貌。

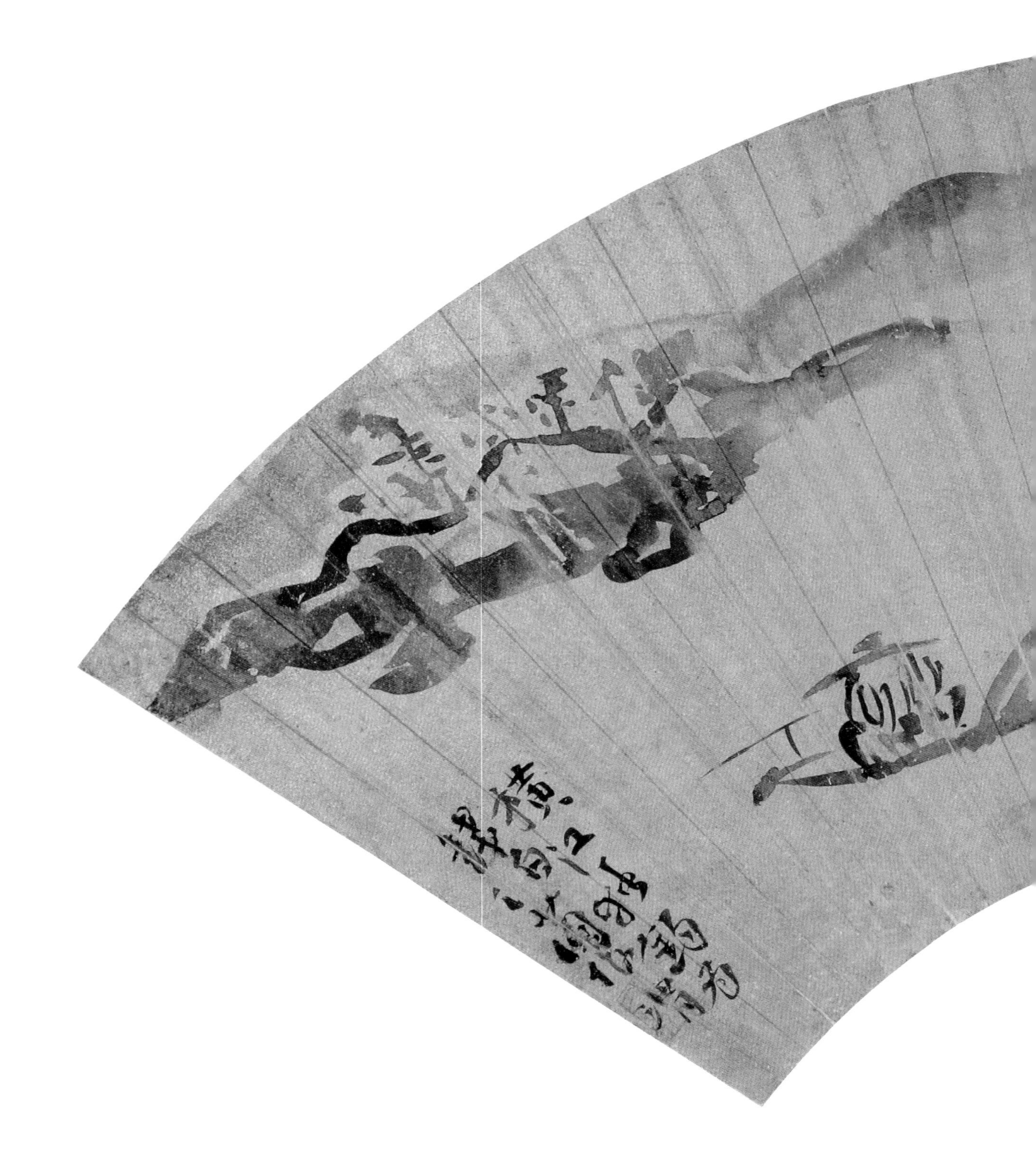

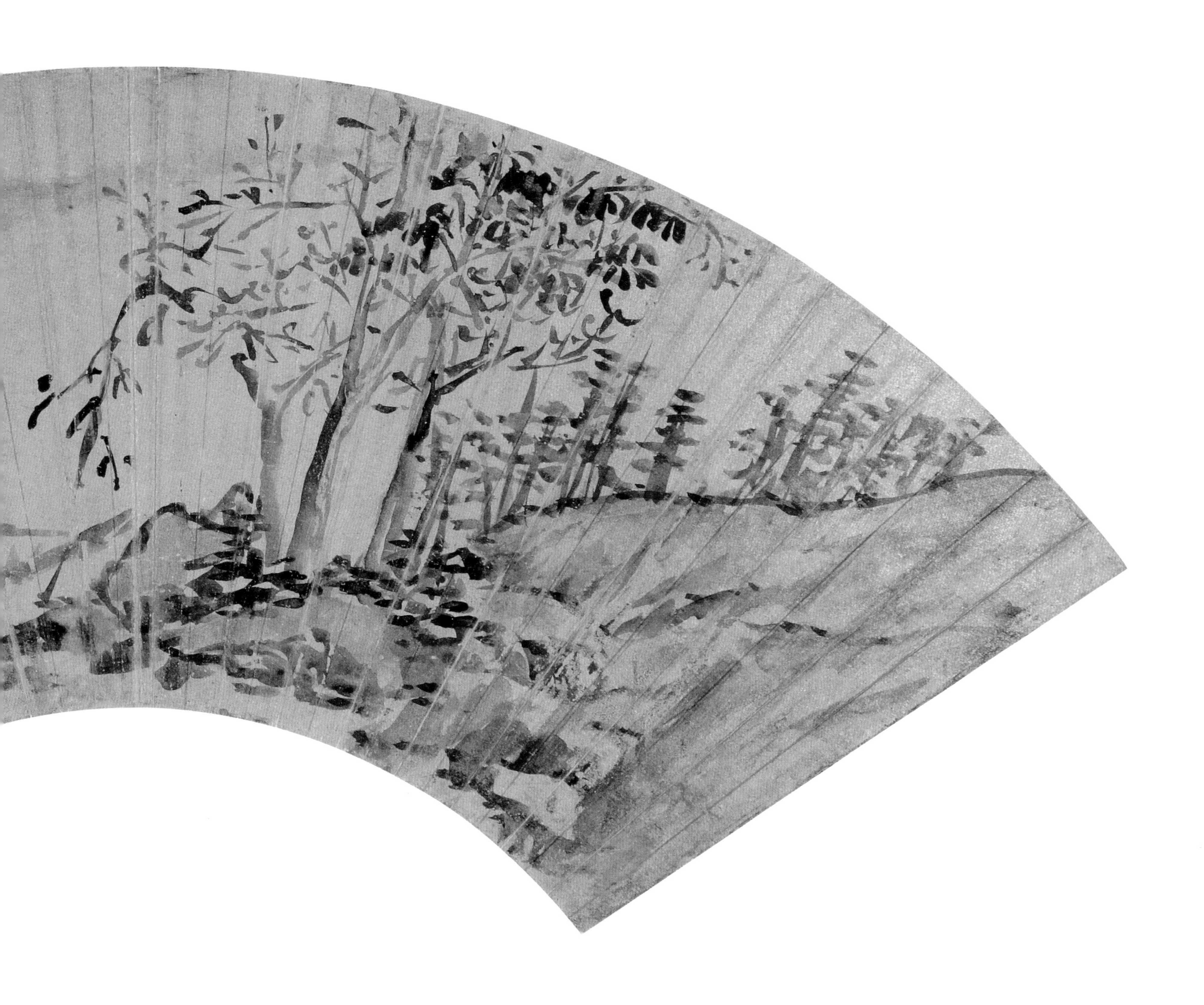

29. 兰竹石图扇页

居节绘　纸本 墨笔

纵 14.6 厘米　横 45 厘米

扇页有自题："居节戏墨。"钤"居士贞"白文印。

居节（约 1524～约 1585 年），字士贞，一作贞士，号商谷、西昌逸士，吴县（今江苏苏州）人。能诗善画，文徵明弟子，明姜绍书《无声诗史》称其"画品绝得徵仲心传，字与诗亦自师门来。"其山水、兰竹于工细中见质朴，沉着中寓灵动，气格之高雅也与文徵明的相仿佛。著有《牧豖集》。

此图自题"戏墨"，当属居节自娱自乐之作。图中兰、竹笔力劲健，线条舒展柔媚。山石以枯笔勾轮廓，干笔皴擦石面，显现出坚实方硬的质感，在秀雅中含有一种凛然难犯的韵味。居节是位注重气节的画家，其人品犹如石品的坚硬和兰、竹的清雅。他曾因刚直不阿的倔强性格，受到织监孙隆的诬陷，但是他无怨无悔，最后竟以穷死。

30. 武陵仙境图扇页

宋旭绘　纸本 设色

纵 17.5 厘米　横 53.5 厘米

扇页有自题：“武陵仙境。万历癸未秋九月，为桃源兄制，檇李宋旭。”钤“石”、“门”朱文联珠印。“癸未”是明万历十一年（1583年），宋旭时年 59 岁。

宋旭（1525～1606 年），字初阳，号石门。后为僧，法名祖玄，又号天池发僧、景西居士。浙江嘉兴（一说为湖州人）人，寓居松江（今属上海）。工绘山水、人物，近师沈周，远法元黄公望诸家，笔墨苍浑，画风高雅古拙，其艺术影响主要在松江地区，赵左、沈士充、宋懋晋均为其弟子，对“苏松派”、“云间派”的形成有着重要的影响。

此图是作者送给友人“桃源”的画作，故特选绘晋代武陵人陶渊明《桃花源记》的场景，以示美意。图绘“武陵人捕鱼为业，缘溪行，忘路之远近。忽逢桃花林”的画面。图中渔舟的划动、浮云的飘动及梅枝的扭动皆与高山的静穆构成强烈的反差，避免了画面的板滞。笔墨精到少皴擦，设色明洁淡雅，将桃花源作为仙境而无世间喧嚣的幽静之美刻画得淋漓尽致。

31. 林塘野兴图扇页

宋旭绘　金笺 墨笔

纵 18.5 厘米　横 55.2 厘米

扇页有自题："林塘野兴。丙戌夏日，宋旭。"钤"石"、"门"朱文联珠印。"丙戌"是明万历十四年（1586 年），宋旭时年 62 岁。

此图仿佛是一幅大画上截下的局部，其树林、稻田、坡地以及水域的画意均不完整，如此的构图，反而增强了想象空间，达到了"画外有画"的特殊效果。画面用笔粗犷，不求形似，唯求达意，颇得沈周晚年画作沉郁苍茫的风貌。

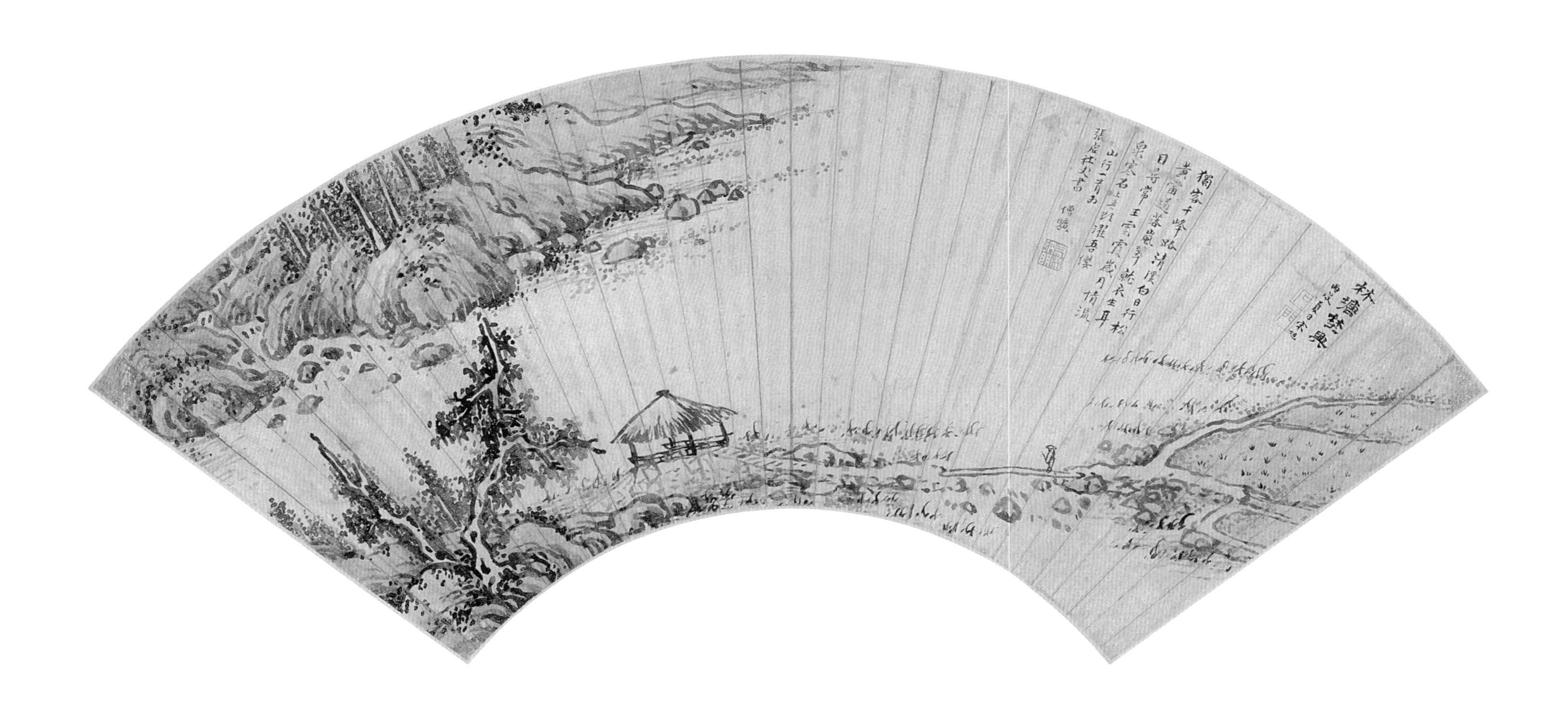

32. 梧竹蕉石图扇页

周之冕绘　金笺 设色

纵 20 厘米　横 55.5 厘米

扇页有自题："汝南周之冕。"钤"服"、"卿"朱文联珠印。

周之冕（生卒年不详，活动于 16 世纪末），字服卿，号少谷，长洲（今江苏苏州）人。他注重以写实的笔法来表现花鸟世界的多彩风貌。他在宗法陆治、陈淳的基础上，创立了先以线勾勒后以色、墨点染的"勾花点叶法"，丰富了花鸟画的表现技法。

图绘秋池小景、鸳鸯戏水的场面。构图虚实相生，具有远近空间层次的变化。线条工细而不呆板，敷色艳丽而不媚俗。此为周之冕早期的画作，其"勾花点叶法"尚未运用到其中。

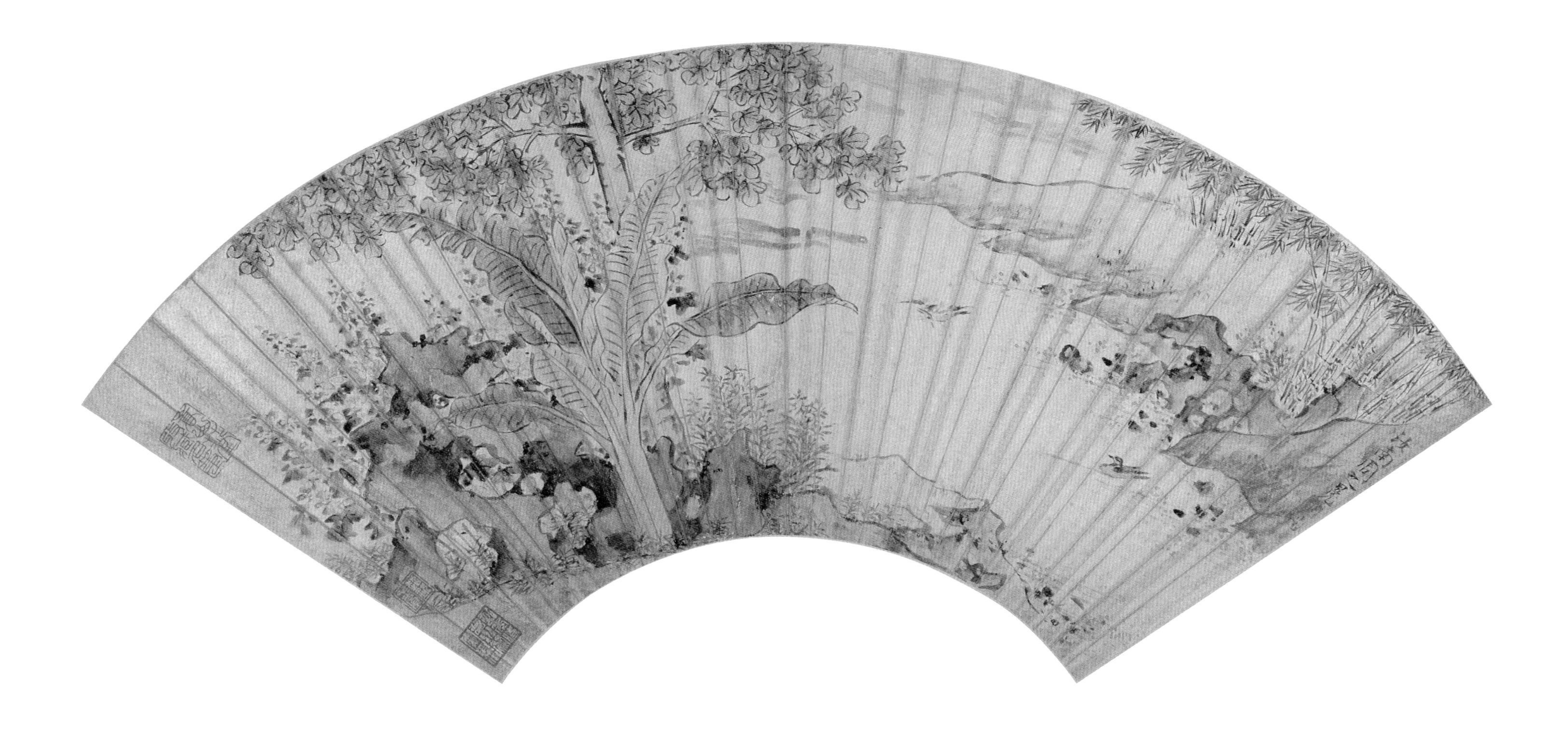

33. 花卉图扇页

周之冕绘　金笺 设色

纵 17.5 厘米　横 51.3 厘米

扇页有自题：“己丑仲春，周之冕写。”钤“服卿”白文印。“己丑”是明万历十七年（1589 年）。

图绘玉兰、海棠等折枝花卉。周氏作为注重写生的画家，曾为了创作，亲自喂养禽鸟、种植各种花卉，以便观察鸟儿的饮啄飞止体态和花儿的成长过程，因此，画史上称陈淳的画是“妙而不真”，陆治的是“真而不妙”，只有周之冕的画是“即真且妙”。此图以工细而不呆板的线条，艳丽而不浓腻的敷色，将花儿描绘得栩栩如生、光彩奕奕，在写实的基础上颇得文人的雅秀之趣。

34. 梅花图扇页

孙克弘绘　金笺 墨笔

纵 15.7 厘米　横 48.5 厘米

扇页有自题："秋日为师我先生写，孙克弘。"钤"汉阳太守"白文印。

孙克弘(1532 或 1533～1611 年),字允执，号雪居，松江（今属上海市）人。礼部尚书孙承恩子。以父荫入仕，官至汉阳太守。生性巧慧，工书画，山水、梅竹、人物皆能，学仿宋人，笔墨简逸，富有书卷气。

此扇页构图奇巧，上部绘横向出枝的梅树，花儿绽放。下部绘流过崖壁的水域，浪涛滔天。历史上以绘梅为主题的作品无数，在表现上，它们通常或与同有"君子"之称的兰、竹、菊相伴，或与有清物之名的湖石相佐，或者是单绘同种类的梅树，总之，将梅与水浪相联的作品极为少见，此图可谓别具新意。作者为了将上下部分联为一整体，巧妙地将浪花绘成层层向上翻滚的样式，它们既给画作带来动感，也成为画扇的中间过渡段，起到了联结上下的重要作用，保证了画作构图的完整。

35. 梅竹寒雀图扇页

孙克弘绘　金笺 墨笔

纵 15.7 厘米　横 47.5 厘米

扇页有自题："克弘。"钤"孙克弘印"白文印。

图绘一只雀儿栖息于梅枝上。雀儿笔墨简约，造型生动，它警觉地侧目张望的神态扩展了画意，给人以想象的画外空间。梅树的花以线描空勾，竹叶为墨笔写意，它们既是突出雀儿的点景之物，也以自身的风采，为画作增添了神采。

36. 春游图扇页

丁云鹏绘　纸本 设色

纵 18.5 厘米　横 56.2 厘米

扇页有自题："丙戌秋日写，丁云鹏。"钤"南"、"羽"朱文联珠印。"丙戌"是明万历十四年（1586 年），丁云鹏时年 40 岁。

丁云鹏（1547～1628 年后），字南羽，号圣华居士，休宁（今安徽休宁）人。善画人物、佛像和山水。早年人物画用笔细秀严谨，取法文徵明、仇英，中年以后画风转为粗放，自成一格。曾为名墨工程君房、方于鲁画墨模，影响颇大。

图绘桃花盛开时节，女子们赏花游春的小景。仕女以工细的笔法勾描，表现出她们轻盈的体态。山石、树木以淡雅的青绿色晕染，其温润的色调与仕女端庄文雅的气质相契合，散发着天真烂漫的气息，渲染出春游之愉悦的氛围。画作反映了作者早期笔墨板拙的面貌。

丙戌秋日寫
丁雲鵬

37. 竹石云泉图扇页

丁云鹏绘　金笺 墨笔

纵 17.8 厘米　横 55.9 厘米

扇页有自题:“乙未夏日为环海先生写,云鹏。”钤“南”、“羽”朱文联珠印。“乙未”是万历二十三年(1595 年),丁云鹏时年 49 岁。

此图最醒目的是绘有大面积的竹林，竹竿挺拔俏立，竹叶青翠欲滴，它们整齐地沿河岸分列，构筑出一个典雅清幽的自然环境。图中的竹以工细的笔法，一丝不苟地精心刻画,竹节笔笔分明,竹叶施墨有近浓远淡之分,它们于虚实相映中扩展了画面的空间层次,也显现出作者工而不板的竹画功底。此幅是作者送给友人环海先生的画作，通过表现有“四君子”之一美誉的竹子，来赞赏友人具有像青竹一样高风亮节、虚怀若谷的品格。

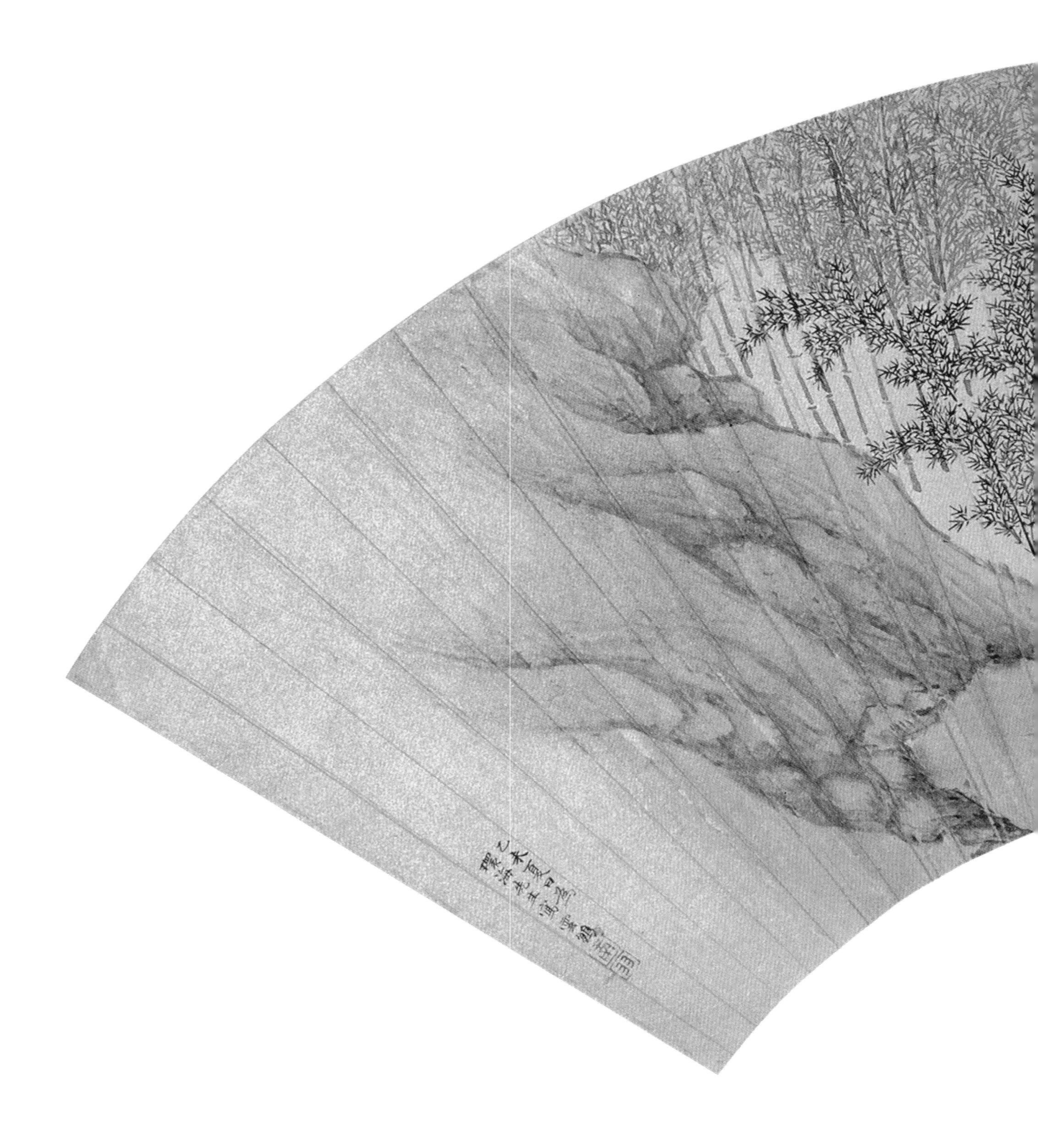

38. 兰竹石图扇页

马守真绘　金笺 墨笔

纵 17.8 厘米　横 49.8 厘米

扇页有自题：“甲午中秋日写，湘兰马守真子。”钤“湘兰”白文印、“守真玄玄子”朱文印。“甲午”是明万历二十二年(1594 年)，马守真时年 47 岁。

马守真(1548～1604 年)，小字玄儿，又字月娇，号湘兰，秦淮名妓。擅绘兰，有君子之称的兰花已成为她内心情感的一种象征，绘画成为她“言志”、“寄怀”的一种手段，同时她也通过画兰来交友助兴。因此，她的作品不太重视对兰外在形态的细致刻画，而重在写出兰的内在精神，借以抒发心中之逸气。马守真以画兰之精、画兰之专而名扬江南，因此自号“湘兰”。

马守真凭借聪颖机敏和才情往来于文人墨客间，构筑了广泛的文化圈，王穉登、陆弼、姚旅、梅鼎祚、何震以及梁辰鱼等人都与之有着密切的交往。其中王穉登(1535～1612 年，字伯穀，在文徵明逝世后，以诗文声华煊赫，主掌吴门文坛 30 余年。)是与马守真交往最密切的著名文人。王穉登作为吴门地区文化圈内的核心人物，同许多文徵明弟子都保持着密切的关系，如钱谷、王穀祥、周天球及文徵明的次子文嘉、侄子文伯仁等。马守真在绘画风格上自然深受“吴门画派”影响。如果将马守真画作与故宫博物院藏文徵明《兰竹拳石》卷、《兰竹石》卷、《墨兰》扇、《兰石》扇、《竹石》扇，辽宁省博物馆藏文徵明《漪兰竹石图》卷，上海博物馆藏文徵明《兰竹图》扇以及故宫博物院藏钱谷《兰竹》卷、陈元素《兰花》扇、周天球《兰花图》轴、《丛兰竹石图》卷、朱之蕃《竹石图》卷，四川省博物馆藏文嘉《兰竹石图》扇等人的画作相比较，不难看出在马氏的作品中，有许多与吴门画家相通的笔墨。如可见在主体物象兰的处理上，兰叶的笔法皆相同：通过笔的提、按变化，表现出叶片的翻转、舒展与折合；线条在一气呵成的运笔中，追求粗与细之间的渐变；此外，还注重通过贴近物态的行笔走线，显现出兰叶飘逸洒脱的风致和自然物态之美。

39. 兰竹图扇页

马守真绘　金笺 墨笔

纵 15.8 厘米　横 48.2 厘米

扇页有自题："癸卯仲秋日写，湘兰马守真。"钤"湘兰"白文印、"守真玄玄子"朱文印。"癸卯"是明万历三十一年（1603 年），马守真时年 56 岁。

马守真最擅画野生兰，它们具有旺盛的生命力和不受任何拘束、自然率朴的真性美。此图是马守真晚年之作，绘坡土地上的兰与竹，其双勾的白描兰、墨笔的竹，运笔率意洒脱，线条舒展飘逸；墨色在行笔中自然显现出浓淡、干枯的变化，展现出春风下叶片随风而舞的摇曳之姿。地面苔草信手点染，墨点聚散有致，增添了画面的朴素无华之美。

40. 仿倪瓒山水图扇页

董其昌绘　金笺 墨笔

纵 17 厘米　横 50.5 厘米

扇页有自题："云林作画，简淡中自有一种风致，非若画史纵横习气也。因拟其意为宏伍丈，玄宰。"钤"董其昌印"白文印。

董其昌（1555～1636 年），字玄宰，号思白、香光居士，华亭（今上海市松江）人。万历十六年（1588 年）进士，官南京礼部尚书，谥"文敏"。工书擅画，精鉴藏。他的山水画出入宋人及五代董源、元代倪瓒诸家。其以禅喻画的"南北宗"美学思想，对晚明以后的画坛影响深远。著《画禅室随笔》、《容台集》、《画旨》等。

在画学上，董其昌对倪云林（瓒）最为推崇，原因正如他题中所言："云林作画，简淡中自有一种风致。"这种"风致"是指云林画作中"墨萧淡而气浓"、"笔疏散而意厚"的画格。他认为只有这种画格显现出的"逸品"美学，才能体现绘画中的最高境界。

此作从构图到用笔均仿自倪瓒。构图取倪氏标准的"一河两岸三段"模式，平波无浪的辽阔水域将近景的树木与远景的山峦分列，令画面空间层次鲜明，又得平远之势。山石行笔仿倪氏折带法，线条勾勒以侧锋为主，笔墨整体苍逸，表现出疏朗清雅而又超逸萧疏的意境。此图当是董其昌仿倪瓒画风的代表作。

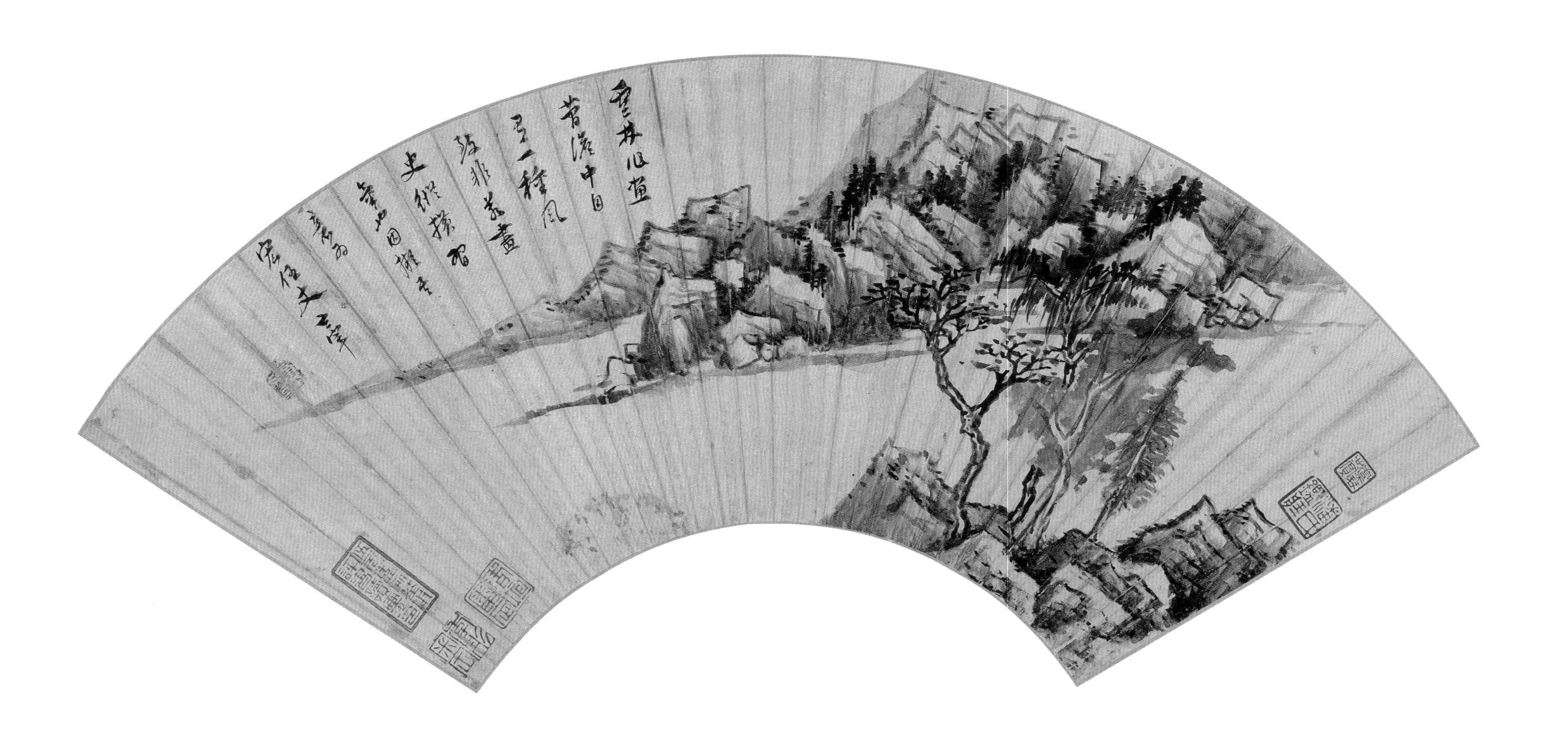

41. 梅花图扇页

陈继儒绘　金笺 墨笔

纵 17.3 厘米　横 51 厘米

扇页有自题："甲子春至写，眉公。"钤"眉公"朱文印、"一腐儒"白文印。"甲子"是明天启四年（1624 年），陈继儒时年 67 岁。

陈继儒（1558～1639 年），字仲醇，号眉公，华亭（今上海松江）人。不求仕途功名，潜心于诗文、书画，工绘山水及花卉，其作品意态萧疏，笔墨湿润松秀，颇具情趣，反映了明末文人闲居弄笔、不求工拙、"以画为寄"的态度。他与好友董其昌共同倡导文人画，他们的"南北宗"论，对明清画坛有着巨大的影响。著有《妮古录》、《陈眉公全集》、《小窗幽记》。

此图是陈氏最擅长的以墨梅为题材的画作。他基于对梅树的了解，在创作上，已达到信手拈来皆成趣的地步。此扇面构思巧妙，所绘梅不是按照通例自下而上或者是左右横向出枝，而是以"下探上扬"的方式布局，梅树给人以横空出世的新意。作者为了弥补画扇左侧的空白，除在左侧上方书写墨题外，还在左侧的下角绘一杈花枝，它的出现不仅起到补白的作用，而且增添了"节外生枝，画外生意"的妙趣。

42. 雪梅图扇页

陈继儒绘　金笺 设色

纵 16.1 厘米　横 49.9 厘米

扇页有自题："顽仙庐对月写此真景，眉公。"钤"醇"、"儒"朱文印二方。

据自题而知，陈继儒画的是月光下的梅花。陈氏在父亡后，移居东佘山，在山上筑"东佘山居"，其中有顽仙庐、来仪堂、晚香堂、一拂轩等房舍。他在这里会三吴名士，以读书作画为乐，死后，亦在此葬身。此图笔墨简约，布景舒朗清新，梅枝呈"U"形，一枝月季斜插而入，似欲与梅争奇斗艳，富有生趣。作者为了表现雪意，在梅枝、月季、杂草的四周留白，并以淡墨晕染笺面，清光静谧之气顿现。

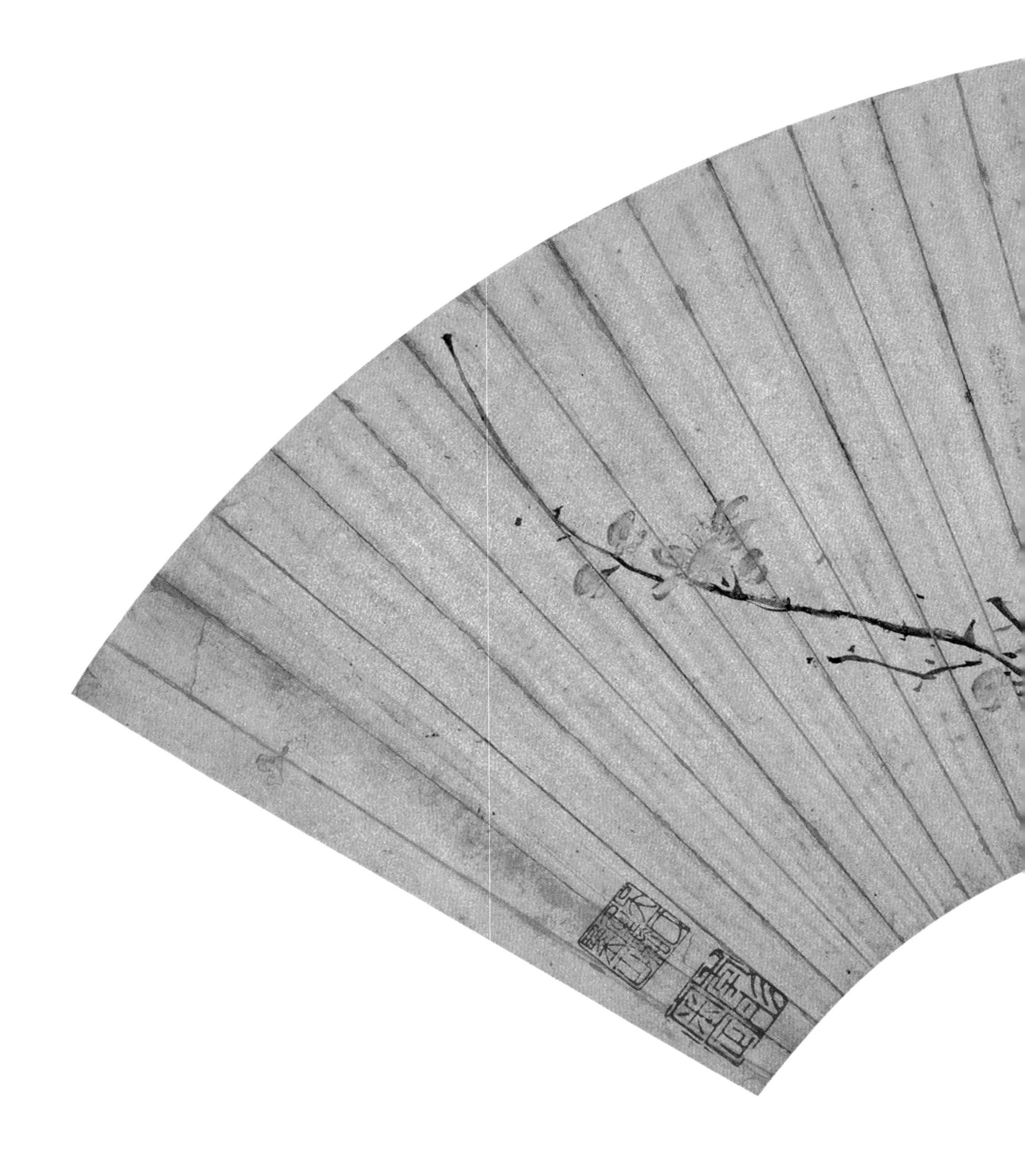

43. 墨兰图扇页

薛素素绘　金笺 墨笔

纵 15.8 厘米　横 45.3 厘米

扇页有自题：“辛丑夏日戏笔，薛素素。”钤“薛”、“素”朱文联珠印。“辛丑”是明万历二十九年（1601 年）。

薛素素（生卒年不详，活动于 17 世纪初），字素卿、润卿、润娘等，号雪素。江苏苏州人，寓居金陵（今南京）为妓。从良后，先后为沈德符、李征蛮所娶。她姿容艳雅，多才多艺，除擅书画外，还工箫、弈、马术、刺绣等多种技艺。在绘画上，她既能工笔重彩又能墨笔写意，具有江南“吴门画派”之风。著诗集《南游草》。

本幅中的丛兰，没有居于扇面的中心，而是偏居一侧。作者通过以兰叶向空白处舒展伸延的方式，将不可见的“风”有了可视的形象，同时令画面于空灵中不失充实。其绘兰叶的笔法豪放洒脱，没有过多的修饰，但是意蕴十足，正如明胡应麟《甲乙剩言》评其兰竹画：“下笔迅扫，各具意态，虽名画好手，不能过也。”

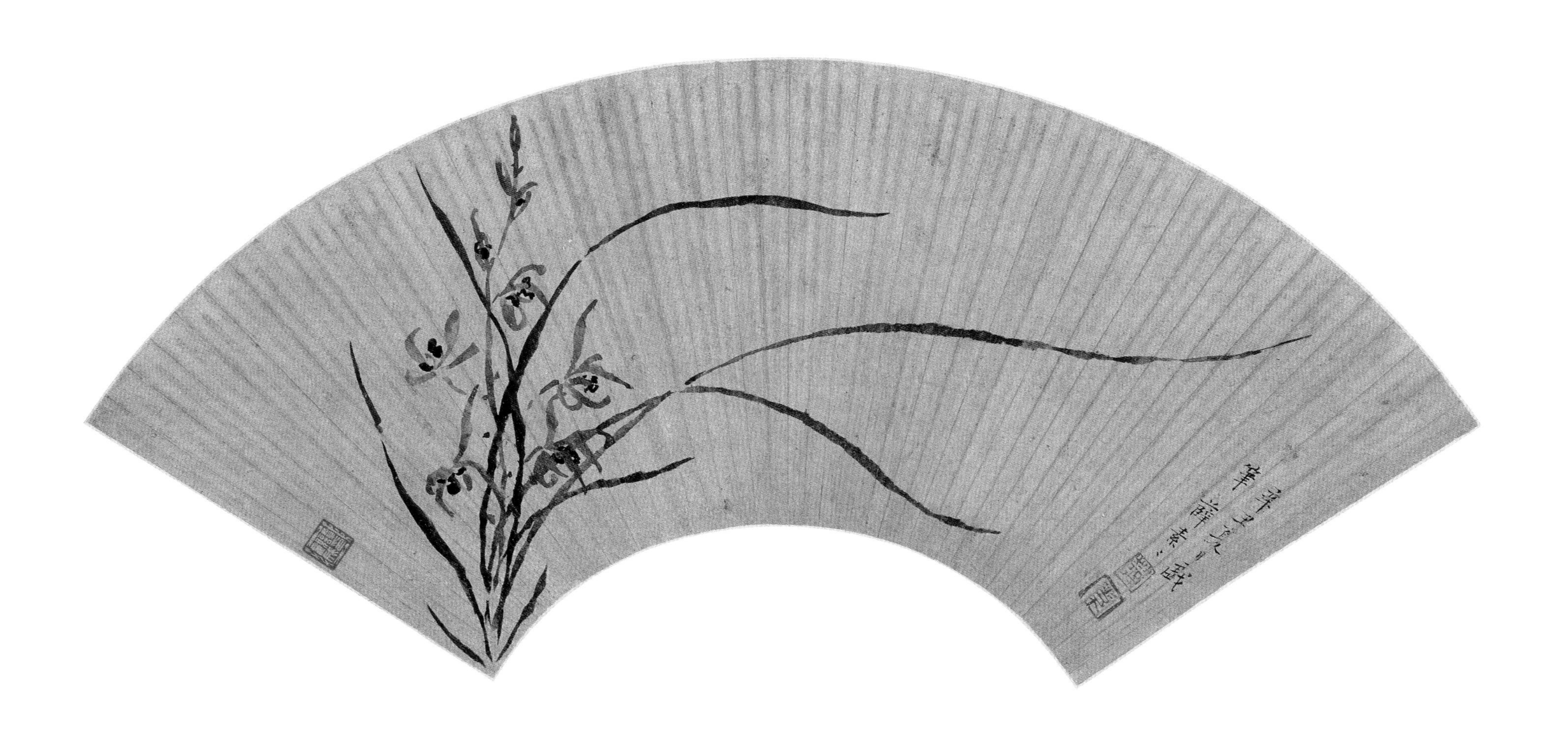

44. 古柏图扇页

姜廷翰绘　金笺 墨笔

纵 18.3 厘米　横 53 厘米

扇页有自题："霜皮溜雨四十围，黛色参天二千尺。戊戌秋日写为百翁老年台词宗，姜廷翰。"钤"姜廷翰"白文方印、"绮季"朱文印。"戊戌"是明万历二十六年(1598 年)。

姜廷翰(生卒年不详，活动于 16 世纪)，字绮季，山阴(今属浙江绍兴)人。风流倜傥，工于诗文书画，擅绘花鸟山水，是陈洪绶挚友，画学曾得陈氏面授。

作者以树喻人，赞友人像历经岁月磨难的古柏一样，具有顽强的生命力。此幅思致巧妙，树枝随扇面的上弧线，向下自然地垂落。地上的杂草沿扇面的下弧线，向上密集地伸展。树与草自然地形成上下空间的呼应，同时以浓淡墨擢点的树叶和以线条勾描的杂草，形成点与线在笔墨样式上的呼应。全图于简约中达到空而不虚的和谐之美。

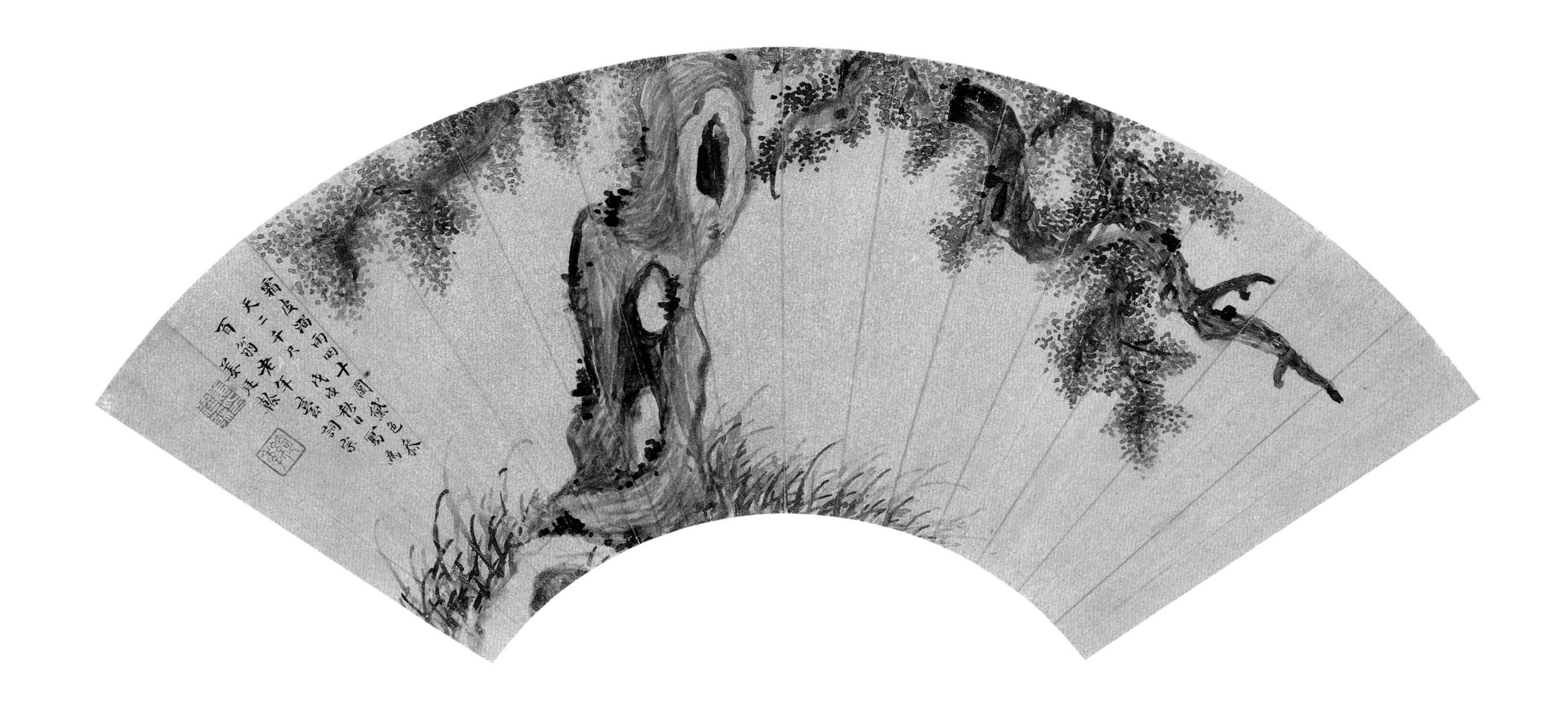

45. 墨梅图扇页

刘世儒绘　纸本 墨笔

纵 16.1 厘米　横 46.8 厘米

扇页有自题："雪湖。"钤"刘世儒印"朱文印。

刘世儒（生卒年不详，活动于 16 世纪），字继相，号雪湖，山阴（今浙江绍兴）人。工画梅，他在学仿元王冕梅花画法的基础上，又至名山幽谷，遍访梅花奇古之姿，因而其笔下的梅以妙于写生、具有神采为人称道。著《雪湖梅谱》。

图绘一株饱经风霜的古梅。作者将盘曲嶙峋的梅树主干居于扇面的中心，成为画作的主体。它左右是带有绽放梅花的花枝，墨色浓重的树干犹如指挥家，与不畏严寒的花朵共同吟唱一曲冬天里的赞歌。刘世儒从大自然中汲取画梅的创作灵感，其笔下的梅不仅富有生机，而且构图以奇巧取胜。

46. 花溪游鸭图扇页

陈遵绘　纸本 设色

纵 17.8 厘米　横 53.8 厘米

扇页有自题："陈遵。" 钤 "陈遵" 白文印。

陈遵（生卒年不详，活动于 16 世纪末），字汝循，浙江嘉兴人，寓居吴县（今江苏苏州）。擅绘花鸟，运笔工细，设色清丽，有"吴门画派"之风。

图绘秋天池塘一隅。构图左实右虚，岸上各色野花竞相绽放，一派繁茂昌盛的景象。水塘内闲鸭结伴浮游，一派怡情逍遥的景致。"繁"与"简"在视觉上形成鲜明的对比。同时，作者巧妙地将图中鸭子停止划水的"游动"表现成浮在水面上的"静"，阳光下花草的"平静生长"，通过其勃勃生机表现成欣欣向荣的"动"，"动"与"静"形成反向的对比，增强了画作的趣味。陈遵擅长绘笔墨写实的花鸟，此图中的花草及鸭子的造型重在写意，尤其是鸭子，没有具象的刻画，只是以白粉一点表示身形，红色一抹以示嘴部，笔墨简约到极致，展现了陈遵写意画亦不失生动的风貌。

47. 山水图扇页

宋懋晋绘　金笺 设色

纵 16.7 厘米　横 54.8 厘米

扇页有自题:“壬子春日写似求仲老先生，宋懋晋。”钤“明之”朱文印。“壬子”是明万历四十年（1612 年）。

宋懋晋（生卒年不详，活动于 17 世纪），字明之，松江（今属上海）人。工画山水，受业于宋旭，推崇李成、关仝及范宽山水。其笔墨苍健润泽，意境幽静清远，绘林麓山峦，颇有气势。他与赵左齐名，受到董其昌赏识，对沈士充诸人绘画有较深的影响，是“松江派”代表画家。

此图刻画的题材不是宋氏最擅长表现的崇山峻岭，而是初春时节各种树木的生命状态：有的枯木槎枒交错，有的新枝吐绿，有的则已枝繁叶茂。由此可见作者对树木有着细致的观察，并且能够娴熟地运用笔墨表现树木的枯华之貌。扇页的正中绘一茅屋，内坐一人，他悠然闲坐的状态，正是作者所要表达的画作主题，这种反映文人野逸情怀的画作在晚明极为普遍，沈士允、赵左等人多有创作。全图工写结合，既有“吴门画派”的文人遗韵，又有“松江画派”松秀明丽的格调，较宋氏通常笔墨浑厚的画法，别具风貌。

48. 柳溪钓艇图扇页

吴彬绘　金笺 设色

纵 17.7 厘米　横 50 厘米

扇页有自题："一叶扁舟泛五湖，鸱夷妙策实吞吴。黄金铸像今何在，美我重模此画图。吴文中。"钤"文中子"朱文印、"吴彬之印"白文印。

吴彬（生卒年不详，活动于 17 世纪初），字文中，号枝隐庵主、枝庵发僧，莆田（今属福建）人，流寓金陵（今属江苏南京）。工画人物、佛像，造型诡怪古朴，独具一格。绘山水，以自然为师，取景生动，山石多变形奇特，迥异前人。明万历年间他以画家身份供奉内廷，官工部主事，其画作受到了万历皇帝明神宗的赞赏和贮藏，外传者甚少。

图绘树木茂密成荫、水草随风摇曳的江南湖景。明朱谋垔《画史会要》称吴彬"善山水，布置绝不摹古，皆对真景描写。"此作正是一幅带有真实情节的写生图。图中的扁舟横水而行，打破了传统山水画舟与水间"随波逐流"的表现格局，给人耳目一新的美感。图中人物、树木、山石的造型平实，没有特别的夸张变形，因此，该图从笔墨上推断应是吴彬早年尚未形成自身特色的画作。

49. 芦艇笛唱图扇页

程嘉燧绘　金笺 设色

纵 16.5 厘米　横 51.2 厘米

扇页有自题："崇祯己卯八月，为远公词兄画，孟阳。"钤"孟阳"朱文印。"己卯"是明崇祯十二年(1639 年),程嘉燧时年 75 岁。

程嘉燧（1565～1643 年），字孟阳，号松园、偈庵,晚年皈依佛门,释名海能。休宁（今安徽休宁）人。初寓武陵（今杭州），后侨居嘉定（今上海市），晚居虞山（今江苏常熟）。能书善画，亦工诗文。其山水宗法元人倪瓒、黄公望，笔墨清劲疏秀。一生矜重其画，不轻易点染。与董其昌、邵弥、张学曾等合称"画中九友",又与唐时升、李流芳、娄坚合称"嘉定四先生"。著有《松园浪淘集》。

图绘高士乘篷船在芦塘行进之景。此图运用大片空白表现水天一色和辽阔的水域，给人以开阔的视野。远处山丘以细净而枯淡的笔墨勾染，颇得黄公望笔意。图中高士悠然吹笛的形象给画卷平添了几分浪漫的情趣，也表现出画家清雅高逸的情怀。

50. 秋游赏月图扇页

程嘉燧绘　金笺 设色

纵 16.6 厘米　横 51.3 厘米

扇页有自题：“庚辰七月晦，孟阳作。”钤“孟阳”方印。“庚辰”是明崇祯十三年（1640 年），作者时年 76 岁。

本作又名《柴门送客图》，是幅气韵清和的小品画。绘明月高悬的晴朗夜，高士乘舟离岸，友人倚柴门相送的情景。此图虽然树木笔笔松散，枝叶交待不清，人物形象简约概括，不拘泥于细节，但是，作者画意不画形，于逸笔草草中画出了孤寂萧淡的意境。全图行笔劲峭，具有程嘉燧晚年的绘画风格。

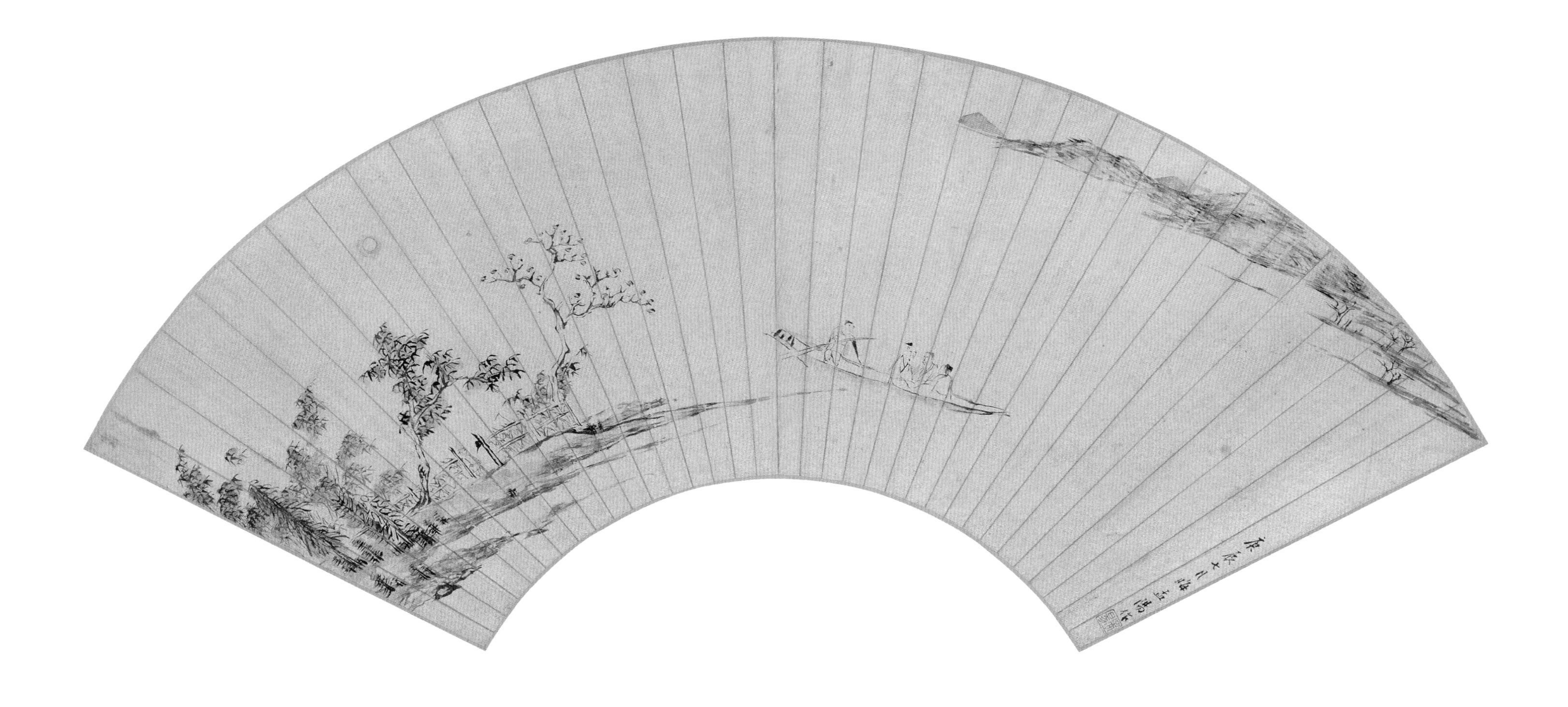

51. 桃源洞天图扇页

袁尚统绘　金笺 设色

纵 16.5 厘米　横 52.5 厘米

扇页有自题：“桃源洞天。丙子秋日写于竹深处。袁尚统。”钤“袁尚统印”、“叔明氏”白文印二方。“丙子”是明崇祯九年(1636 年)，袁尚统时年 67 岁。

袁尚统（1570～？），字叔明，吴县（今江苏苏州）人。擅绘山水、人物，虽然笔墨技巧相近于文人画，但是迥异于文人画家笔墨秀雅的审美情趣，多表现江南民俗中的世态百相，其颇为野放的画风在晚明画坛中独树一帜。

此图根据东晋陶渊明《桃花源记》中的情节，绘“林尽水源，便得一山，山有小口，仿佛若有光。便舍船，从口入。初极狭，才通人。复行数十步，豁然开朗。土地平旷，屋舍俨然，有良田美池桑竹之属……”的美景。全图用笔劲峭，景色奇险，设色清丽，其所呈现的静谧祥和意境，成功地表达了桃花源乃是人间仙境的创作主题。

52. 兰花图扇页

陈元素绘　金笺 墨笔

纵 17.7 厘米　横 53.7 厘米

扇页有自题：“拟杯当晓起，呵镜可微寒。隔箔山樱熟，褰帷桂烛残。书长为报晚，梦好更寻难。景响输双蝶，偏过旧畹兰。己未清和既望戏为启扬仁兄并书。陈元素。”钤“元素”朱文印。“己未”是明万历四十七年（1619 年）。

陈元素（生卒年不详，活动于 17 世纪初），字古白、孝平、金刚，号素翁、处廓先生等，长洲（今江苏苏州）人。神宗万历三十四年（1606 年）应乡试不第。工诗文书画，尤善绘兰，笔墨于疏放中具力沉之气，是“吴门画派”中重要的画兰名家。著《古今名将传》、《南牖日笺》。

图绘一丛无根兰，旁录唐李商隐《晓起》五律诗。偃仰的兰花为兰叶所掩，花与叶间顾盼呼应，以意到笔不到的内在神韵相连，达到形散神聚的境地。作者画兰的水平被公认在同时代的绘兰名家王榖祥、周天球之上。

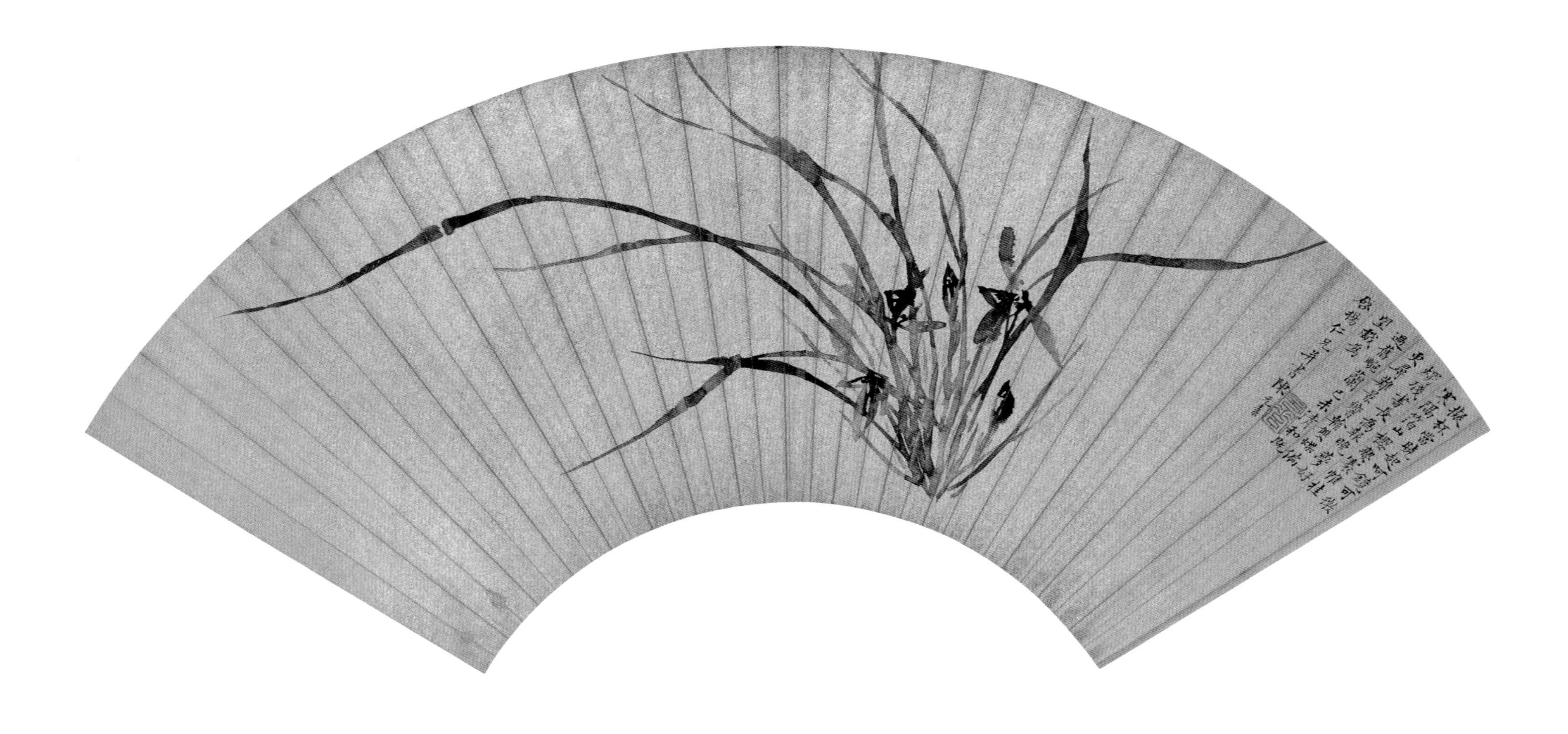

53. 问道图扇页

崔子忠绘　金笺 设色

纵 20.8 厘米　横 60.2 厘米

扇页有自题：“崔子忠。”钤“子忠”朱文印。

崔子忠（？～1644 年），初名丹，字开予，改名子忠，字道母，号北海、青蚓（一作青引）。北海（山东省莱阳市）人，移居顺天（即北京）。为人孤高，自甘清贫，李自成攻克北京后，绝食死。擅绘人物、山水、花鸟，尤以取材于佛画及传说故事的人物画见长。其笔墨高古，画风标新立异迥于前人，董其昌评崔子忠：“其人、文、画，皆非近世所见。”与同时代在南方活动的陈洪绶合称“南陈北崔”。

图绘一年轻男子正向老者作揖行礼，老者则举手指点的场景，因此，本幅又名《说法图》。崔子忠的人物画在师法顾恺之、陆探微、阎立本、吴道子等传统笔墨的基础上而有创新。他注重人物表情的刻画，在故宫博物院所藏其《洗象图》《藏云图》及《渔家图》中，都能准确地画出不同身份的人物特征。在此图中，他将年轻人问询时谦卑的表情和老者自信淡定的神态均表现得生动传神。衣纹用笔圆润细劲，线条颤掣，虬折多变，突出了衣料的柔软质感和随风飘起的动势。树木的枝叶，以双线勾边填色，用笔工细，富装饰性，是崔子忠人物画的代表作。

54. 山水图扇页

李流芳绘　金笺 墨笔

纵 18.5 厘米　横 55.3 厘米

扇页有自题："丁卯早春，为九万词兄作，李流芳。"钤"李流芳印"白文印。"丁卯"是明天启七年（1627 年），作者时年 53 岁。

李流芳（1575～1629 年），字长蘅，又字茂宰，号檀园、香海、慎娱居士、六浮道人等。歙县（今属安徽）人，侨居嘉定（今属上海市）。明万历三十四年（1606 年）举人，闻宦官魏忠贤专权，排斥异己，遂绝意仕途，专心诗文书画创作。他擅画山水，学仿元倪瓒、吴镇、黄公望诸家笔墨，又能对景写生，尝绘西湖景，别有意趣。其画作以笔墨苍劲清标为人赞誉，时与王时敏、王鉴、董其昌等并称"画中九友"。又与归昌世、王志坚并称"三才子"，与唐时升、娄坚、程嘉燧合称"嘉定四先生"。

此扇面构图是由近至远的平远法，笔法疏淡秀简，从中既可见追仿倪瓒高逸的画风，又可见他对倪氏画法的变格。作者在仿倪氏笔墨之余，亦注重创新，这正是他"自谓稍存笔墨之性，不复寄人篱壁"，学古而不成古画学思想的体现。他的这种思想在当时崇古之风盛行的画坛颇为难得。

55. 仿米云山图扇页

李流芳绘 金笺 墨笔

纵 17.7 厘米 横 54 厘米

扇页有自题：“丁卯秋日仿米家山，李流芳。”钤“李流芳印”白文印。

此图与故宫藏李氏《山水图》扇绘于同一年，即明天启七年（1627 年）。它是李氏晚年仿宋代米芾、米友仁“墨戏法”绘制的烟雨变幻山水图。扇面中的远山运用“落茄皴”（即“米点皴”）点染，饱含水分的墨笔横点，点点相叠，积染成形，不仅增强了画面的水气迷蒙感，丰富了山峦的远近层次，同时也表现出群山于苍茫中的雄伟气势。近景的树木亦以墨气淋漓的卧笔横点，灵动的墨点既各自独立又彼此联结成片，它们以不求形似的笔墨，表现出的是“数树新开翠影齐，倚风情态被春迷”诗意。

56. 山水图扇页

赵左绘　金笺 设色

纵 14.8 厘米　横 43.9 厘米

扇页有自题："甲辰秋日，华亭赵左。"钤"赵左之印"白文印。"甲辰"是明万历三十二年（1604 年）。

赵左（？～1636 年后），字文度，华亭（今上海松江）人。工诗文，擅绘山水，初师宋旭，兼得倪瓒、黄公望遗意，与董其昌是翰墨挚友，是董氏绘画重要的代笔人之一。其笔墨苍劲秀逸，设色雅淡清丽，偶用焦墨枯笔，以皴染精工见长。对叶有年、吴振、释常莹、陈廉等人影响较大，是"松江画派"领袖。

图绘柳溪放舟的江南水乡。构图以平远为主，通过层层推进的手法，表现远中近景，首先由近景的芦苇推出狭长的河道，涟漪的水面上一高士驾舟独行，悠然自得，点出逍遥游的主题。河道向后又推出沙坡土地，其上生长有一排排茂密的柳树，柳叶相互交叠，一派兴盛的景致。柳树之后可见房舍及远山，表明此处是可居可游的高士遁隐之地。全图景物虽多，却错落有致，疏密有序，显示出作者对空间层次的掌控力。是赵左成熟期的山水画代表作。

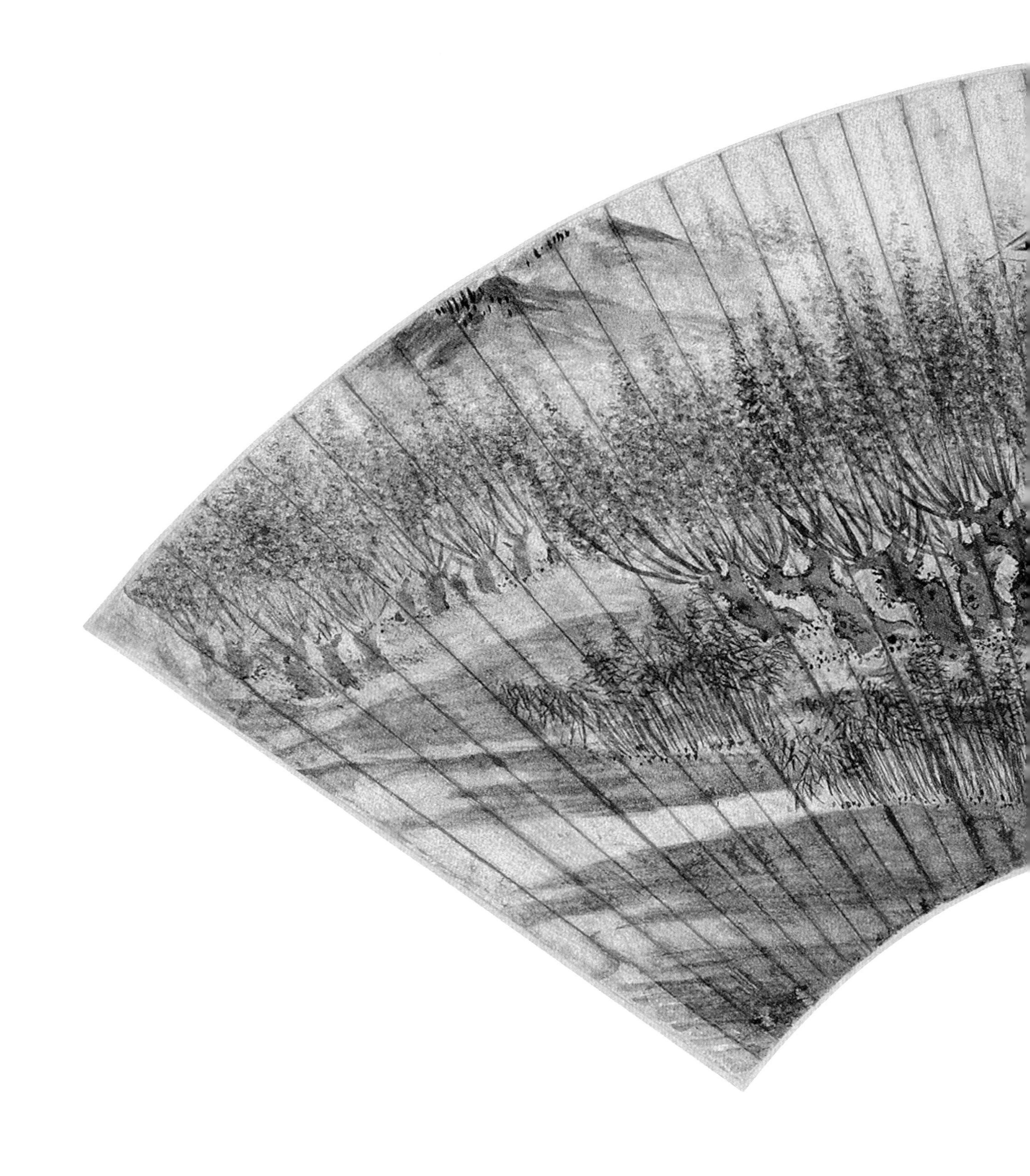

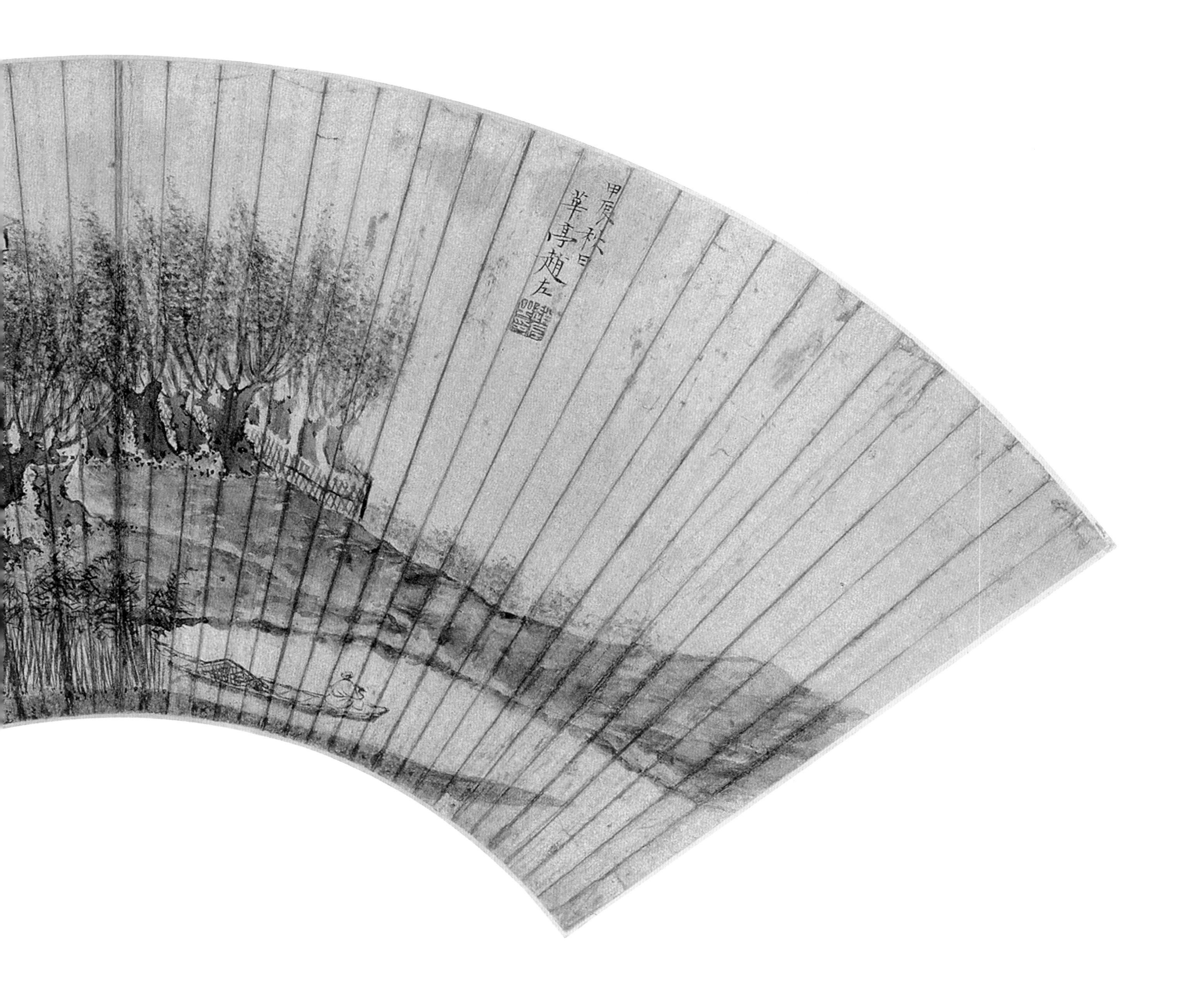
甲辰秋日
華亭趙左

57. 阊关舟阻图扇页

张宏绘　金笺 设色

纵 16.7 厘米　横 51.6 厘米

扇页有自题："丁亥中秋，寓蒋氏酿花斋，同友游虎丘，返棹阊关，舟阻不前。偶有便面作此图以记其兴。呵呵。张宏时年七十有一。"钤"张宏"、"君度氏"白文印二方。"丁亥"是清顺治四年（1647 年），张宏时年 71 岁。

张宏（1577～？），字君度，号鹤涧，吴县（今江苏苏州）人。是位擅写意人物和山水见长的画家。他创作出的一系列现实主义风俗画，有助于后人对 17 世纪江南民俗生活史的研究。其山水画，注重写生，在宗法沈周的基础上，能够再师造化，遂自成运笔劲峭、墨色润泽、构图繁复的画风，是晚明苏州地区著名画家之一。

此图是张宏在游玩虎丘归来，目睹阊门关前小舟争抢进城的情景，在"便面（即扇面）"上随手图成的风俗画。全图采用俯视下观的构图法，将繁杂的舟船，以及房舍、树木、关口等统统纳入图画中，充分显示出其细致的观察力和娴熟的笔墨表现功力。

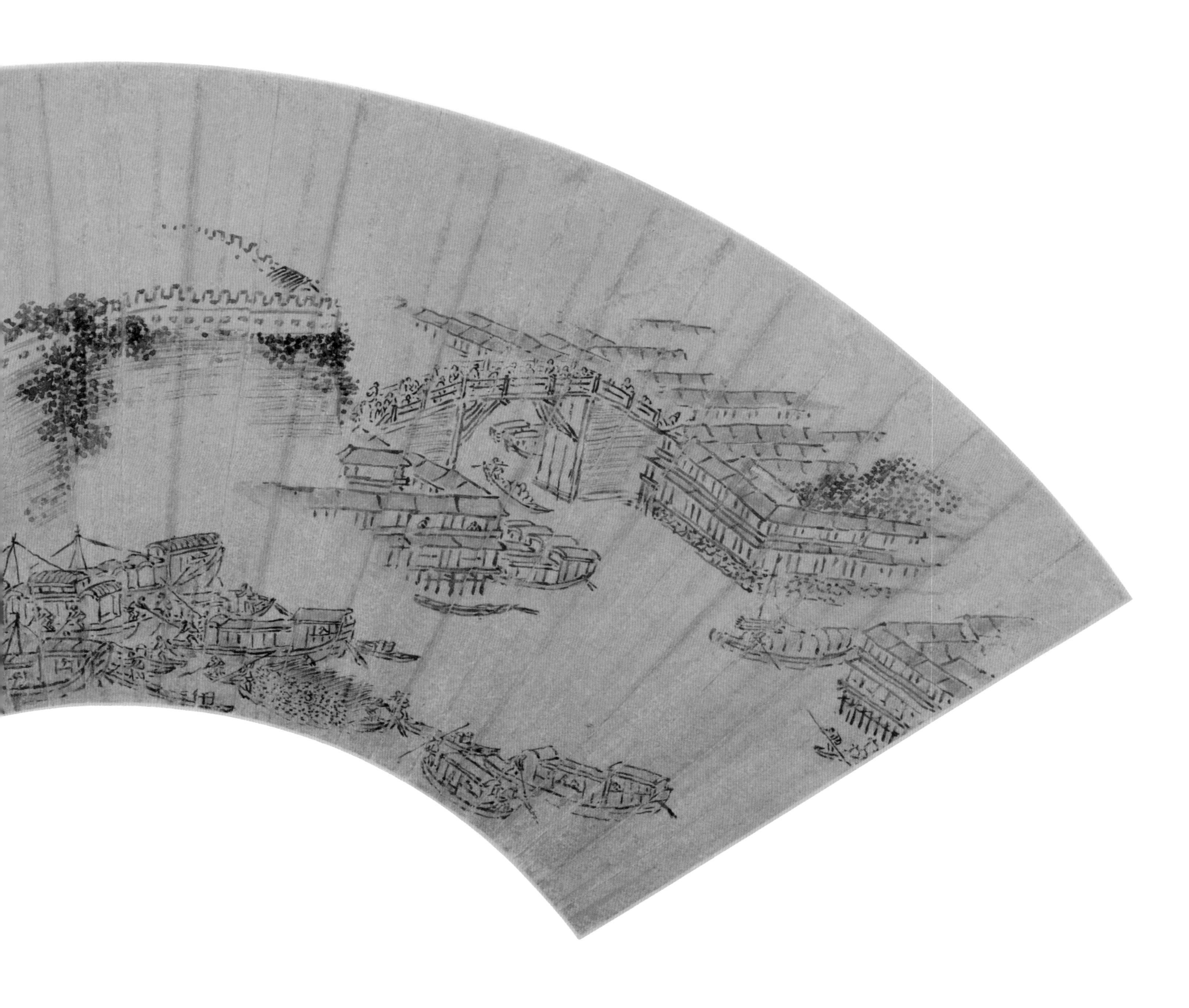

58. 农夫打架图扇页

张宏绘　金笺 设色

纵 16.2 厘米　横 51 厘米

扇页有自题：“丁亥秋日写于横塘草阁，张宏。”钤白文印二方“张宏”、“君度氏”。“丁亥”是顺治四年（1647 年），张宏时年 71 岁。

此图与张宏《阊关舟阻图》扇绘于同一年。图绘酷暑时节，农夫在稻田边争斗的场景。折扇自明代普遍流行以来，除了具有驱暑纳凉的日常功用外，更是书画艺术的表现载体，是人们出入怀袖的雅物，因此，以社会最底层的农夫为表现主题的画扇，实属罕见。此图人物众多，情节非常生动，有斗殴的双方、劝架者、观望者，还有受场面刺激狂吠不已的黑犬。彼此通过“争斗”的主线有机串联，组成一个相互呼应的整体。图中各类人物虽为小写意，造型不够精确，但是人物形象的刻画高度精练，神态表现得细致入微，因此，是一幅难得的带有戏剧性情节的画作。

丁亥秋日寫于
横塘草閣
張宏

59. 竹鹑图扇页

朱统鍷绘　金笺 设色

纵 18 厘米　横 52.2 厘米

扇页有自题："己巳又四月写，朱统鍷。"钤"朱统鍷印"、"嗣宗父"白文印二方。"己巳"是明崇祯二年（1629 年）。

朱统鍷（生卒年不详，活动于 17 世纪初），号嗣宗，江西南昌人，明皇族宗室。工画，擅绘花鸟。

图绘在翠竹成荫、野菊盛开的时节，一只鹌鹑突然发现蚂蚱的瞬间。情节描绘生动，图中鹌鹑不敢移身，正强扭着脖子，紧盯着前行的蚂蚱。作者在创作上巧妙地运用了对比的艺术手法，鹌鹑因发现美食蚂蚱而兴奋，蚂蚱因没发现天敌鹌鹑而淡定，由野菊、翠竹营造出的静寂空间，反衬出即将发生追杀的残酷气氛。弱肉强食是自然界最基本的生物规律，也是画家笔下最生动的表现题材，本作与宋人李迪《枫鹰雉鸡图》有着异曲同工之妙。创作方面，作者继承了北宋崔白以来的院体花鸟传统，以小写意绘制物象，造型准确生动，可见作者虽然是业余画家，但是有着敏锐的洞察力和写生传神的笔墨功力。

己巳又四月寫
朱統鍨

60. 青山红树图扇页

蓝瑛绘　金笺 设色

纵 17.3 厘米　横 49.5 厘米

扇页有自题："壬辰花朝拟范长寿法，为九一辞盟画，蓝瑛。"钤"田叔"朱文印。"壬辰"是清顺治九年(1652 年)，蓝瑛时年 68 岁。

蓝瑛(1585～1666 年)，字田叔，号蜨叟、石头陀等，钱塘(今浙江杭州)人。善画山水、人物、花鸟等，力追唐宋元古法，并能融会贯通，自成落笔纵横奇古、气象崚嶒一格，对明末及清初画坛有很大影响。从其学者有刘度、蓝深、冯湜等，合称"武林画派"。

此图以"没骨重彩法"绘青山、红树、白云等景致。作者自言拟唐没骨山水画的肇始者张僧繇的弟子范长寿(生卒年不详，活动于公元 7 世纪，曾任武骑尉职。画学梁张僧繇，善绘道释、人物、山水树石等各类题材，能涉笔成趣，各尽其妙)法，表明他对传统绘画的继承与重视。图中冷暖色调和谐，石青、石绿、朱砂等矿物质颜料的运用独具特色，于争妍斗丽中营造出明媚亮丽的秋景，富有强烈的视觉冲击感染力，显示出作者对色彩的敏感识别力与巧妙搭配的能力。蓝瑛是继董其昌之后创作"没骨山水"别有新意的画家。

61. 雪山行旅图扇页

刘度绘　金笺 设色

纵 18.2 厘米　横 51.2 厘米

扇页有自题："仿王右丞画法。甲申长至刘度，惟时词兄正。"钤"叔宪"白文印。"甲申"是明崇祯十七年（1644 年）。

刘度（生卒年不详，活动于 17 世纪），字叔宪，一字叔献，钱塘（今浙江杭州）人。蓝瑛弟子，宗法宋元人名迹，工界画楼台，多作青绿山水，画风细密精妍。

图绘寒冬雪景。作者通过在树木弯如蟹爪的梢尖上敷白粉、山石留白少皴擦的技法，成功地表现出白雪压枝和山舞银蛇的雪意。作品构图别具匠心，以起伏峻拔的山峦作为前景树木的衬景，其平整硬朗的石壁，既提亮了整个画面，又令画面不因树的枝杈过于细碎而显得零乱。

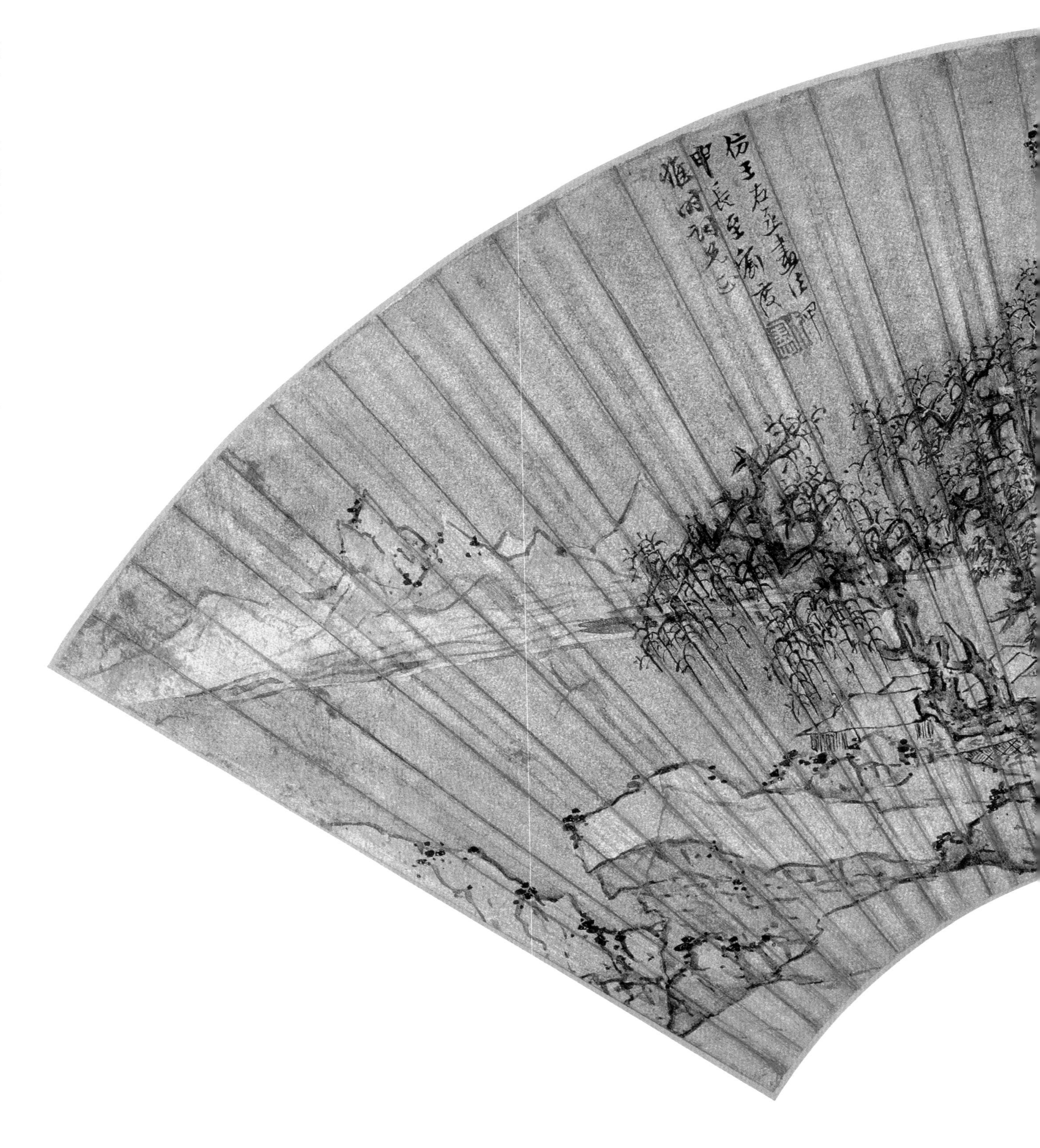

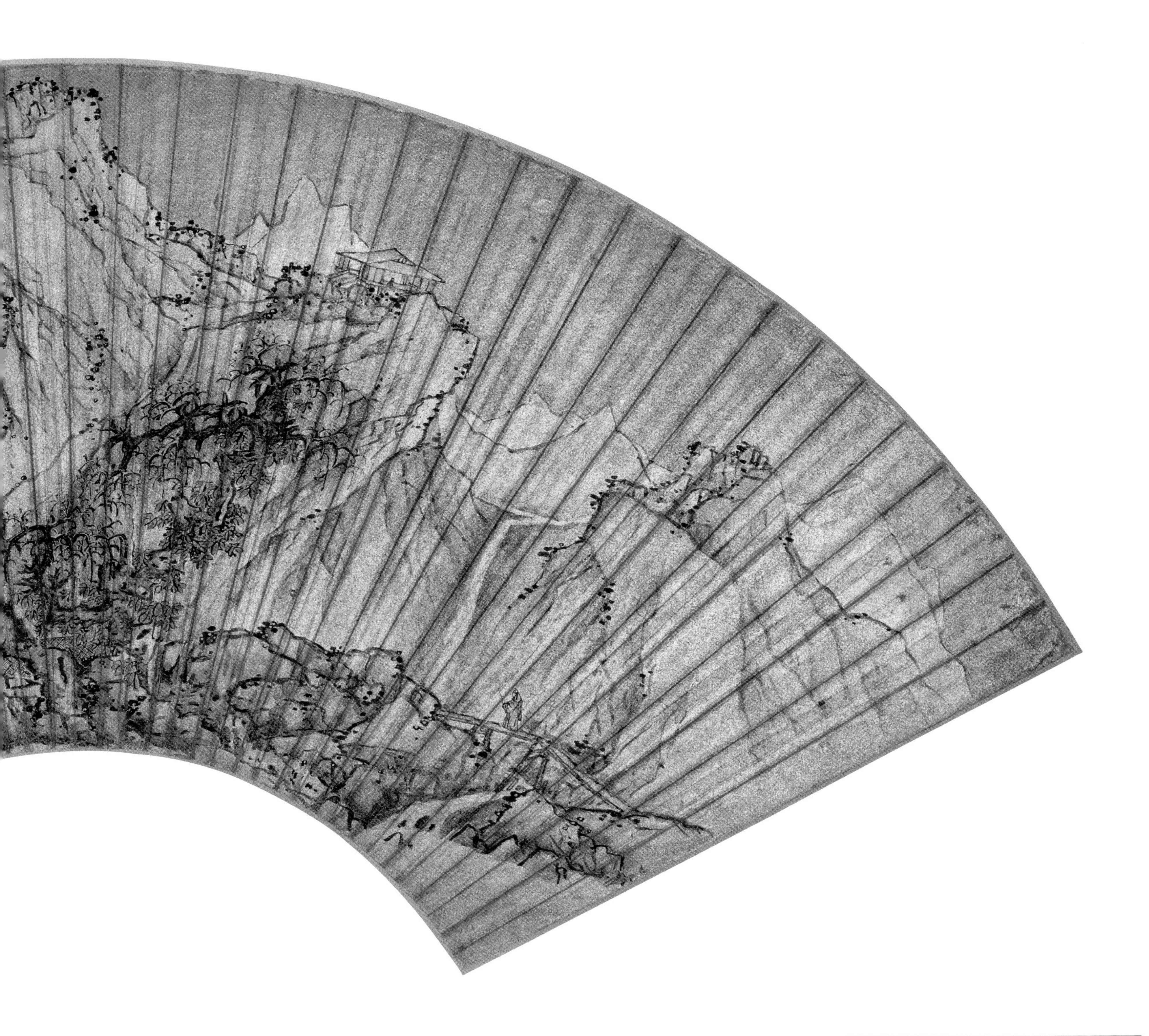

62. 危楼秋雁图扇页

沈士充绘　纸本 设色

纵 17.1 厘米　横 47.3 厘米

扇页有自题："危楼日暮人千里，歌枕风秋雁一声。沈士充。"钤"子居"朱文印。

沈士充（生卒年不详，活动于 17 世纪），字子居，华亭（今上海市松江）人。山水画学宋懋晋，兼师赵左，画风或墨气氤润，或苍秀雄阔，是"松江派"主要画家，董其昌重要代笔人之一。

此图是作者依宋人"危楼秋雁"诗意所作。图绘隐居者在简陋的茅舍内独身而坐，目视大雁渐行渐远的情景。"危楼"与"秋雁"具有悲凉之意，作者借绘此图表现了他在晚明动荡时局下无奈的心境。

此扇面在构图上匠心独运，虚实相映，互为比衬。茅舍、远山尽为雾霭云气所遮，其形态隐约可见，呈"虚景"。图中绘有二树，一是在山坡上为秋风所染的红叶树，一是在山脚下体态多姿的松树，二者不仅位置有高低之分，而且色调有冷暖之别，古板的造型带有一定的装饰性。它们以其"实"将"虚景"烘托得饶有诗意。

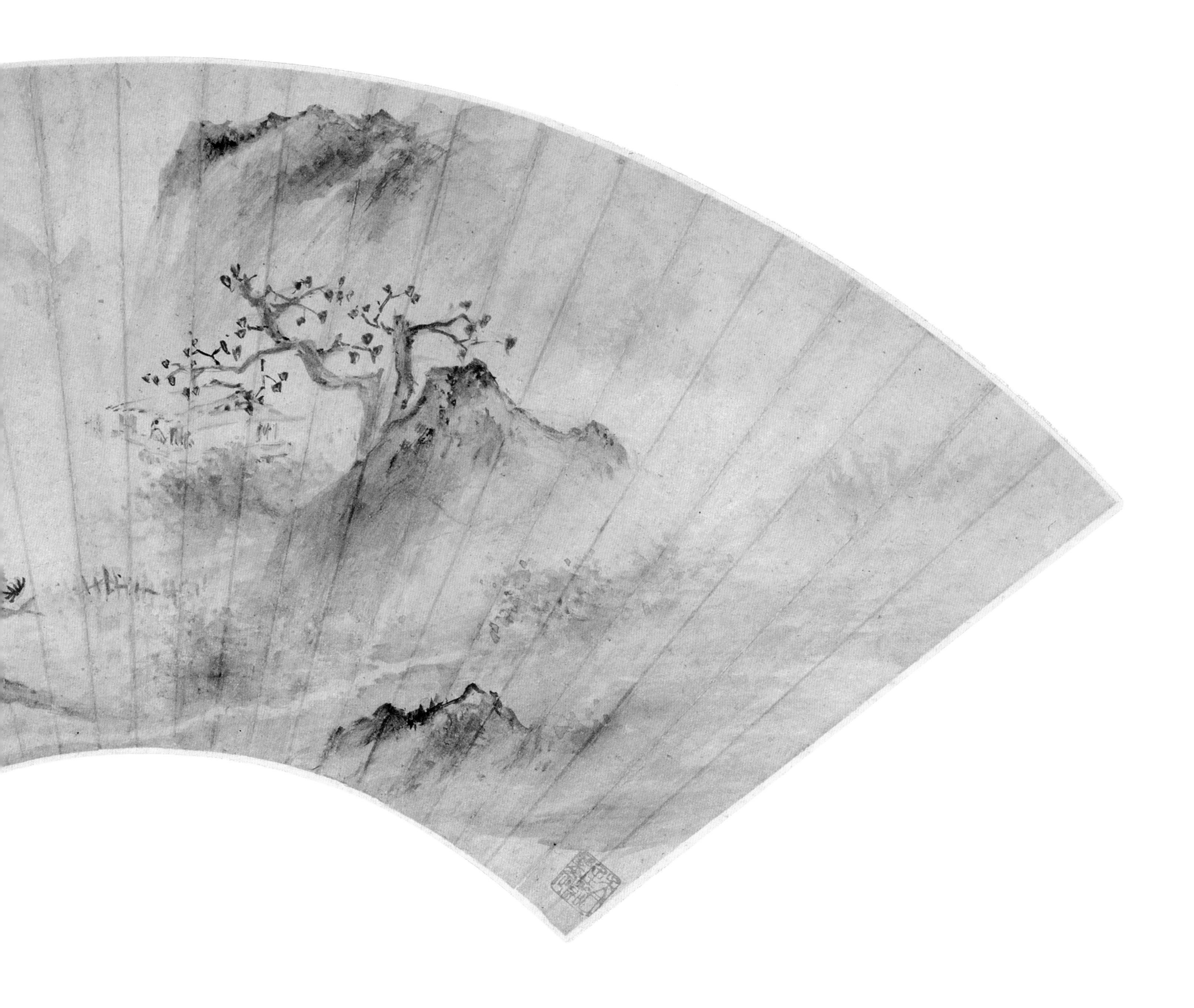

63. 品古图扇页

郑重绘　金笺 设色

纵 15.8 厘米　横 47.5 厘米

扇页有自题："丙戌冬十一月写似裕翁先生词宗，郑重。"钤"千里"朱文印。"丙戌"是明万历十四年（1586 年）。

郑重（生卒年不详，活动于 16 世纪），字千里、重生，号天都懒人、风道人，歙县（今属安徽）人，流寓金陵（今江苏南京）。其山水，取法宋元，笔墨精研。其佛像画，被丁观鹏推为赵伯驹（字千里）后身，故也取字千里。万历四十二年（1614 年），他以绘《法海图》进呈皇室，受到神宗万历皇帝赏识，复传旨画御书莲径（华严径）引首，并赐帛赐宴。又以为东宫画扇得到高度赞赏，遂被拟授待诏中翰职位。他性喜闲居品茶、品古作画，力辞不就，退隐黄山。

图绘在湖石、柏树相衬的环境下，仨位高士围坐在石案处，品鉴古物的雅集活动。作者将扇面分作三个部分，巧妙地展现了高士们鉴古的过程，扇面的左侧是正在观赏图册的高士，扇面的右侧是等待鉴赏的青铜器，连接左右两侧的是抱着器物或者书画轴前来递送的侍者。高士们的鉴古在如此清幽的环境中进行，体现了他们对传统文化的敬仰。

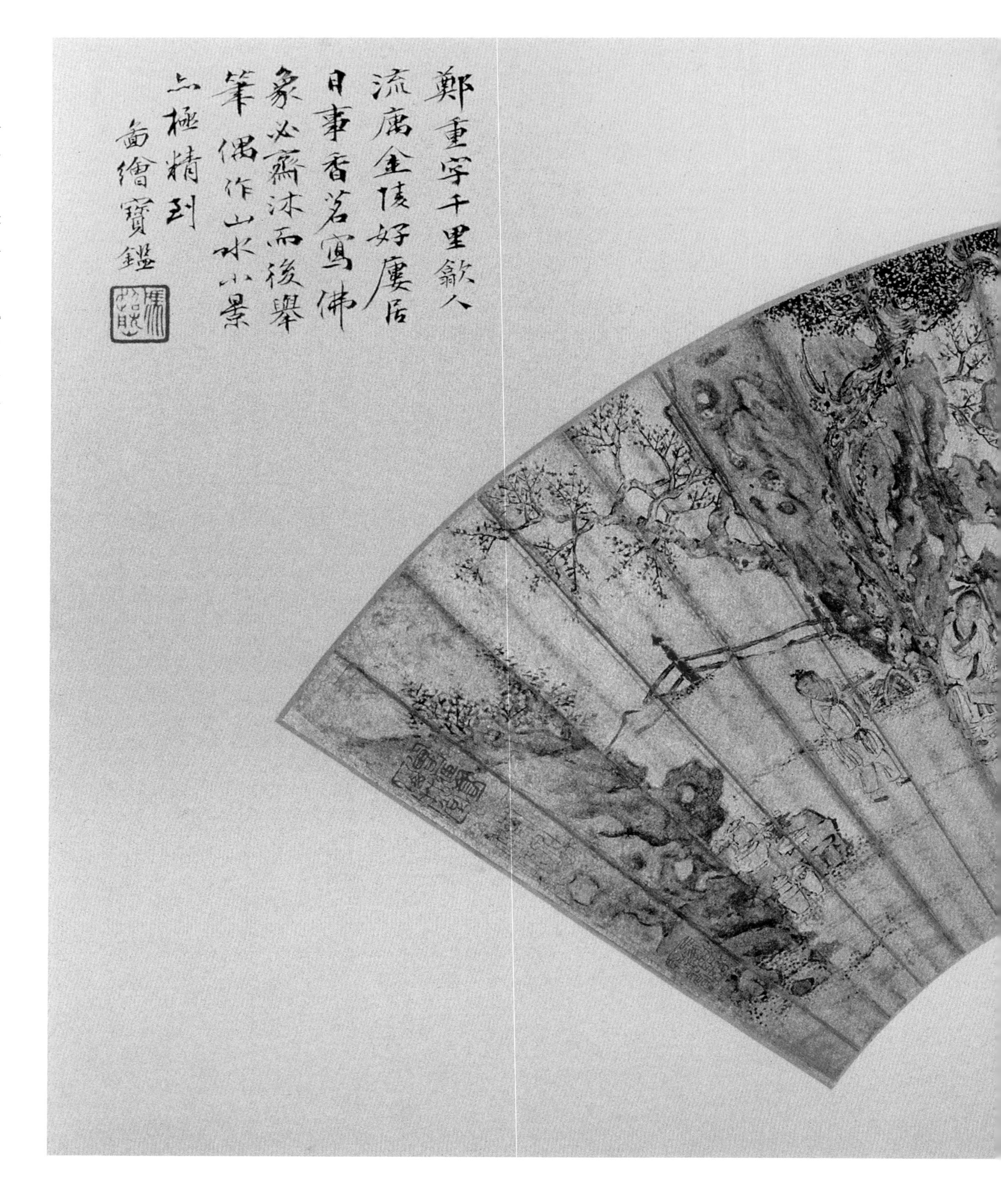

64. 山水图扇页

姚允在绘　金笺 设色

纵 16.3 厘米　横 51.1 厘米

扇页有自题："辛巳二月画，姚允在。"钤"允在"、"简叔"白文印二方。"辛巳"是明万历九年（1581 年）。

姚允在（生卒年不详，活动于 16 世纪末），字简叔，会稽（今浙江绍兴）人。善绘山水，学仿五代荆浩、关仝，以绘全景式山水取势，笔墨遒劲有力，在晚明独树一帜。他亦工人物，以精工秀丽见称。他自矜其画，因此，画作传世甚少。

图绘高山峻岭、草木华滋的怡人景观。突兀的山石先以墨线勾勒，后以粗笔短皴石面，石体坚凝，富有质感。点景的树木，高低错落，刻画精细，它们既充实了画面，也以直拔的造型，增加了山体上升的峭峻之势。此图是作者仿荆、关用笔绘制的北方山水代表作。

65. 仿古山水图扇页

王铎绘　金笺 墨笔

纵 17 厘米　横 51.9 厘米

扇页有自题："己丑四月朔日偶尔仿古不用近派，写于燕台。王铎。"钤"王铎之印"白文印。"己丑"是清顺治六年（1649 年），王铎时年 59 岁。

王铎（1591～1652 年），字觉斯，号嵩樵、烟潭渔叟等，孟津（今属河南）人。明天启二年（1622 年）进士，累官礼部尚书、东阁大学士。工真、行、草体书法，笔力雄劲，结体险峻，享有书名。兼能山水，宗法五代荆浩、关仝，以笔墨高古浑雄见称。刻有《拟山园帖》、《琅华馆帖》。

图绘林木茂密的层峦叠嶂。构图繁复，然而密处却可通风，散乱中饶有法度，具有北宋山水的浑厚气势。用笔如作者的书法点画一样，线条长短、轻重、欹正，富有律动变化，给人以"飞腾跳踯"的美感。

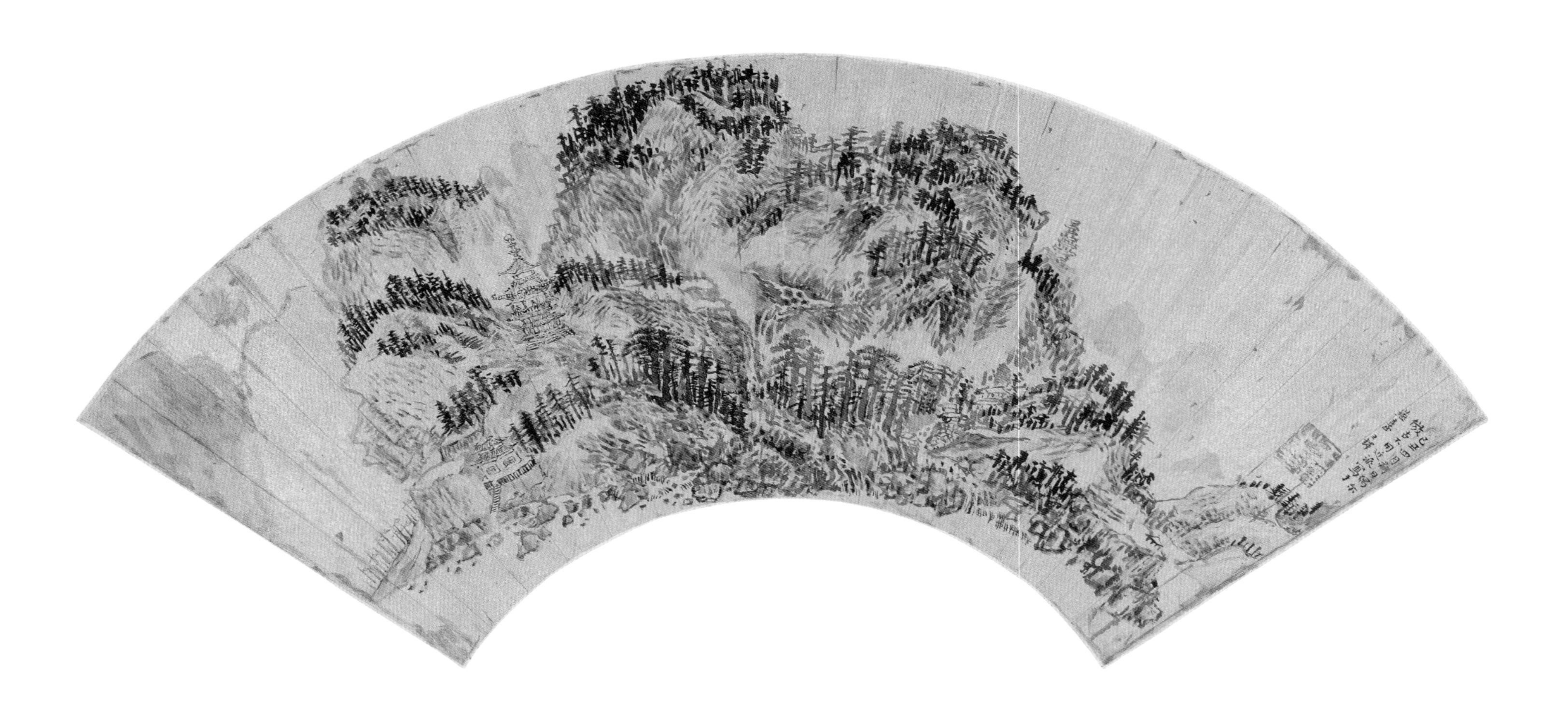

66. 山水图扇页

王铎绘　纸本 墨笔

纵 17 厘米　横 50.5 厘米

扇页有自题："吾家摩诘画初见于许氏次，同三弟见于金鱼池别墅。己丑偶仿之，意象相跂正，不在形似也。庚寅九月夜识于龙松堂中，兄铎六旬笔。"钤"王铎之印"白文印。"己丑"是清顺治六年（1649 年），王铎时年 59 岁。"庚寅"是顺治七年（1650 年），王铎时年 60 岁。

图绘白雪覆盖下的高山峻岭。作者绘雪景采取的是外罩染地法，通过对天空和水面的淡墨渲染，烘托出山峦的雪色银装。山体上绘有一片片寒林，深黑、粗短的枝杈在积雪的映衬下，苍老枯硬，也为寂静的冰雪世界增添些许生趣。王铎不是职业的画家，能如此贴切地表现出雪意，实属难得。

67. 山水图扇页

王时敏绘　金笺 设色

纵 17.2 厘米　横 52 厘米

扇页有自题："乙丑小春画，王时敏。"钤"王时敏印"白文印。"乙丑"是明天启五年（1625 年），王时敏时年 34 岁。画幅上有陈继儒题："窗前树已红，梦笼山犹绿。眉公。"

王时敏（1592～1680 年），字逊之，号烟客、西庐老人等，太仓（今属江苏省）人。明万历朝内阁首辅王锡爵孙，翰林王衡子，明末以荫仕至太常寺少卿，故亦称"王奉常"。工诗文书画，富于收藏。擅绘山水，受董其昌影响较大，精研宋元名迹，摹古不遗余力，尤其对元黄公望山水更是刻意追摹、临仿不怠。他在深究传统画法的基础上，形成墨法醇厚、笔致松秀、意境清幽的画风。与王鉴、王翚、王原祁合称"清初四王"。

此图以润笔为主，受董其昌影响，画仿元人黄公望，水墨与浅绛同染。构图疏密得当，并有高山与低谷的错落之分，于盈实中不失空灵。山峦多以长线条皴擦，侧锋卧笔点苔，既得石体坚硬的质感，又不失山峦葱郁深秀的气韵，代表了王时敏早期山水画的典型风貌。

陈继儒（1558～1639 年），字仲醇，号眉公。工诗善文，通绘画，颇受时任内阁要臣的王锡爵赏识。王时敏自幼学画，深受陈氏影响。

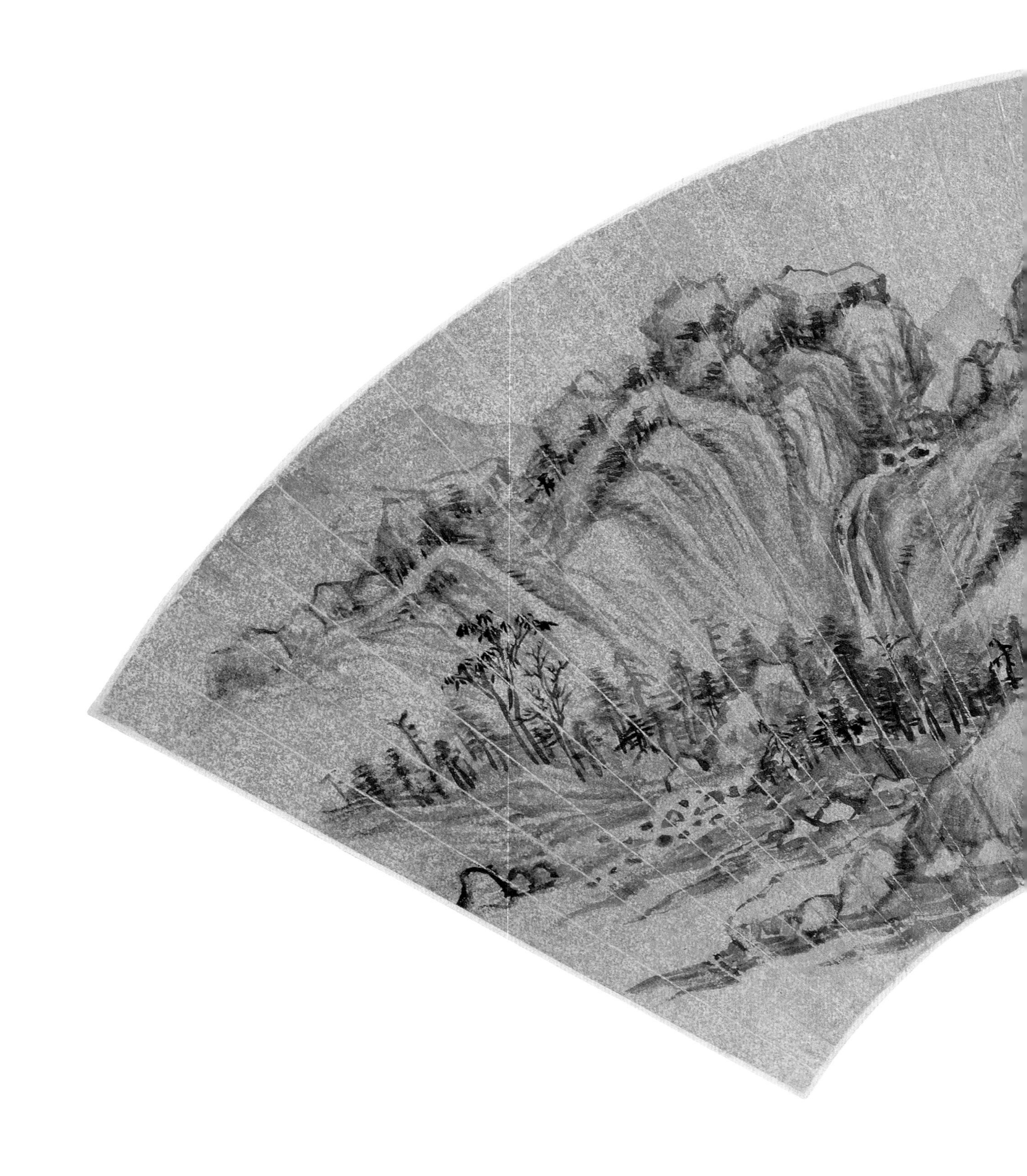

乙丑小春畫
王時敏

68. 仿黄公望山水图扇页

王时敏绘　纸本 设色

纵 15.1 厘米　横 49.3 厘米

扇页有自题："戊戌初秋仿黄子久笔，王时敏。"钤"王时敏印"白文印。"戊戌"是清顺治十五年（1658 年），王时敏时年 67 岁。

此扇页构图以视野开阔的平远法取势，远处重峦叠嶂，草木成荫；近景平湖碧水，蜿蜒曲折。在水际、山坳处有房舍、板桥穿插隐现，俨然世外仙境，深得文人画淡泊怡情的审美意趣。图中景致繁多，但疏密呼应，高低错落，于严谨的章法中不失隽永的形式趣味，是王时敏晚年仿黄公望的代表作。

69. 山水图扇页

王时敏绘　纸本 设色

纵 15.7 厘米　横 49.8 厘米

扇页有自题：“乙巳小春散翁老先生连举两雄，写此称庆。弟王时敏。”钤“王时敏印”白文印。“乙巳”是清康熙四年（1665 年），王时敏时年 74 岁。

由王时敏自题而知，此扇页是他祝友人“散翁老先生连举两雄”之禧所绘，因此，他在创作上颇为用心。图扇以全景式构图绘清溪谷涧，丛林茂树，一派繁荣昌盛的兴旺景象。其画法以黄公望为宗，兼取董源、巨然和王蒙诸家笔意，用笔细腻朴拙，设色清润淡雅，皴染分明，是作者晚年风格的代表作。

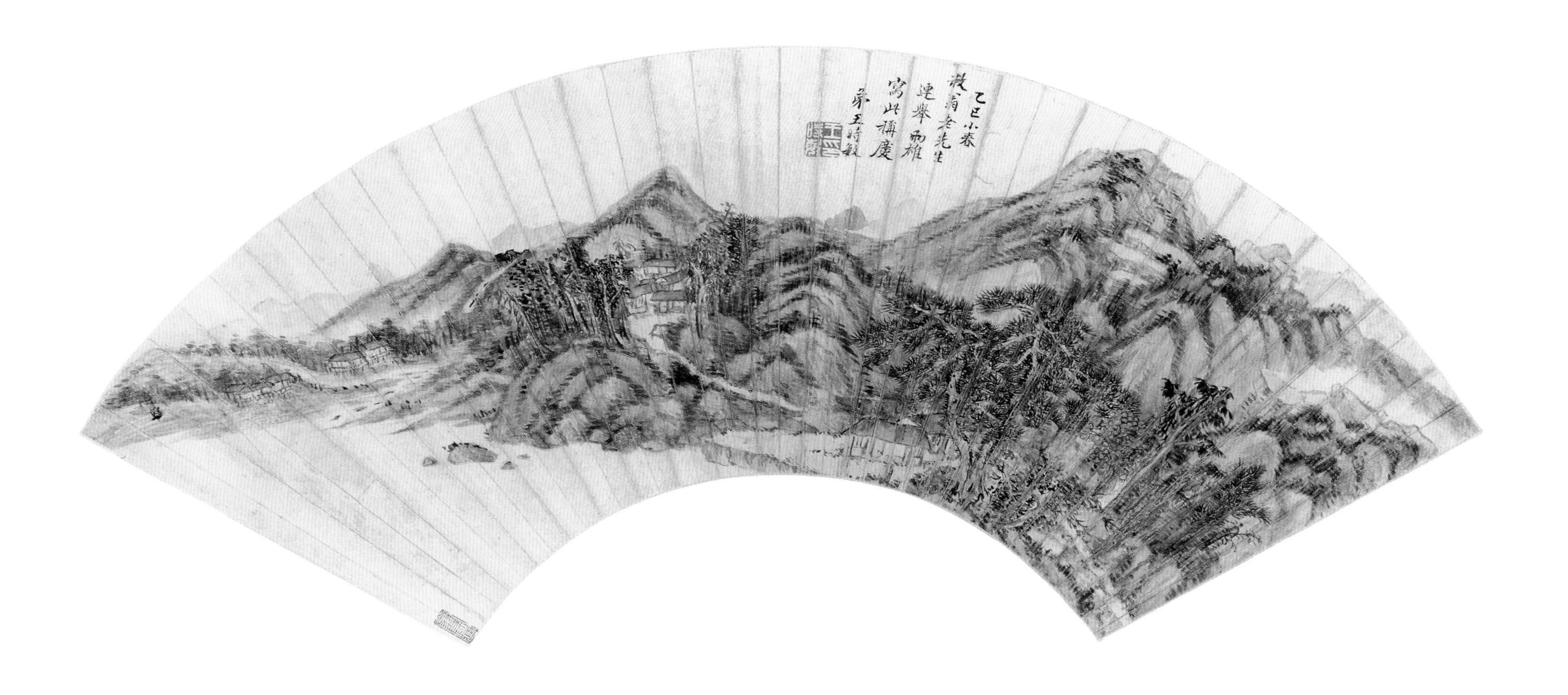

70. 松岩高士图扇页

邵弥绘　纸本 设色

纵 16.8 厘米　横 56 厘米

自题："颐堂无事，静坐焚香，作此松岩高士图以志兴。时壬午春二月也，邵弥。"钤"邵"、"僧"、"弥"朱白文联珠印。"壬午"是明崇祯十五年（1642 年），邵弥时年约 51 岁。

邵弥（约 1592～1642 年），字僧弥，号瓜畴，长洲（今江苏苏州）人。一生布衣，性迂癖不谐俗。工书画，善诗文。画仿宋元诸家，笔墨简括，格调高秀。与董其昌、程嘉燧、张学曾等合称"画中九友"。

图绘孤松垂萝，高士携琴坐于流云浮动的石台上，凝神远眺的景致。此图是邵弥逝世当年画给自己的"志兴"之作，表明了他淡泊高逸的心境，追求与自然山水为伍，以焚香抚琴为乐的生活情趣。全图笔墨劲秀，设色淡雅，代表了他晚年成熟期的风貌。

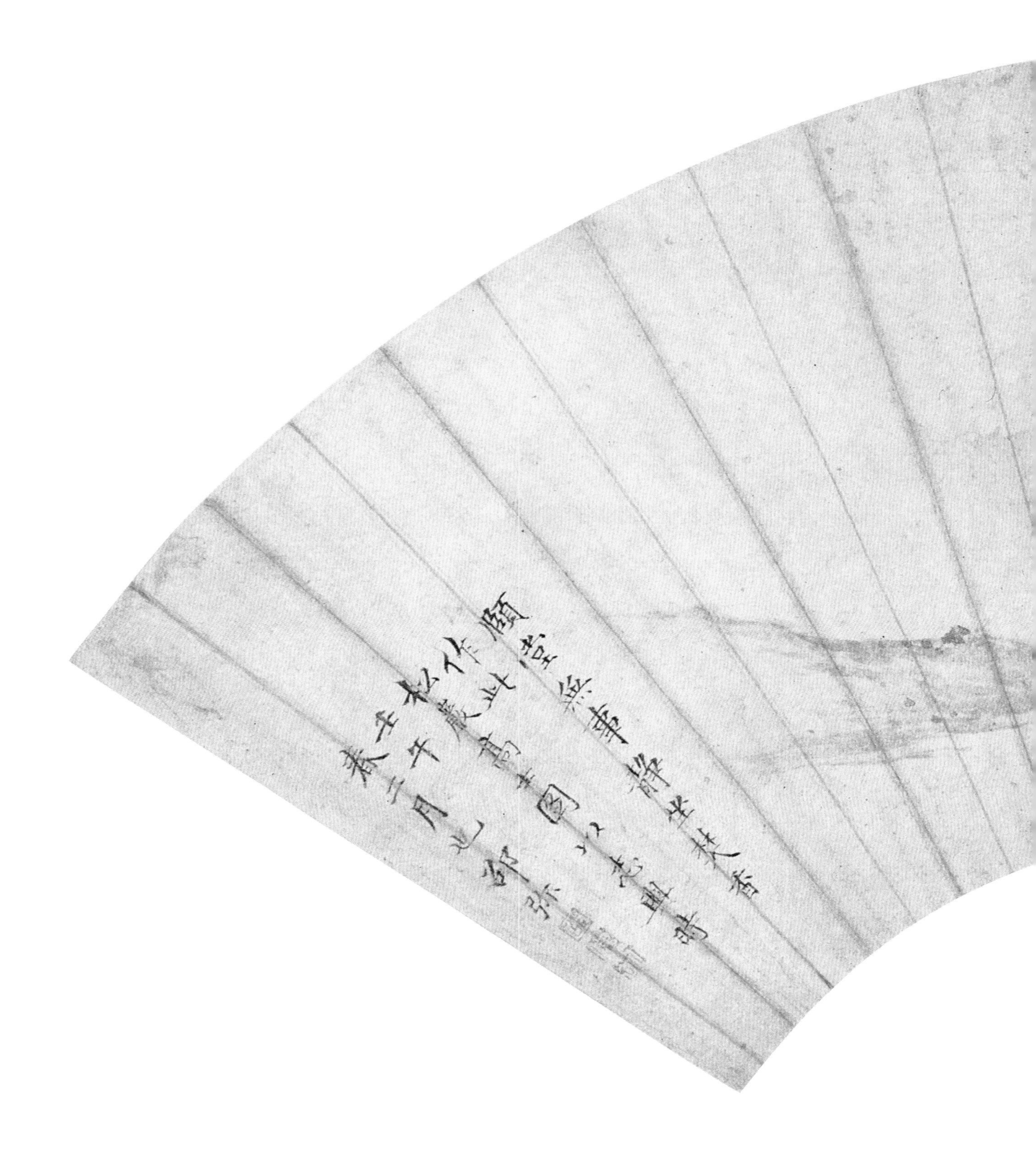

71. 花蝶图扇页

文俶绘　金笺 设色

纵 16.5 厘米　横 52.6 厘米

扇页有自题:“己巳夏文俶画。”钤“端”、“容”朱文联珠印。“己巳”是明崇祯二年(1629 年), 文俶时年 35 岁。

文俶 (1595～1634 年),字端容,长洲 (今江苏苏州) 人，文从简女。来自于有画学渊源的“文氏”世家，以文徵明、文彭、文嘉、文伯仁、文从简、文从昌等为首的画坛名家，为之营造了底蕴浓厚的艺术氛围。她自幼在“文家笔墨”的熏陶下，勤于画作，悉心摹写，终于不负家学，卓有成就。其笔下花草虫蝶勾染精细，笔意淳雅，富有生趣。姜绍书《无声诗史》称她“赋性聪颖，写花卉苞萼鲜泽，枝条荏苒，深得迎风浥露之态。溪花汀草，不可名状者，皆能缀其生趣。芳丛之侧，佐以文石，一种茜华娟秀之韵，溢于毫素，虽徐熙野逸，不是过也”。明末钱谦益则给予文俶更高的评价，言:“点染写生，自出新意，画家以为本朝独绝。”

此图以兼工带写的小写意法绘花蝶。笔法轻快疏秀，设色清丽蕴藉，将花卉枝条随风摇摆，婀娜之姿刻画得生动鲜活，令画面充满温馨而浪漫的诗意。

72. 兰石图扇页

文俶绘　金笺 设色

纵 17 厘米　横 52.2 厘米

扇页无自题，钤“端容”朱文方印、“文俶”白文印。

图绘兰石相伴的田园小景。此图应该是作者在对景写生的基础上，按自己的审美意趣提炼、概括而创作的。因而在构图上人工造作味虽很强，但兰石却表现得真实自然。文俶在设色上不求大红大绿强烈的色彩对比，而是注重冷暖色调的和谐搭配，追求的是以简胜繁、清新淡雅的娟秀之美，具有吴门文人画的特点。

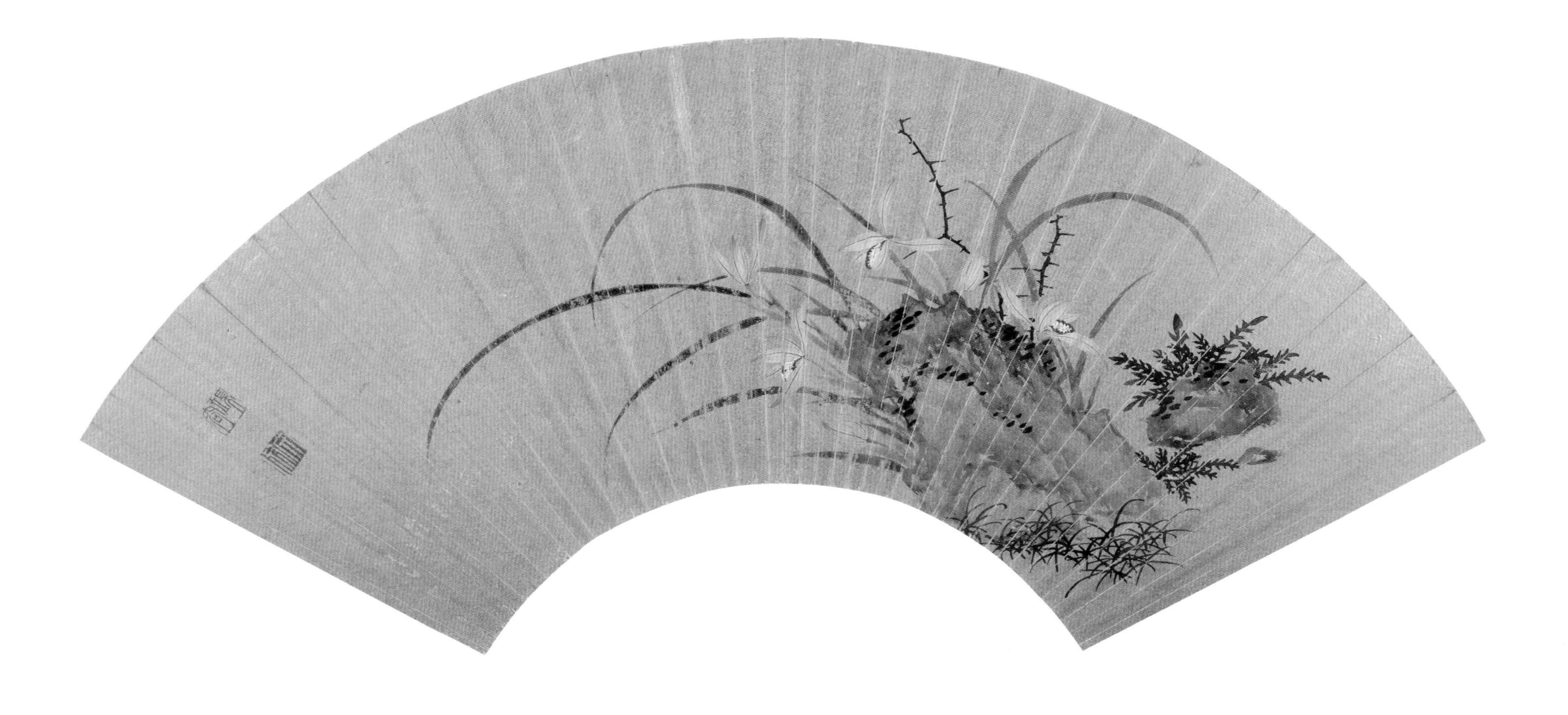

73. 天寒有鹤守梅花图扇页

项圣谟绘　纸本 设色

纵 20.1 厘米　横 54.2 厘米

扇页有自题：“天寒有鹤守梅花，句自苕社微诗。余在松陵赋十有二韵，尔瞻索图应之。辛卯正月，项圣谟。”钤“项氏孔彰”朱文印。“辛卯”是清顺治八年（1651 年），项圣谟时年 55 岁。

项圣谟（1597～1658 年），字孔彰，号易庵、胥山樵等，秀水（今浙江嘉兴）人。收藏家项元汴之孙。擅画山水，初学文徵明，远法宋人以及元代诸家，画风细密，秀逸雅致。兼工花木竹石和人物，尤擅画松，有“项松”之誉。著《朗云堂集》。

图绘在梅竹掩映的茅舍前，孤鹤不畏严寒，迎风而立的情景，形象地表现了“天寒有鹤守梅花”的诗意。梅以遇寒不败的品格，鹤以具有健康长寿的寓意，成为世人推崇的对象，宋代的林逋曾以梅为妻、鹤为子，相守一生。项氏借此图表明他作为明遗民，在清初腥风血雨的恶劣环境下，格律自守，不肯向清政府屈从的心迹。他这类画作还有著名的《大树风号图》轴。

天寒有鶴
守梅花
句自茗
社徵
詩余在
松陵
賦十有
二韻
爾瞻索
圖應
之辛卯
正月 項聖謨

74. 山水图扇页

黄应谌绘　金笺 设色

纵 17.5 厘米　横 45 厘米

扇页有自题："己酉中秋为河图年翁写，黄应谌。"钤"应""谌"朱文联珠印。"己酉"是清康熙八年(1669 年)，黄应谌时年约 73 岁。

黄应谌（约 1597～1676 年后），字敬一，号创庵，顺天（今北京）人。世居京师，擅长画人物、鬼神、婴孩等，傅染一遵古法。顺治中期被召入宫廷供奉，是重要的宫廷画家。

这是一幅带有生活情趣的画作，近景是高士静坐在草堂内品酒，水面上是渔民撒网的劳动场景，一静一动构成一幅生动的民俗风情图。

图中远峰仿宋人米氏云山画法，以浓墨点染山头，表现出云蒸霞蔚的深秀景致。中景和近景所绘物象较多，作者通过合理的穿插，将山石、树木、草阁以及渔舟等统一在清溪的转折延伸中。全图小写意笔墨具有"吴门画派"秀雅的遗风。

己酉中秋爲
河圖年翁寫
黃應諶

75. 人物图扇页

陈洪绶绘　金笺 墨笔

纵 16.5 厘米　横 52.2 厘米

扇页有自题："丙辰八月，子婿陈洪绶写寄槎菴翁岳父为寿。"钤"陈洪绶印"白文印。"丙辰"是明万历四十四年（1616 年），陈洪绶时年 19 岁。

陈洪绶（1598～1652 年），字章侯，号老莲、悔迟等，诸暨（今属浙江）人。聪颖机敏，仕途坎坷。工诗擅画，山水、人物、花鸟无一不精。其画初受同时期的蓝瑛影响，后广泛临学唐周昉、宋李公麟等古人笔意，并大胆突破创新。所作人物、花鸟形象古拙、变形，富于装饰情趣，是晚明变形主义绘画大家，与崔子忠合称"南陈北崔"。著《宝纶堂集》等。

此图是作者为自己的岳父来斯行（1567～1634 年，字道之，号槎菴）50 岁寿辰绘制的祝寿图。来氏曾任工部主事，一生狂放，博览群书，富有收藏。他对陈洪绶艺术修养和人生观的形成有着很大的影响，对陈洪绶后来结识众多上层人物及开阔眼界也有很大的帮助。图中行走于祥云间身着红袍的壮汉，当是来氏的化身。此图是作者早期工笔重彩人物画佳作，与同年所绘《九歌图》画风相近。陈洪绶早年人物画受宋李公麟影响最深，用笔圆中带方，人物多以游丝、铁线描勾画，气韵生动且富有情趣。

76. 秋江泛艇图扇页

陈洪绶绘　金笺 设色

纵 16.3 厘米　横 51.8 厘米

扇页有自题：“乙酉暮春为素中盟兄画，即请鉴。老莲洪绶。”钤“陈生”朱文印。“乙酉”是清顺治二年（1645 年），陈洪绶时年 48 岁。

此图通过木叶丹黄的秋天景色和人物悠闲划艇的活动，展现出宁静清逸的意境，给人以远离尘俗之感。清初期，陈洪绶面对明王朝为清人所灭，友人相继殉国的情境，深感亡国离乱之痛，产生了隐遁避世的情致。此图绘成后的第二年六月，他就在云门寺剃发为僧，改号“悔迟”、“悔僧”、“秃翁”，亦号“云门僧”、“迟和尚”等。图中山石、树木法自蓝瑛，多以中锋行笔，笔致粗犷，点染生动，于雄浑中见朴拙蕴藉，加强了画面的视觉效果。

77. 水仙竹石图扇页

陈洪绶绘　金笺 墨笔

纵 16.5 厘米　横 52.2 厘米

扇页有自题："庚寅孟冬，与张展老、荆丝老过公治道友天香邸中，斗酒之会画此，兵戈中得此良少。洪绶。"钤"章侯"朱文印。"庚寅"是清顺治七年（1650 年），陈洪绶时年 53 岁。

图绘水仙、翠竹与山石相伴的园林小景。石以侧锋勾线并作皴擦，笔力劲爽，显现出石材坚硬的质感，衬托出水仙及竹的娇柔之美。据自题而知，此图是作者与友人酒酣后趁醉所绘。由于作者晚年写意花卉技法已达至炉火纯青的地步，因此从构图到运笔施墨，一气呵成，守规守矩，毫不凌乱。

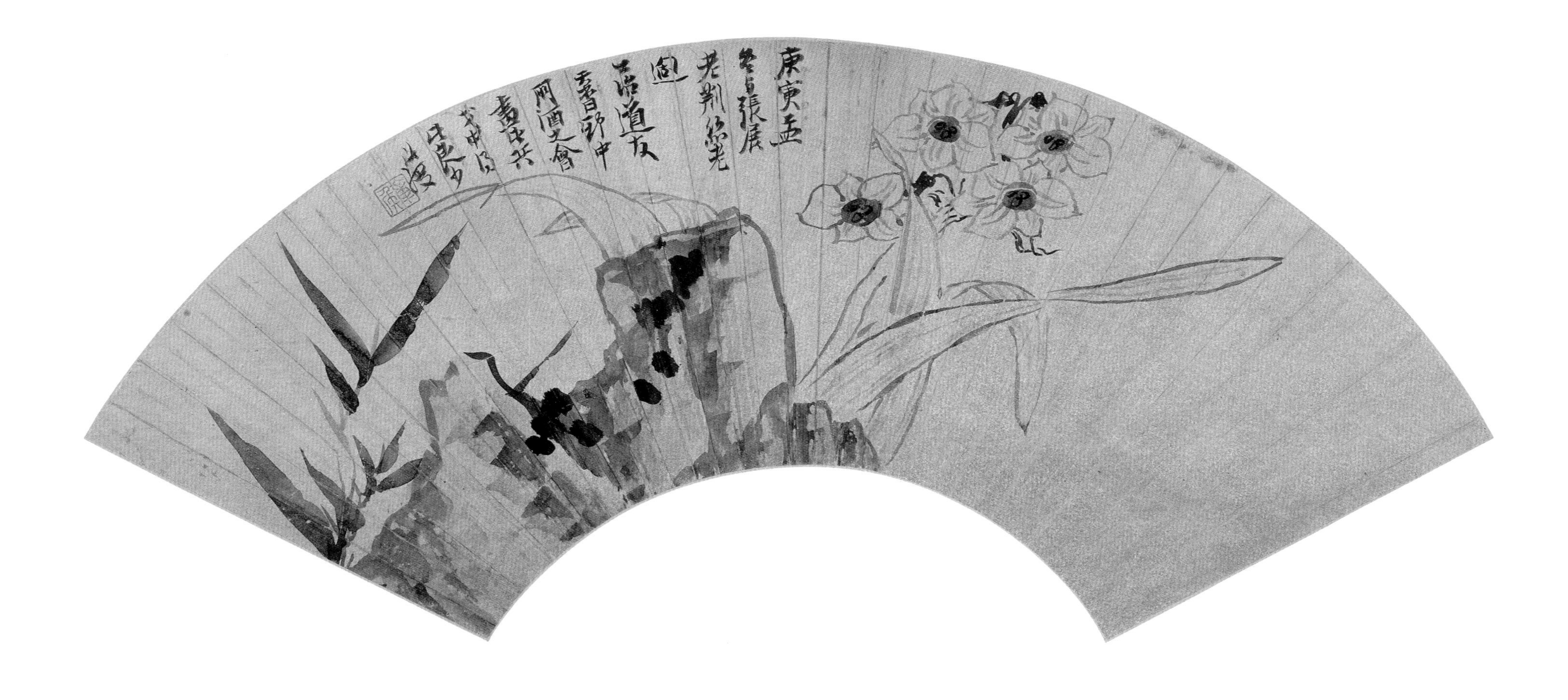

78. 梅石图扇页

陈洪绶绘　金笺 设色

纵 17.1 厘米　横 50.6 厘米

扇页有自题："秉之道盟兄属，洪绶画。"钤"章侯"朱文印。

图绘粗壮的梅树与湖石相佐的田园景致。构图简约平实，设色淡雅，用笔工整略带刻板，具有装饰性和笔意古雅的特点，属于陈氏艺术成熟期的花卉画代表作。

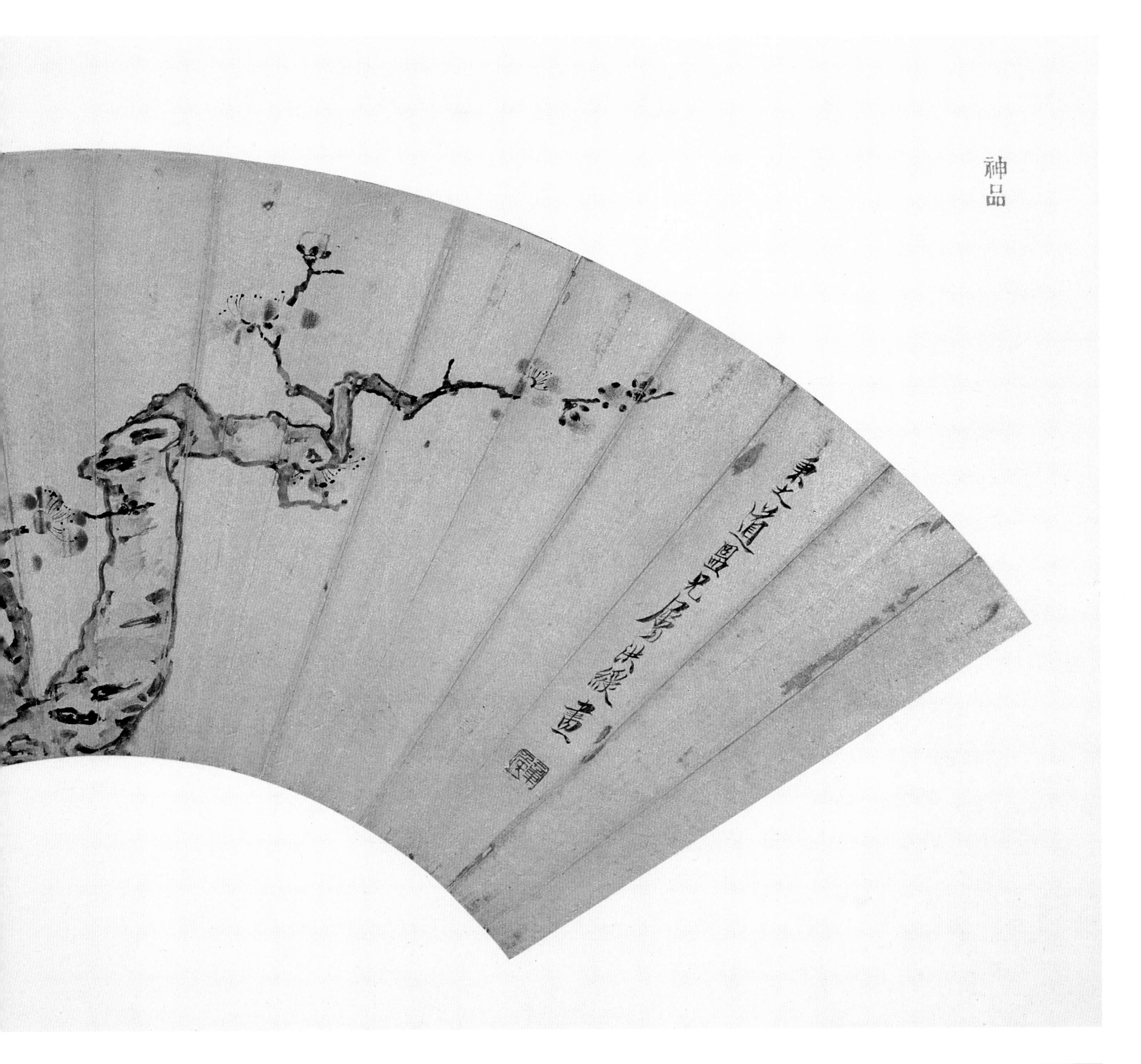

神品

79. 花石蝴蝶图扇页

陈洪绶绘　金笺 设色

纵 16.1 厘米　横 50.7 厘米

扇页有自题："洪绶写于玉兰客馆。"钤"章侯"朱文印。

图绘蝶恋花小景。作者在晕染上注重色彩的深浅变化，以及冷暖色的对比，色调间的净洁映衬。在线条勾描上，注重以不同的线条表现不同品质的物象。花儿的勾线细劲而流畅，以此表现其秀媚之姿。石头的勾线多为方硬用笔，随意顿、折，以此表现其坚实稳重的品质。作者在创作时具有严谨认真的态度以及丰富多样的表现手法，从而令本是小品画的扇页不失端庄大气的审美张力。

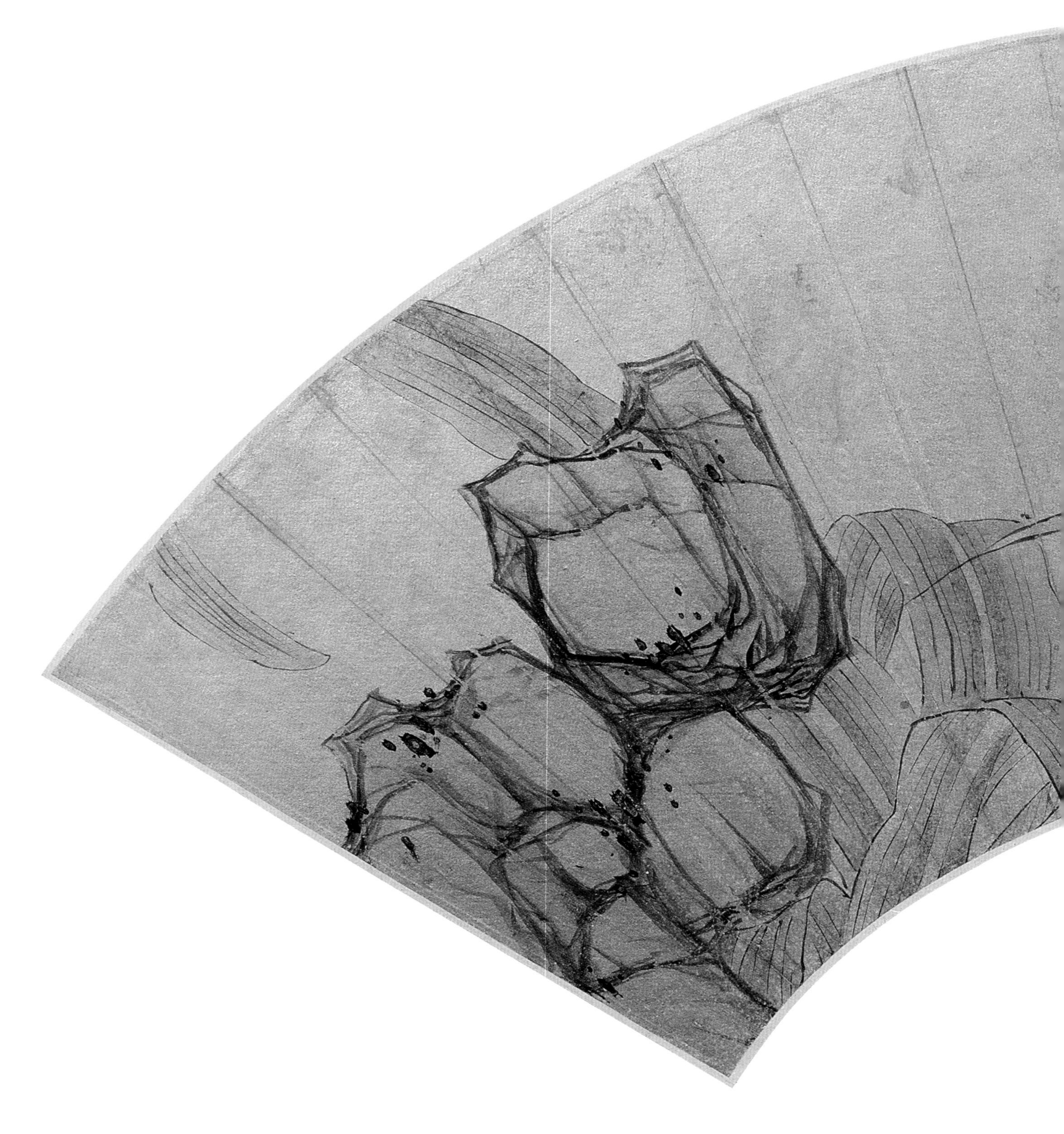

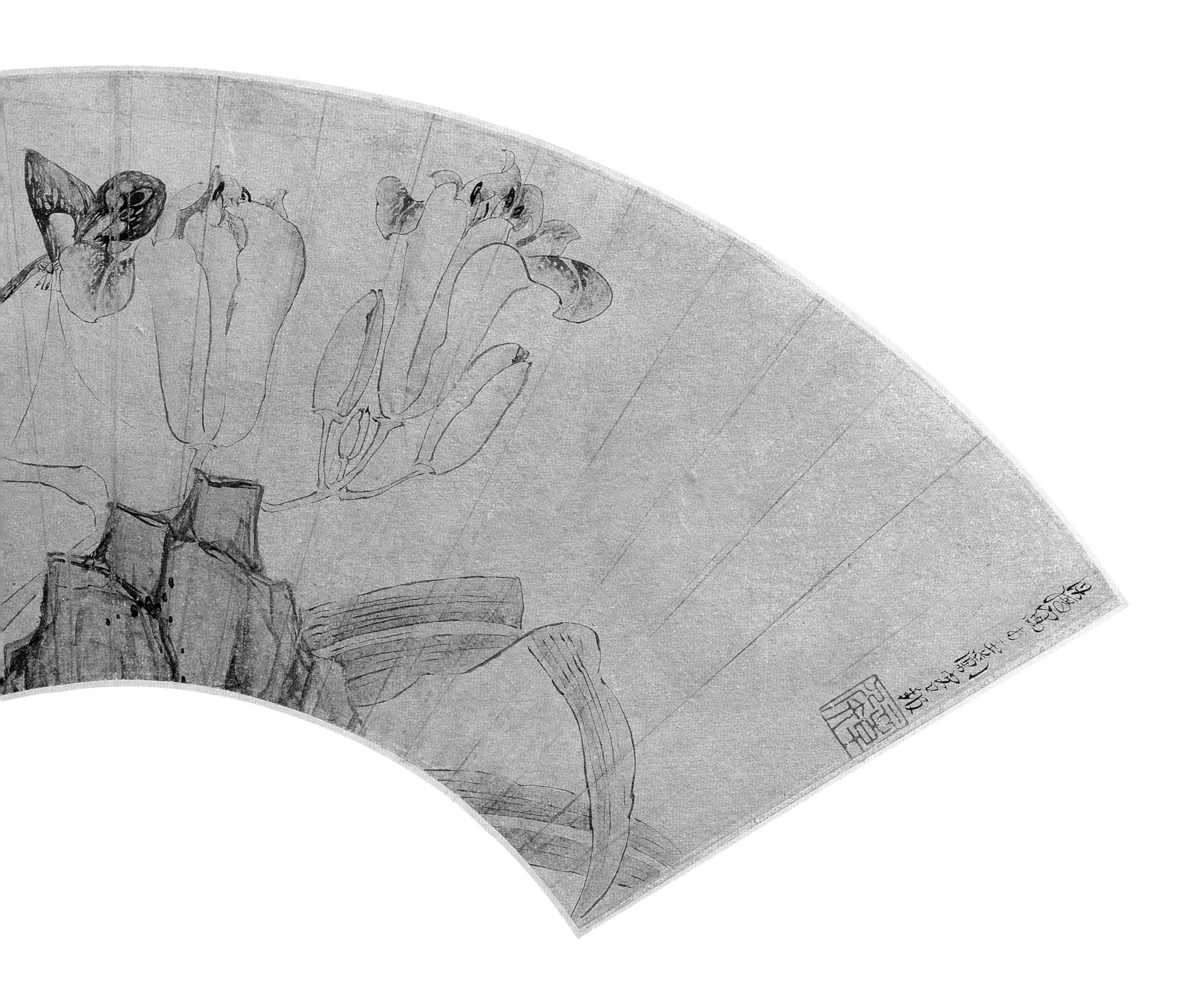

80. 花溪渔隐图扇页

王鉴绘　纸本 设色

纵 15.7 厘米　横 51.8 厘米

扇页有自题："甲午年余同张约菴使君联舟南下，蓬窗相对，出惠崇《花溪渔乐图》见示。日夕展玩，不欲去手。今使君墓木已拱，不知此画流落何处。余犹倦息人间，追思往昔，不禁人琴之感。偶仿其遗意，以志不忘故旧耳。染香遗老鉴。"钤"鉴"朱文印。"甲午"是清顺治十一年（1654 年），王鉴时年 57 岁。

王鉴（1598～1677 年），字玄照、圆照，号湘碧，太仓（今属江苏省）人。因明末曾官廉州知府，故亦称"王廉州"。擅绘山水，宗法五代董源及以黄公望为首的"元四家"，画风清润，具有古意，与王时敏、王翚、王原祁合称"清初四王"。著《染香庵集》、《染香庵画跋》。

王鉴在画坛上以崇古、摹古、仿古著称，他四处寻访传世佳构，只要过目的名作，往往要摹写或者背临下来，毫不倦怠。据自题而知，此图扇是王鉴对友人张约菴（名学曾）所藏北宋惠崇《花溪渔乐图》的背临。图画桃花盛开时节，渔家行舟打鱼的情景。其疏朗简约的构图、秀逸婉转的线条、清新淡雅的设色，均展现出惠崇所绘江南春景的情趣，亦可见王鉴深厚的仿古功力。对此，王时敏对王鉴摹古画本领之高佩服至极，曰："今廉州继起，董(源)、巨(然)、李(成)、范(宽)、三赵(赵令穰、赵伯驹、赵孟頫)以暨元四大家皆得心印，非但肖其形似，兼能抉其精髓，不待标记，即知为某家笔意。"(《王奉常书画题跋》)

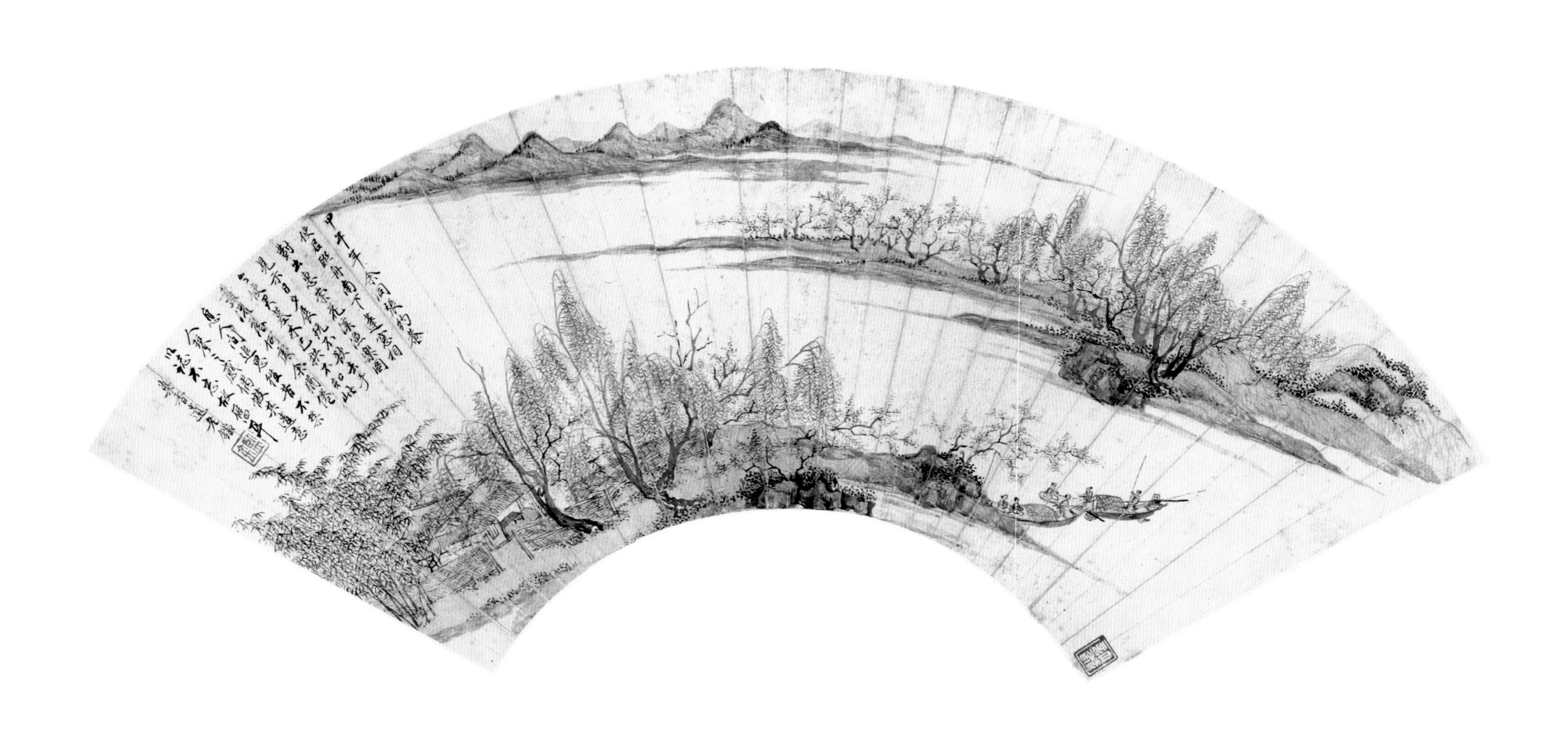

81. 山水图扇页

王鉴绘　纸本 墨笔

纵 16 厘米　横 49.7 厘米

扇页有自题："丁酉春为藻儒世兄画。王鉴。"钤"鉴"朱文印。"丁酉"是清顺治十四年（1657 年），王鉴时年 60 岁。

据款文而知，此图是作者为朋友"藻儒"所画。藻儒名王掞，号颛庵，是王鉴好友王时敏的第八子，与王鉴交谊甚厚。

图绘江河交错地带的秋日景观。王鉴画学元人笔墨，最擅长烘染，此图水与墨融为一体，皴法细密，呈一片深灰色调，表现出草木苍郁葱茏之美，是王鉴的墨笔精品画扇之作。

82. 仿惠崇水村图扇页

王鉴绘　纸本 设色

纵 16.7 厘米　横 52 厘米

扇页有自题："辛亥冬仿惠崇，王鉴。" 钤"王鉴"朱文印。"辛亥"是清康熙十年（1671年），王鉴时年 74 岁。

王鉴对宋代画家惠崇的艺术推崇备至，直至晚年，仍然悉心临仿，毫不懈怠。此图是他仿惠崇《水村图》的佳作。全图以青绿色为主调，表现了江南清丽明洁的山光水色。其笔墨精巧，设色淡雅，意境虚和，既得青绿山水的工丽，又具文人画的气韵。

辛亥冬仿
惠崇
王鑑

83. 山水图扇页

黄媛介绘　金笺 墨笔

纵 16.2 厘米　横 50.5 厘米

扇页有自题：“断檐偏趁日，高树不妨云。皆令画。”钤“媛介”白文印、“字皆令”朱文印。

黄媛介（生卒年不详，1650 年左右在世），字皆令，秀水（今浙江嘉兴）人。出身于儒学世家，黄葵阳族女。能诗擅绘，极具才情。明亡之际，黄媛介与其夫杨世功为躲避战乱不得不背井离乡，在江南的吴越间四处漂泊。颠沛流离的生活令黄氏居无定所，难得安逸，但是，这种生活也给其艺术的发展创造了难得的机会，无论是流徙途中的亲身经历，还是所见所闻自然景观，都丰富了她的写作和画作的素材，使得她比一般的女性有更多的机会云游自然山水，从中获得创作灵感，促使其山水画日臻成熟。其山水追仿晚明文人画中盛行的简淡画风，推崇元倪瓒、明董其昌的笔情墨趣，运笔纤弱中内含筋骨，墨色浓淡有致，多为淡赭晕染的浅绛山水。所绘景致疏简，文人野逸之情溢于清幽空寂的画境中。

图绘二株阔叶梧桐树相伴偎依，树下一座空房，杳无人迹，一块巨石，摇摇欲坠地位于房屋的左侧。构图简略，险中有稳巧于布势。笔墨法董其昌，粗犷简率中不失古雅秀润。

84. 山水图扇页

黄媛介绘　金笺 墨笔

纵 16.2 厘米　横 51.2 厘米

扇页有自题：“媛介画。”钤“皆令”朱文印。

图绘远山二座，不见笔痕皴擦，为淡墨轻抹，隐约欲现。近景一船工正划篷船离岸，船中端坐二人。水际处有一株分枝柳，又有沿岸而生的芦苇丛，与江中摇曳的芦苇相呼应。全图以简取胜，占全幅一半画意的江面，却没画一笔水，水意全是通过水中的物象——船、芦苇等暗示出来的，这可谓全图的巧妙之处，亦是作者以虚应实、以点示面匠心独运的表现。全幅带有较强的文人画韵味，着重表现文人所追求向往的隐逸意境。

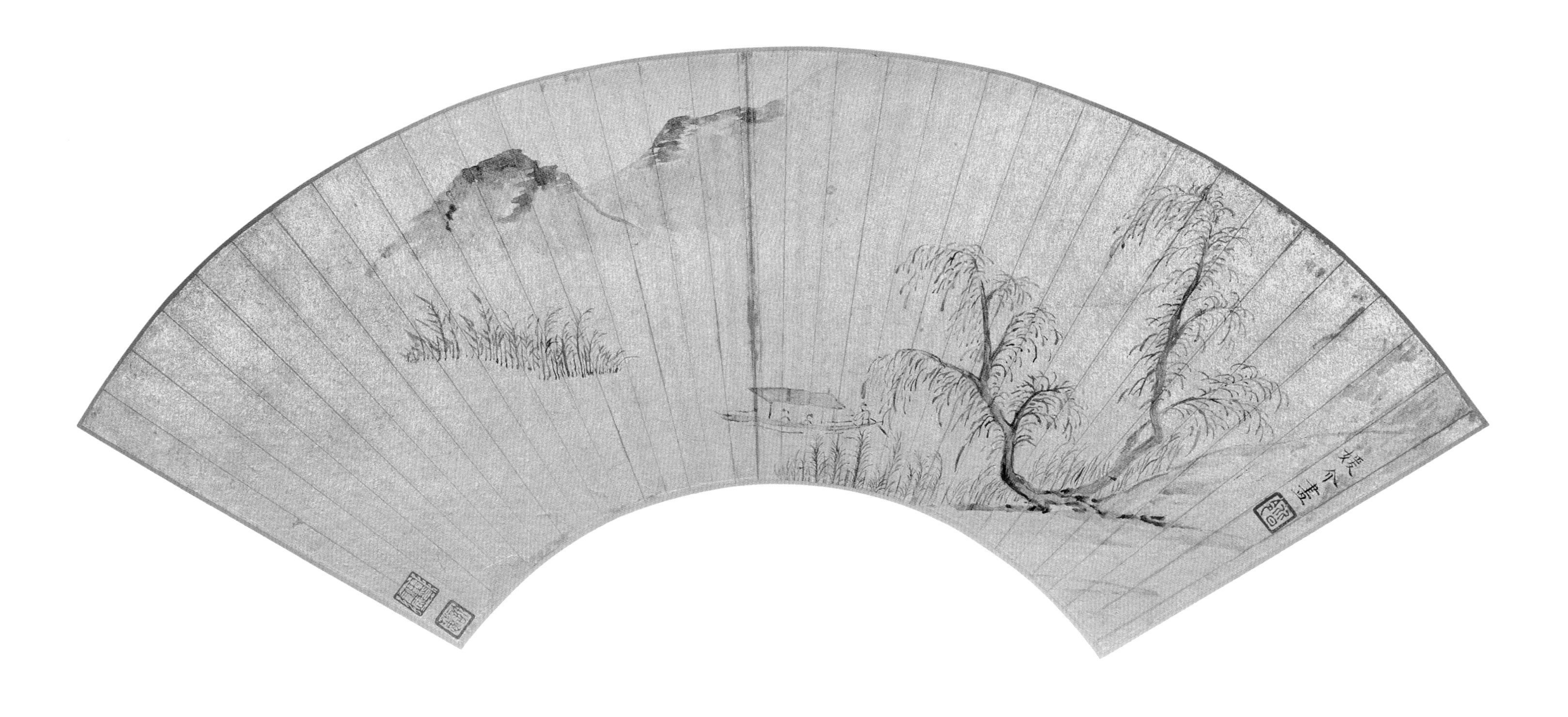

85. 兰石图扇页

范珏绘　金笺 墨笔

纵 17.2 厘米　横 51.8 厘米

扇页有自题："壬申秋日写似叔昭词兄，范珏。"钤"双玉"朱文印。"壬申"是明崇祯五年（1632 年）。

范珏（生卒年不详，活动于 17 世纪），字双玉，青溪人。南京地区名妓。虽为妓，但其以志向高洁及拥有较高的笔墨造诣，为时人称道。余绍宋《板桥杂记》言她"静廉寡所嗜好，一切衣饰歌管、艳靡纷华之物，皆屏弃之。惟阖户焚香，沦茗相对，药炉经卷而已。性喜画山水，模仿大痴、顾宝幢，槎枒老树，远山绝涧，笔墨间有天然气韵，妇人中范华原也"。余绍宋将范珏比作了宋代山水名家范华原（宽），对其艺术给予了高度的肯定和赞赏。可惜她留存的作品不多，仅有故宫博物院藏《兰石图》扇、《山水图》册页及无锡市博物馆收藏的《兰花合卷》（与顾眉作品合装）等。

此扇页构图别具一格。作者紧贴着扇面的上部边缘，绘俯探下垂的幽兰，一反兰自下而上生长的态势。兰叶每片均一笔绘成，线条飘逸舒展，穿插有致，生动地表现出兰娇柔的质感和在轻风吹拂下的风韵，具有"吴门画派"文人笔墨的特征。

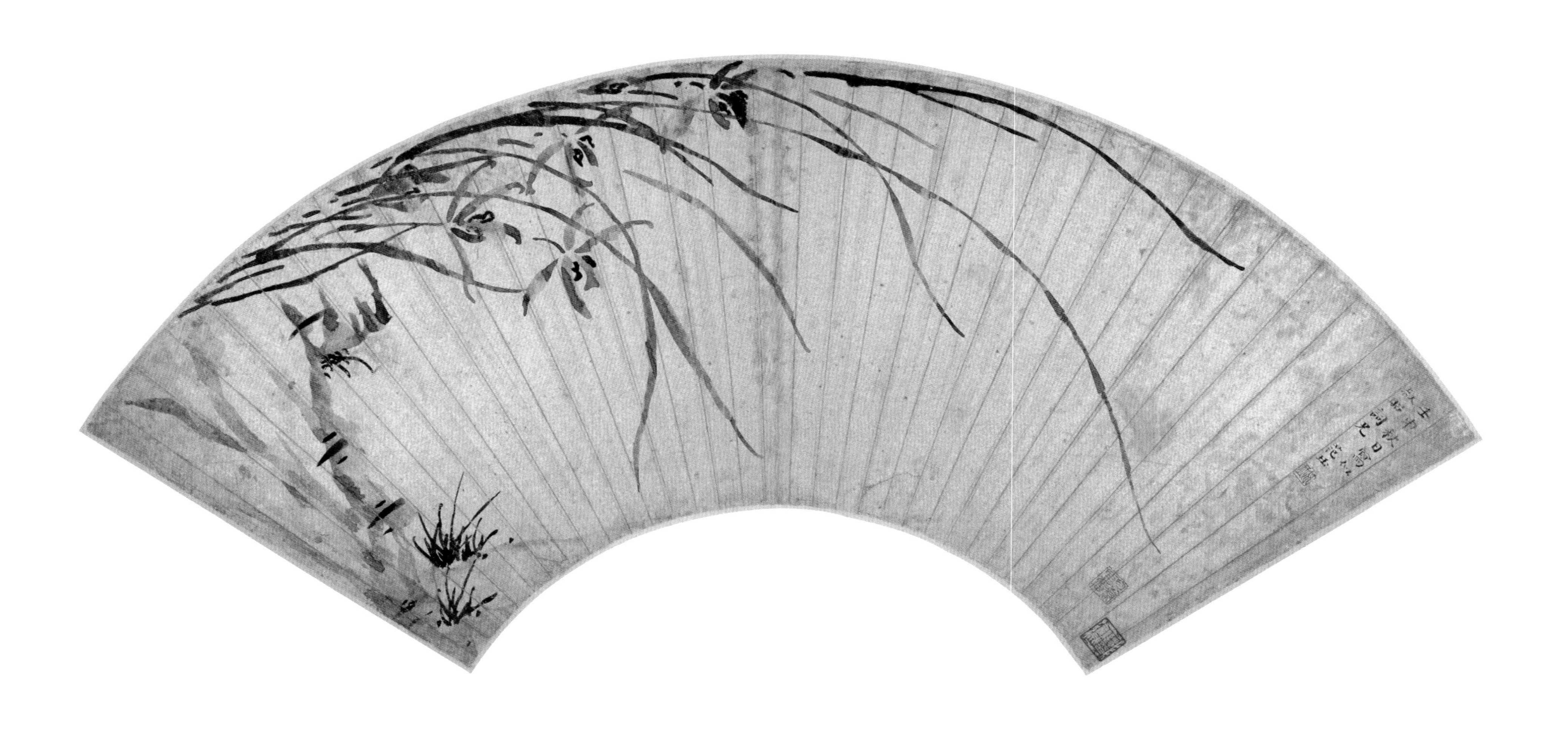

86. 黄山诗意图扇页

张风绘　金笺 设色

纵 16 厘米　横 51.2 厘米

扇页有自题："高下龙松石笋撑，白云影里老僧行。薰风五月吹残雪，开遍山花不记名。友人游黄山归，道其胜，诗以纪之。辛丑初夏作图请正栎翁老先生。张风。"钤"张大风"朱文印。"辛丑"是清顺治十八年（1661 年）。

张风（？～1662 年），字大风，号升州道人、上元老人，江苏上元县人。工绘山水、人物、花鸟，张庚《国朝画征录》记他："无师承，以己意为止，颇有自得之乐，笔墨中之散仙也。"他的画不受画风画派的约束，注重以画言情，直抒心声，因此，笔墨间多有新意。著《双镜庵诗钞》、《上药亭诗馀》等。

据自题而知，此图是作者根据友人口述五月游黄山的经历所画。扇面采取上下开合式构图，不落前人窠臼，景致奇险。全图以七上八下的山石为主，石面皴染结合，看似松散率意的用笔，实则笔法多变不失章法。张风虽然没有亲历黄山，但自 1644 年明亡以后，他曾经佩剑走北都，出卢龙、上谷，纵览昌平、天寿诸山，攀登过许多名山大川。当晚年的他耳闻黄山的神采时，能够准确地画出自身对黄山萧森郁茂壮美的感悟。

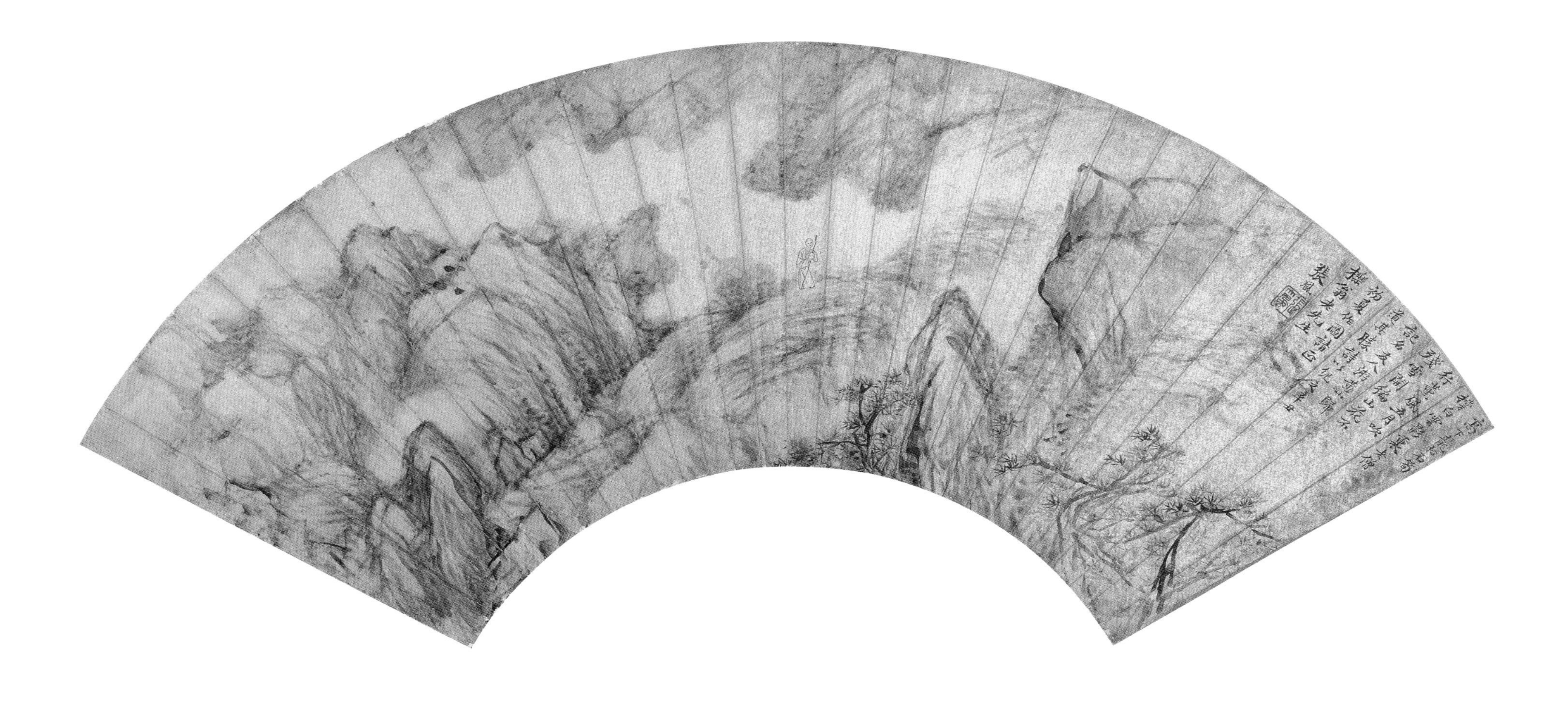

87. 探梅图扇页

谢彬绘　金笺 墨笔

纵 18.5 厘米　横 55 厘米

扇页有自题：“康熙乙卯画于止园之玉树堂，古香谢彬时年七十有四。”钤“彬”白文印、“文侯”朱文印。“乙卯”是清康熙十四年（1675 年）。

谢彬（1602～1681 年），字文侯，号仙臞，上虞（今属浙江）人，寓居钱塘（今浙江杭州）。工人像写真，师事曾鲸，寥寥数笔，便可形神兼备，为“波臣派”重要画家。间作山水，宗法宋元，笔墨疏放，饶有韵致。

图绘高士们结伴出游，寻梅探春的隐逸生活。近景的山石采用富有力度的斧劈皴，以侧锋行笔皴擦石面，有宋人画苍劲的笔意。人物刻画生动传神，通过简约的勾染，便将人物“探梅”时彼此交流的动态表现得惟妙惟肖，由此可见作者对生活有着细致的观察，在人像创作上有着深厚的功底。

88. 山水图扇页

程正揆绘　纸本 设色

纵 17 厘米　横 52.7 厘米

扇页有自题：“青溪道人为山长社翁图。”钤“正揆”白文印。

程正揆（1604～1676 年），字端伯，号鞠陵，晚号青谿道人，孝感（今属湖北）人，来自官宦世家。明崇祯四年（1631 年）进士，入清后官工部右侍郎，54 岁时遭革职，遂返乡。早年得董其昌指授，后云游庐山、黄山等大山名川，自出机杼，喜以秃笔点擦，干湿墨并用，于平淡中具真率，与石谿并称“二谿”。

程正揆是一位在宗法宋元人传统笔墨的基础上注重写生的山水画家。此图绘江南暮霭笼罩的山川景色。全图以交杂的树木为主体，配以远山、石桥及茅舍，整体布局气脉连贯，自然而严谨。其用笔骨格松秀，施墨、设色淋漓蕴藉，皴擦点染于相互交融中呈现粗头乱服之美，是其山水画代表作之一。

89. 山水图扇页

吴伟业绘　金笺 设色

纵 16.4 厘米　横 50.9 厘米

扇页有自题：“甲午初夏画似行翁老先生一笑。伟业。”钤“吴伟业印”朱文印、“下云”朱文葫芦印。“甲午”是清顺治十一年（1654年），吴伟业时年 46 岁。

吴伟业（1609～1671 年），字骏公，号梅村等，太仓（今属江苏）人。明崇祯四年（1631 年）进士。清初征为国子监祭酒，清顺治十四年（1657 年）辞官南归。善书画，山水宗法元人，笔墨温润秀雅，具有文人书卷气，与张学曾、王时敏、邵弥等书画家友善。精诗词，是娄东诗派开创者。与钱谦益、龚鼎孳并称“江左三大家”，著《梅村集》。

吴伟业是位有着多方面兴趣爱好的著名文人，社交圈子广泛。他与绘画界的名流杨文骢、程嘉燧、张学曾、卞文瑜、邵弥、王时敏、王鉴等保持着亦师亦友的密切关系。受这些画界名流的影响，其画风亦随时尚，具有“南宗”笔墨的时代特点。此图为开合式构图，绘一河两岸的夏日风光。长松杂树，葱茏苍翠。山石圆浑秀润，呈雨后苔滑状。意境净洁平和，明显带有怡悦性情的文人写意画情趣。

90. 菊花图扇页

李因绘　金笺 墨笔

纵 16.6 厘米　横 51 厘米

扇页有自题:“是菴。”钤“李因”白文印、“是菴”朱文印。

李因（1610～1685 年），字是菴，自幼家贫，沦落为妓，17 岁脱籍，成为葛征奇妾。工绘墨笔山水、花鸟，尤以写意花鸟为人称道。其画作受业于叶大年（字寿卿），推崇陈淳、徐渭画风,《国朝杭郡诗辑》言她:“洒然落笔，则花竹之夭斜，禽鸟之飞跃，高淡生动，净洗铅粉妍媚之习”。陈维崧《妇人集》评她“作水墨花鸟，幽淡欲绝”。窦镇《国朝书画家笔录》则言其“水墨花鸟苍古静逸，颇得青藤、白阳遗意,所画极有笔力,无轻弱态”。著《竹笑轩吟草》、《续竹笑轩吟草》。

图绘一枝盛开的菊花由左下角斜插入扇面。叶片以浓淡墨晕染，将双勾白描的花瓣烘托得如珠似玉，清纯脱俗，深得陈淳疏爽隽逸的意趣。

91. 松竹幽亭图扇页

弘仁绘　金笺 墨笔

纵 16.1 厘米　横 50.5 厘米

扇页有自题："夜卧时闻啸聚声，钓天幽梦总难成。晨兴抚几闲涂抹，藉此松筠滌秽尘。己亥八月，下榻德翁先生介石书堂画正。渐江学人弘仁。"钤"渐江"白文印、"弘仁"朱文印。"己亥"是清顺治十六年（1659 年），弘仁时年 50 岁。

弘仁（1610～1664 年），俗姓江，名韬，字六奇，明亡后入武夷山为僧，名弘仁，号渐江学人等，安徽歙县人。善画山水，画学萧云从，又取法元倪瓒、黄公望诸家，构图洗练简逸，线条瘦劲精整，善用折带皴和干笔渴墨，风格冷峭。与原济、梅清同为"黄山画派"的代表人物。与查士标、孙逸、汪之瑞并称"海阳四家"，是"新安派"的开派画家。同时，与原济、朱耷、髡残合称"清初四僧"。

根据自题而知，此图是弘仁在"己亥八月"下榻德翁先生处，晨起后乘兴所绘，画的目的是"藉此松筠滌秽尘"。"己亥"是中国社会大动乱的一年，清军攻取滇都，桂王（永历帝）出走缅甸。郑成功、张煌言与清军在安徽、南京一带不断交战，纷乱的事态使得弘仁"夜卧时闻啸聚声，钓天幽梦总难成"。因此，他希望通过画松竹清雅之物去"滌秽尘"。图绘由孤亭、修竹和松木营造的隐居之所。图中两棵各具形态的松，非常引人注目，一棵纠结盘曲，另一棵挺拔瘦削。弘仁多次游览以松、石之美著称的黄山，对松的状态及生长规律有着细致的观察和研究，所以他笔下的松都特别的生动有韵味。该图扇笔法轻快疏秀，构图疏简，是弘仁随手而成的小品山水画代表作。

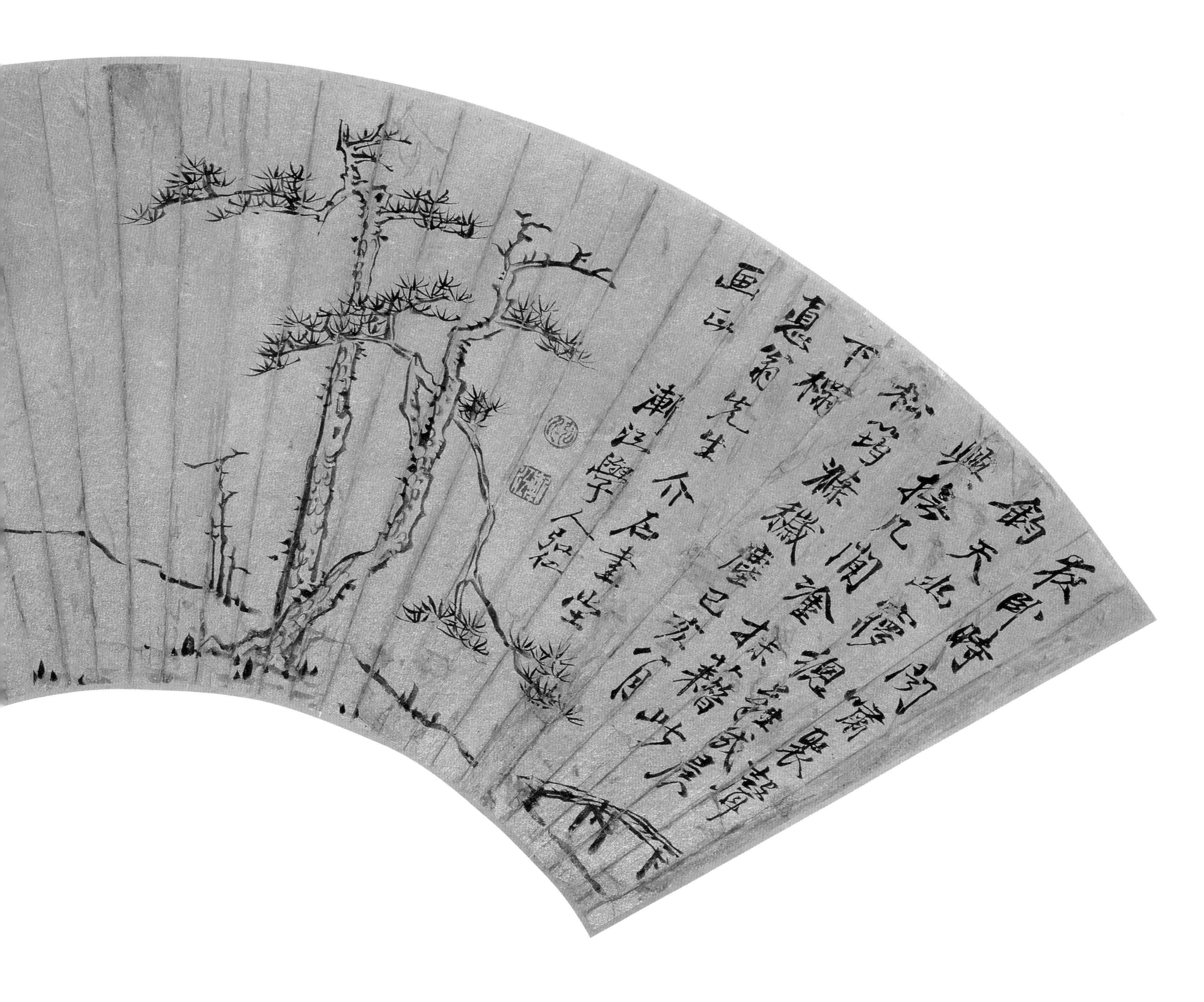

92. 南冈清韵图扇页

弘仁绘　金笺 墨笔

纵 17.6 厘米　横 50.4 厘米

扇页有自题：“南冈清韵，为洪起居士写。弘仁。”钤“渐江”白文印。

此图构思巧妙，作者通过将前后叠嶂的山石绘成气势宏大的石壁，推出友人洪起居士的敞轩；通过绘秋林响泉，点出周围环境的古雅幽静。此图意在通过清旷高洁的山水景观揭示出洪起居士的淡泊高隐之心。山石以勾勒为主，线条仿倪瓒的折带皴，笔墨于瘦削处见腴润，体现了弘仁学倪瓒而又有变化的风格。

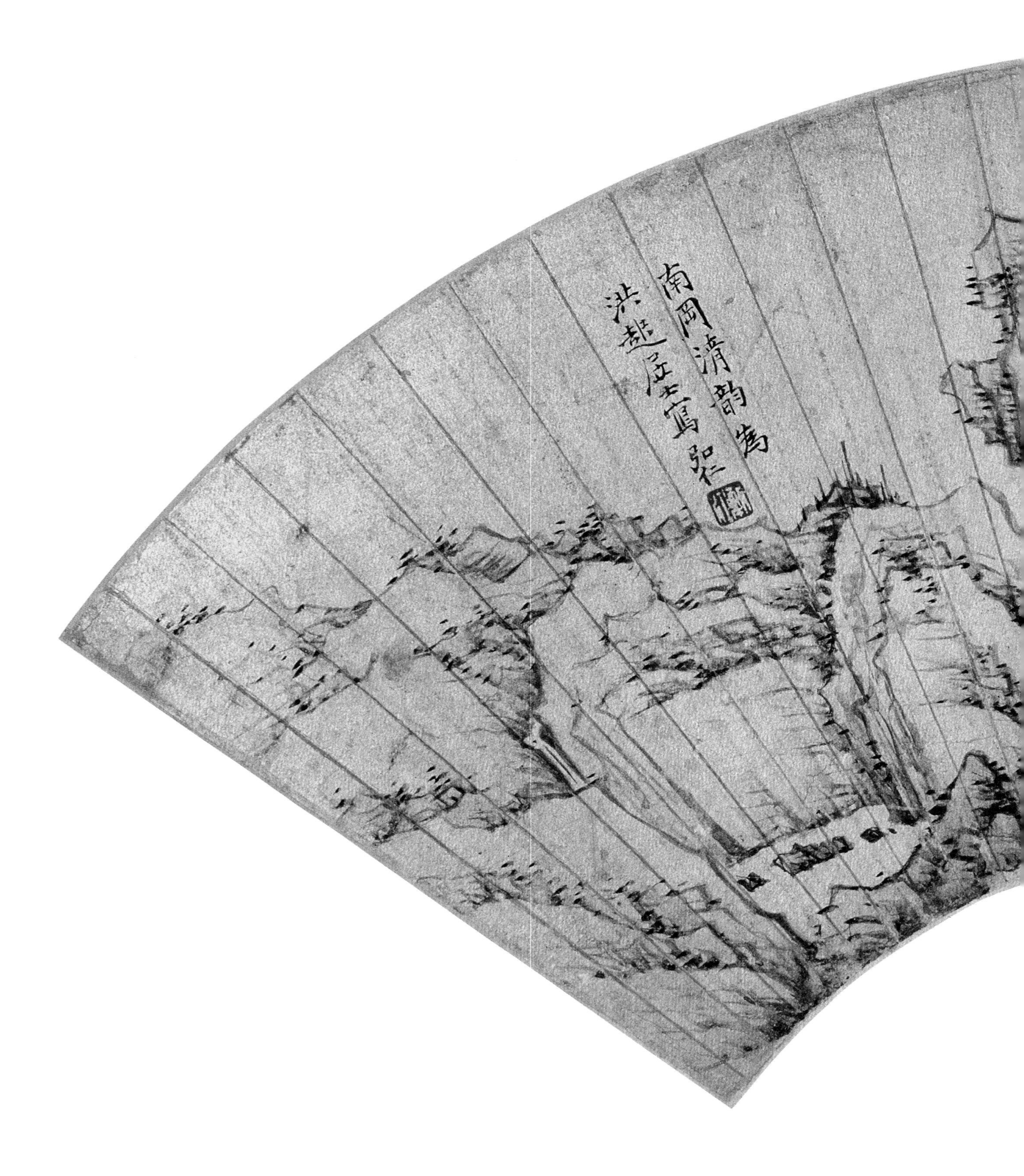

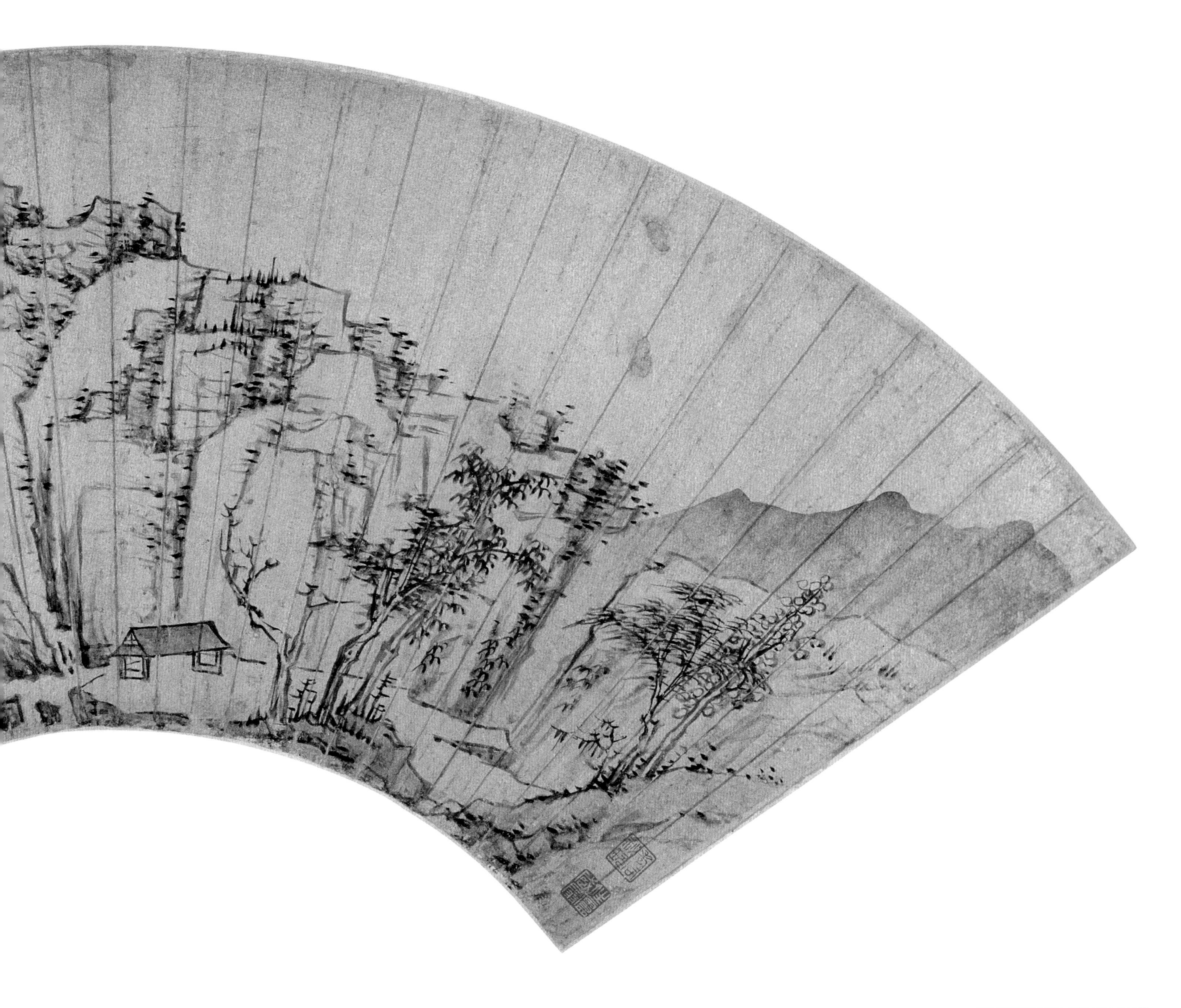

93. 溪阁读书图扇页

髡残绘　纸本 设色

纵 16.6 厘米　横 52 厘米

扇页有自题："山中云雾深，不识人间世。偶然出山游，还是山中是。戊申冬十月行脚武昌，遇山长大居士，握手论廿年心交，别时举此以志相感云耳。石道人。"钤"石豀"白文方印。"戊申"是清康熙七年（1668 年），作者时年 57 岁。

髡残（1612～1673 年），俗姓刘，武陵（今湖南常德）人。青年时出家为僧，法名髡残，字介丘，号石豀、白秃、石道人、残道者等。长期寓居南京，修禅弘佛之暇潜心于山水画的创作。他承袭元人王蒙，明人沈周、文徵明诸家笔法，结合自身感悟，形成独特的山水画风。善用秃笔，以线造型，在深浅、断续、粗细线条的相互交叉、转换、顿挫中表现幽僻景致。其意境苍莽，画格高逸而古拙。他与同时代的程青豀合称"二豀"；与原济（石涛）合称"二石"；与朱耷、弘仁、原济并称"清四僧"。

由自题而知，此图是髡残离开久居的山野行至武昌，赠别"山长大居士（王岱）"所绘。髡残自廿岁削发为僧后，长年隐遁于山光云影间，得以悉心观察大自然的阴晴朝暮，这不仅使得其心灵得到净化，也使得他的艺术从真山实水中悟出画界六法，而更具有神采。本幅以爽快的笔法画出雨后山川清新怡人的景色。构图严谨，虚实互映，空疏的云、水、天与叠嶂的山石、茂密的林木构成疏密明暗的变化，增强了画面的节奏感、空间感以及崇高感。

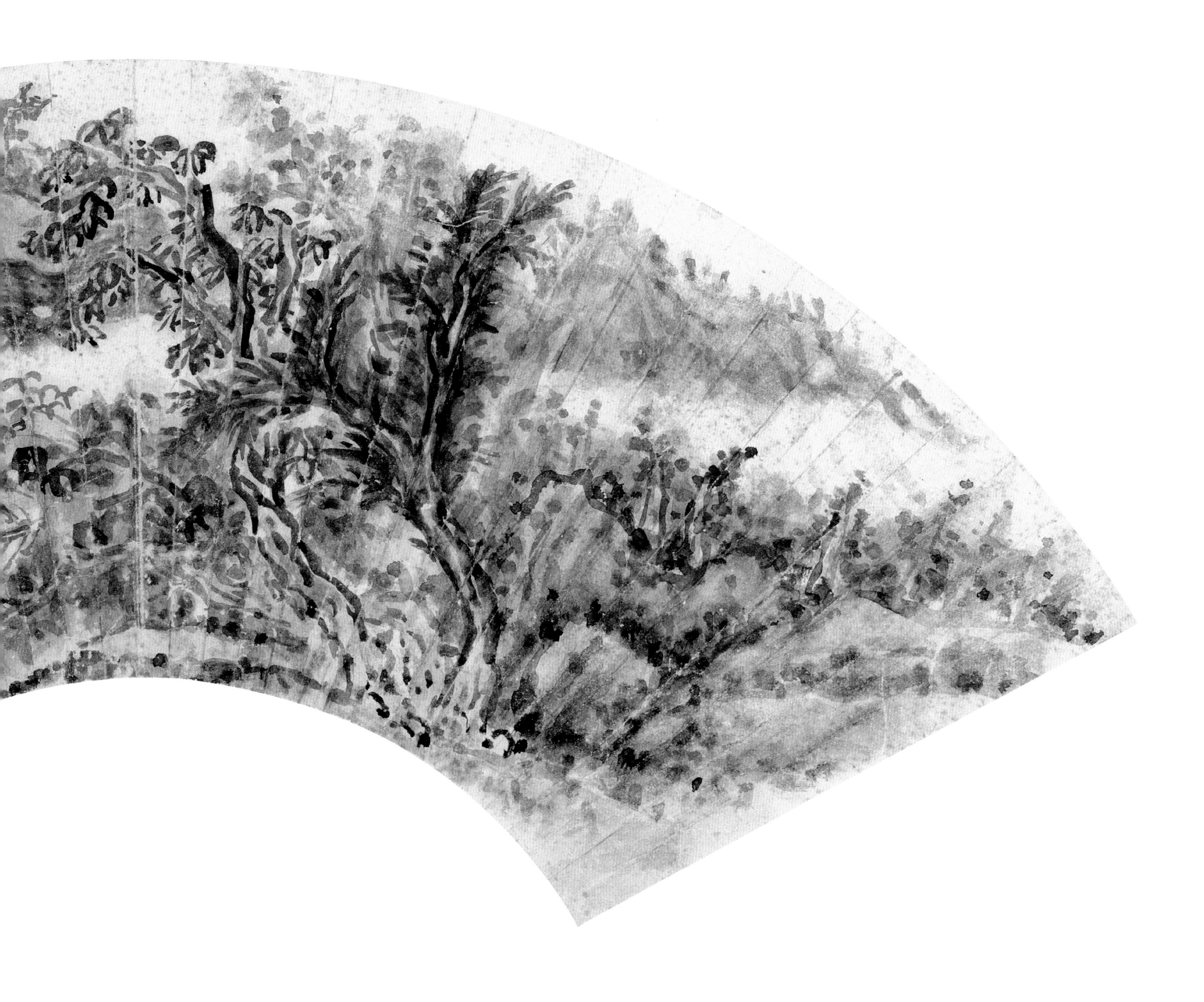

94. 策杖寻幽图扇页

查士标绘　纸本 墨笔

纵 16.8 厘米　横 51.5 厘米

扇页有自题：“画倪法，似卧南道兄正。甲寅秋日，查士标。”钤“二瞻”白文印。“甲寅”是清康熙十三年（1674 年），查士标时年 60 岁。

查士标（1615～1697 年），字二瞻，号梅壑、懒老，休宁（今属安徽）人。家藏多鼎彝、金石篆刻及宋元人画迹，其文化修养深厚。明末，家境因战乱而败落，遂避居于新安山中，或者往来于苏州、扬州。擅山水，宗法元人倪瓒、吴镇，并将自己的遗民思想融入于画作中，其用笔简括超逸，意境荒寒清旷。与渐江、孙逸、汪之瑞并称“海阳四家”，是“新安画派”的代表。著《种书堂遗稿》。

图绘疏林缓坡、浅水平岑、一河两岸的景致。近景的树木株叶秀整，四面出枝；远景的山峦起伏绵延，扩展了左右空间。全幅多以侧锋行笔，线条富有变化和表现力。作者自言此图法自倪瓒，但是在创作上又与倪画有所不同，增添了寻幽觅诗的人物，使观者有了别样的感受。

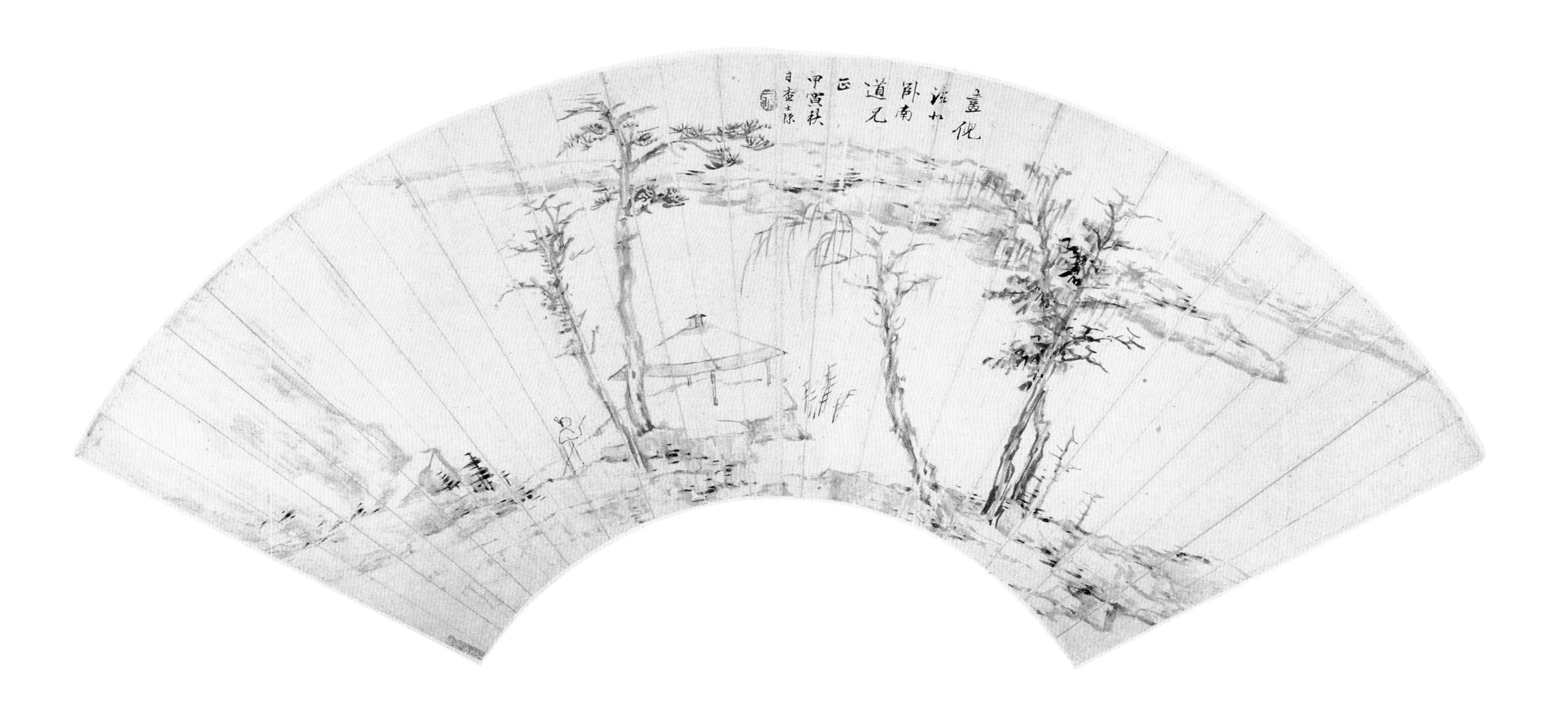

95. 举杯对月图扇页

樊圻绘　金笺 设色

纵 16.3 厘米　横 51.4 厘米

扇页有自题：“一杯在手，世事等闲。乙酉清和月画，似石生先生正。秣陵樊圻。”钤“樊圻之印”白文印、“洽公”朱文印。“乙酉”是清乾隆三十年（1765 年），樊圻时年 50 岁。

樊圻（1616～？年），字会公，更字洽公，江宁（今江苏南京）人。与其兄樊沂均以擅画出名。工绘山水、人物，取法宋元人笔墨，格调穆然恬静，与龚贤、高岑、吴宏等同为南京地区的重要画家，是“金陵八家”之一。

图绘一高士举杯望月的洒脱之景。构图极为简单，创作主题鲜明，以不同的笔法刻画了相应的物象。人物以白描造型，流畅的线条准确地勾勒出童子与高士的站姿和坐姿，以及高士超凡脱俗的隽雅气质。横卧的山石以墨晕为主，深浅不同的墨色，不仅表现出石材厚重的体积和坚硬的质感，而且在画幅中起到以重色稳定画面的作用。不同的笔墨手法与高士以酒为乐、超然物外的情调相切合，吟诵出“一杯在手，世事等闲”的诗意。

96. 秋林读书图扇页

吴宏绘 纸本 设色

纵 15.8 厘米 横 51.8 厘米

扇页有自题："甲辰二月画，为伸甫仁兄正之。竹史吴宏。"钤"吴"、"宏"联珠文印。"甲辰"是清康熙三年（1664 年），吴宏时年 49 岁。

吴宏（1616～？年），字远度，号西江竹史，江西金溪人，寓居金陵（今江苏南京）。工绘山水，曾寻访名山大川，从自然景观中汲取营养。笔墨纵横放逸，不落时蹊，与龚贤、樊圻、高岑、叶欣同为南京地区的重要画家，是"金陵八家"之一。

吴宏在清顺治十年（1653 年），38 岁时曾渡黄河，游雪苑，从此以自然造化为师，画作独具新意。此幅绘秋木掩映下，文士于茅舍内临窗品读的书斋生活。其构思奇巧，画作的主角读书人既非形体高大，也未处于画幅的醒目位置，而是只露上半身且背对着观者。其主体形象的确立，是作者巧妙地将读书人所在的茅舍置于秋木与山石的空隙间，纵横交错、枝杈繁多的树木和以乱柴皴皴擦的石面烘托出了茅舍的齐整，读书人也就自然地成为全幅中最引人注目的对象。

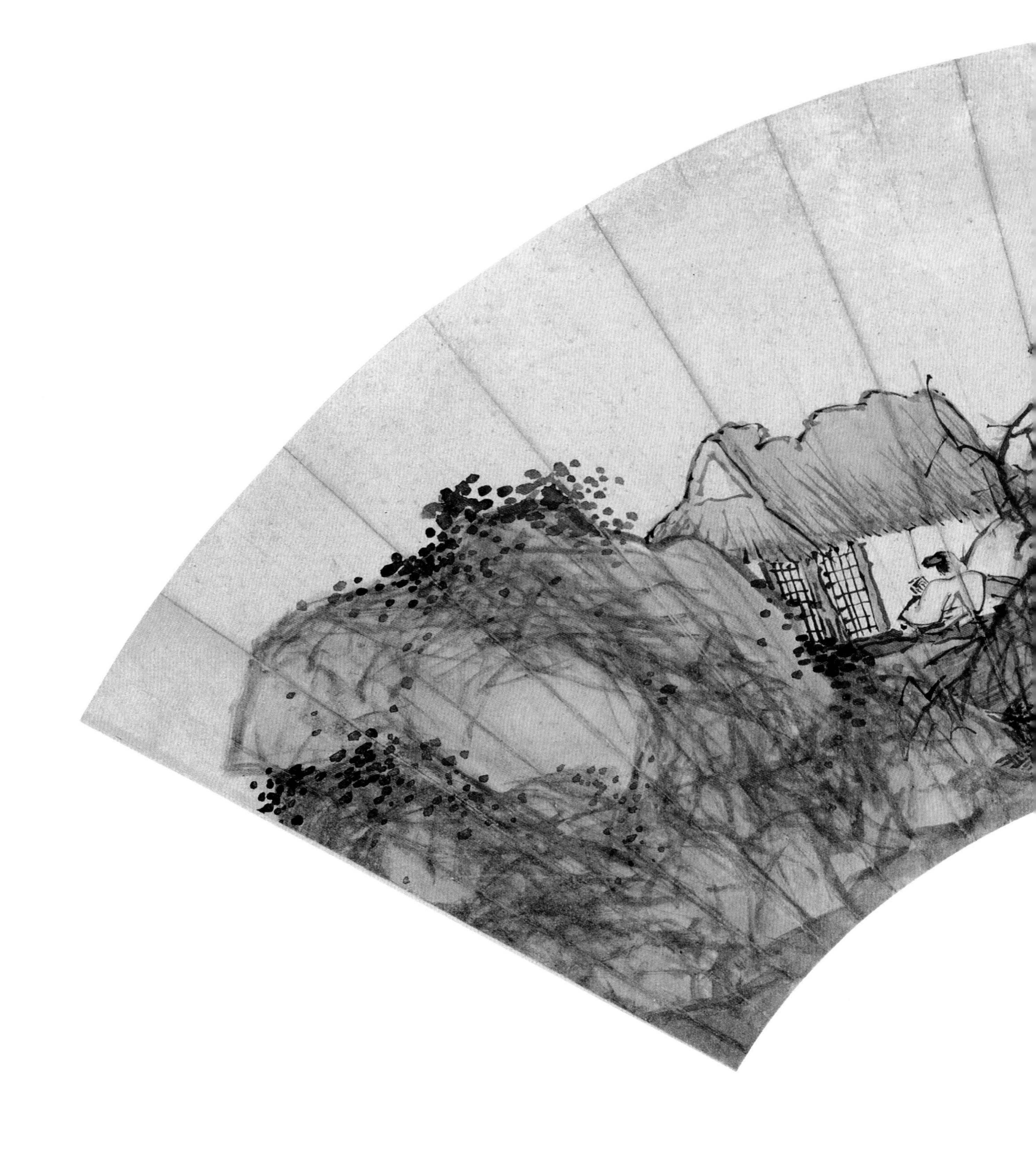

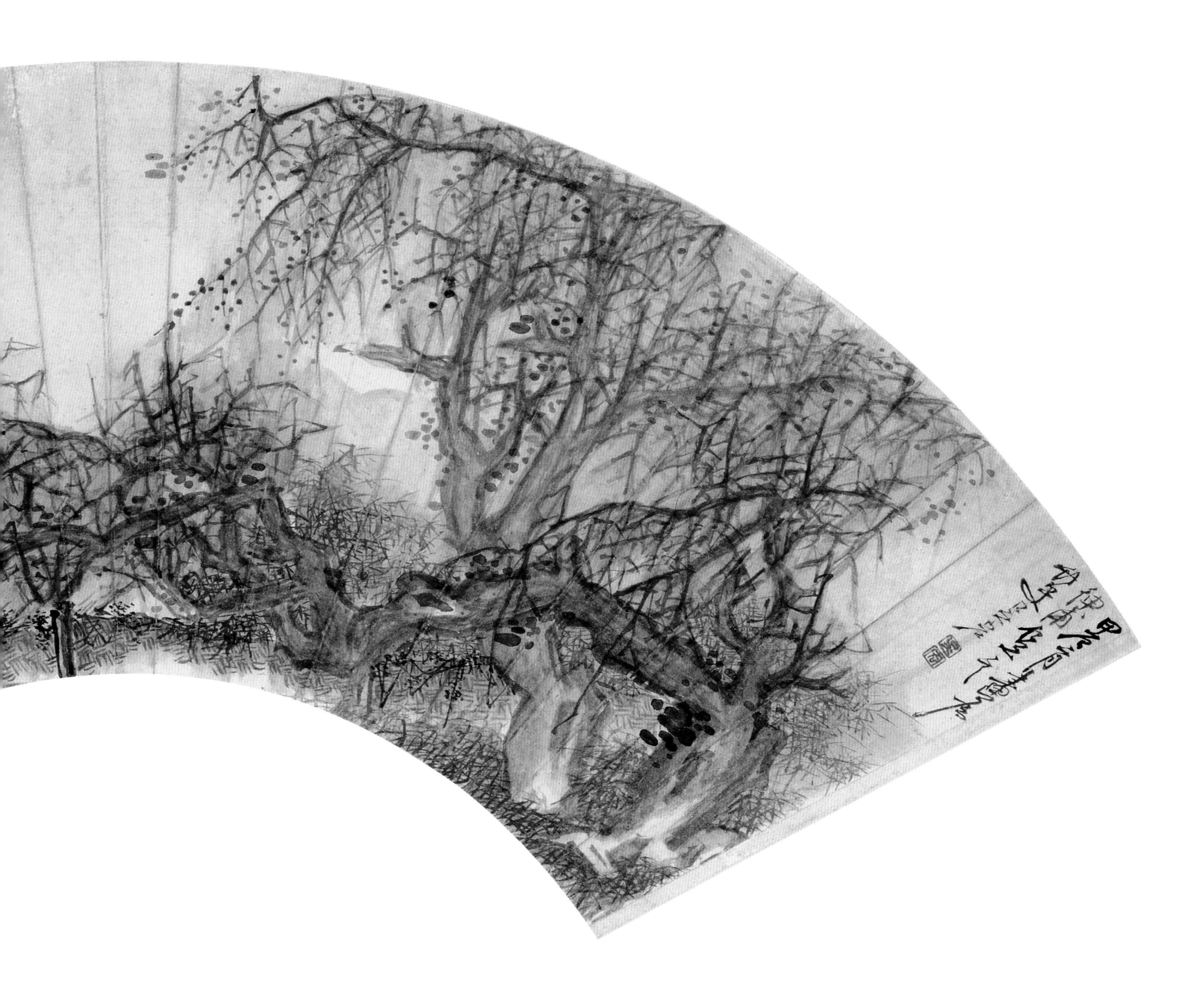

97. 山水图扇页

龚贤绘　金笺 设色

纵 17.6 厘米　横 50.5 厘米

扇页有自题："元末四家虽繁减不同，而笔致相类。兹为叔奇先生摹之，龚贤。"钤"半"、"千"朱白文联珠印。

龚贤（1618～1689 年），一名岂贤，字半千，号野遗、柴丈人等，昆山（今属江苏）人，寓居金陵（今江苏南京）。是位既注重传统笔墨又注重师法造化的山水画家。他在取法五代董源、元代吴镇的同时又云游于山水之间，主张"心穷万物之源，目尽山川之势"。擅以墨层层染渍，发展了"积墨法"。与活跃于金陵地区的画家樊圻、高岑、叶欣等同为南京地区的重要画家，是"金陵八家"的代表人物。著《香草堂集》。

此图中树叶的画法最为奇特，作者以笔笔分明，深浅、纵横不一的墨点表现叶片。它们前后交叠，平整而有变化，并且与远山的苔点相呼应，从而巧妙地构筑出远近空间层次，其景观与意境的丰富令人神往。

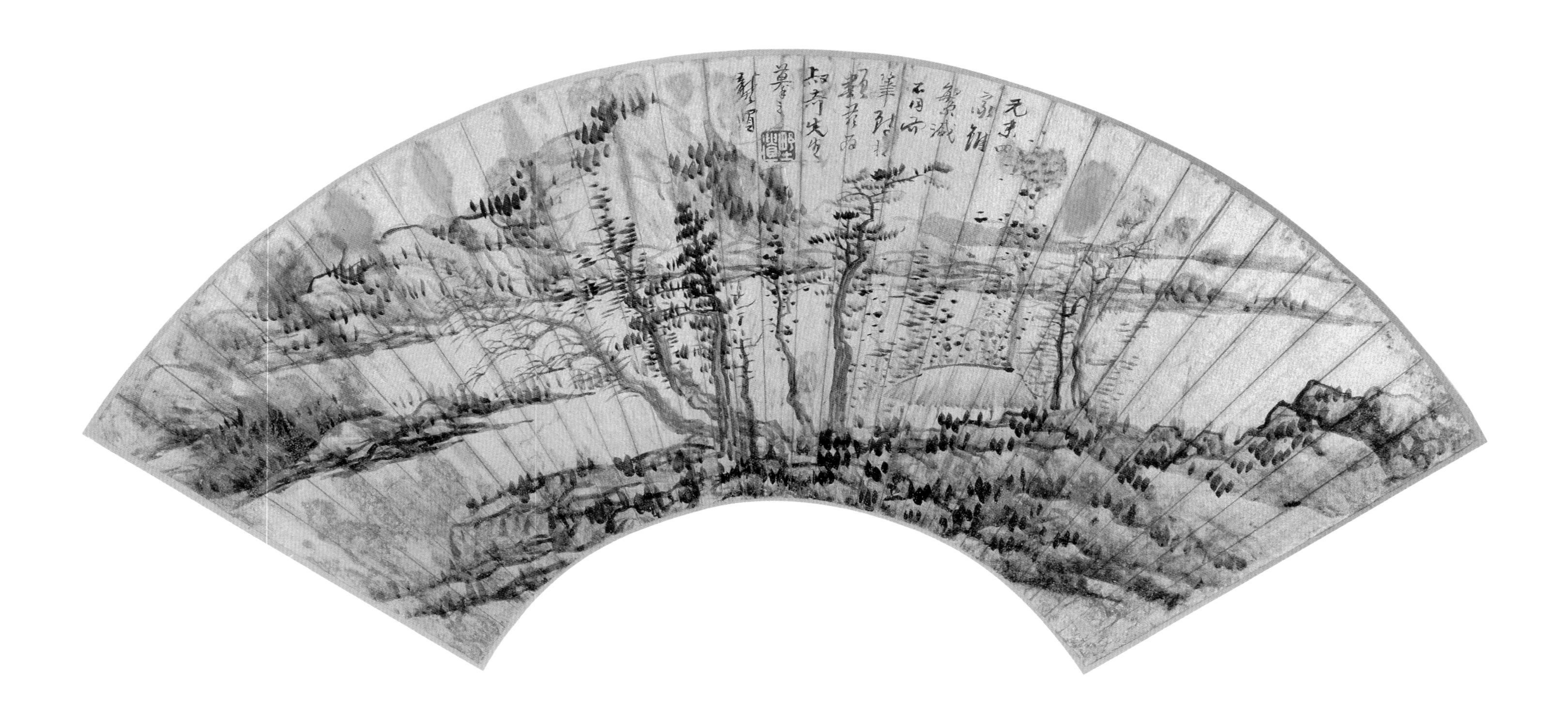

98. 山水图扇页

龚贤绘　纸本 墨笔

纵 18.2 厘米　横 56.3 厘米

扇页有自题：“问酒溪边客路，藏书谷里人家。料得桃源无有，寂寥堪送年华。为筠菽道兄写，龚贤。”钤“半千”朱文印。

图绘山石层叠，杂木枯荣相伴，茅舍数间空无人迹的景象。龚贤的画作有“白龚”和“黑龚”之分，此图扇不属于以积墨法表现的“黑龚”画，是幅典型的“白龚”之作。全图墨点不繁复，重在线条的勾勒，仅对山石略加皴擦晕染。它应是龚贤早期的画作，此时作者对丘壑的重视远在笔墨之上。

99. 山水图扇页

龚贤绘　纸本 墨笔

纵 22.7 厘米　横 63.1 厘米

扇页有自题："此一人家占胜游，树环垂荫水环流。莺来笋候茶新焙，远迓琴师放小舟。贤为天老同学画并题。"钤"柴丈"朱文印。

此图是龚贤画的友人居所：四周碧水漱石，嘉木成荫，一派清幽的景致。龚贤与友人生活的时代正是明清交替的动荡时期，如此宁静的自然环境，正是龚贤与友人理想的隐居之地。图中山石树木多用饱含水分的浓淡墨直接点染，笔法灵动，施墨朴厚明净，表现出江南山水温润的特质。

100. 山水图扇页

邹喆绘　金笺 设色

纵 16.6 厘米　横 51.9 厘米

扇页有自题：“庚子春月写似子玄词宗，石城邹喆。”钤“邹喆”、“方鲁”白文印二方。“庚子”是清顺治十七年（1660 年）。

邹喆（生卒年不详，活动于 17 世纪），字方鲁，吴县（今江苏苏州）人，寓居金陵（今南京）。自幼从父邹典习画，善花卉，兼工山水，笔墨苍劲整洁，富有秀逸清新之感。与龚贤、樊圻、高岑、吴宏、叶欣等同为南京地区的重要画家，是“金陵八家”之一。

邹喆作为民间的职业画家，与金陵画派的龚贤、樊圻、叶欣等人有许多共同之处。他们在艺术上承袭古人的传统，但是反对泥古不化，反对把山水画艺术降低为单纯的皴擦点染的笔墨技术。他们主张在继承传统的基础上，师法自然造化，所以常用画笔表现身边的山形地貌。

此作即是以俯瞰式的构图，绘南京万木争荣的春天景致。作品布局平稳开阔，颇具气势；用笔尖劲，工写结合，墨与色富于浓淡变化，是邹氏的精心之作。

101. 山水图扇页

侯方域绘　金笺 墨笔

纵 16 厘米　横 56 厘米

扇页有自题：“甲申冬日为雅臣大兄，弟域。”钤“侯方域印”朱文印。“甲申”是明崇祯十七年（1644 年），侯方域时年 27 岁。

侯方域（1618～1655 年），字朝宗，河南商丘人。复社社员，能诗文，工墨笔写意画，有文人画的书卷气。明末与方以智、陈贞慧、冒襄齐名，称“四公子”。清初著名戏剧家孔尚任依据他与秦淮名妓李香君的爱情故事，编排出戏曲名剧《桃花扇》。著《壮悔堂文集》、《四忆堂诗集》。

侯方域作为以诗文见长的才子，绘画功力虽然不够，但是在明亡之际，他仍希望通过画笔以寄托亡国的哀怨之痛，其笔下的山水黯然无色，寒江空亭毫无生趣，一派萧寂清凉的景象。图中瘦细的树木以浓墨点叶，点法灵活，与用笔方硬、刻板的山石形成了对比。

102. 兰花图扇页

顾眉绘　金笺 墨笔

纵 16.3 厘米　横 52.1 厘米

扇页有自题："丙子秋望为子寅词宗写，秦淮顾眉。"钤"眉生之印"白文印。"丙子"是明崇祯九年（1636 年），顾眉时年 18 岁。

顾眉（1619～1664 年），字眉生，一字眉庄，上元（今江苏南京）人。秦淮名妓，后为崇祯进士龚鼎孳（字孝升）宠妾，改姓徐，号善财君、梅生，时称横波夫人。她才貌双全，精诗擅画，通晓音律。尤以撇笔画墨兰为人称绝，与马守真难分伯仲。清张庚《国朝画征录》称她"工墨兰，独出己意，不袭前人法"。古代女画家无论闺阁还是妓家，她们的画不为人所重，其原因之一是她们在创作上缺乏新意，而顾眉画兰能不袭前人之法，实属难得。

此图构思新颖，巧妙地借助扇子顶端弧形的边线，绘丛兰嫣然下垂的样子。随风而舞的兰叶不仅显现出兰清幽典雅的特质，而且增强了画作的律动感。全图刚中有柔的用笔、秀润的墨色与兰婀娜飘逸之美，形成完美的统一。

103. 黄河晓渡图扇页

叶欣绘　金笺 设色

纵 18.5 厘米　横 54.3 厘米

扇页有自题："黄河晓渡。秋日为敬可道兄正。叶欣。"钤"叶"、"欣"联珠文印。

叶欣（生卒年不详，活动于 17 世纪），字荣木，云间（今上海市松江）人，寓居金陵（今南京）。山水画宗法宋人赵令穰，擅绘平远小景，笔墨简淡清远。与龚贤、樊圻、邹喆、吴宏、胡慥、谢荪、高岑等同为南京地区的重要画家，是"金陵八家"之一。

此幅表现的是黄河岸边民众生活的场景。图中远山仅以淡花青色一抹，没有勾画出山石的体积感及坚硬的质感；人物仅以精简的线条勾勒出大致的体态动势，面部的五官被略去；辽阔的水域，亦仅以轻柔的笔墨绘数条水纹，借以代表水势的走向。叶欣的山水画素以"工细幽淡"著称。本幅作品中，他没有表现黄河发水时浊浪滔天的一面，而是以简约的笔墨表现黄河风平浪静时的景致。借助黄河山水这一题材，作者表达了其平淡天真的审美情趣。

104. 山水人物图扇页

吕焕成绘　金笺 设色

纵 16.2 厘米　横 51.5 厘米

扇页有自题：“丙寅秋日写似用老道兄，焕成。”钤“焕”朱文印、“吉文”白文印。“丙寅”是清康熙二十五年（1686 年），吕焕成时年 57 岁。

吕焕成（1630～约 1705 年），字吉文，号祉园山人，浙江余姚人。创作题材广泛，人物、山水及花卉皆能。绘画风格多样，既有“吴派”设色秀媚之风，又有“浙派”笔墨豪爽之气。

图绘静谧清旷的山水间，文人雅士拱手相见的场景。山石仿浙派以侧锋行笔，作斧劈皴皴擦石面，树木及青竹仿吴派以工细的笔致勾描填色，人物造型生动，衣纹线条为颤笔描，表现出材质面料的柔软。作者能够在一幅画中娴熟地运用不同画派的笔法表现物象，显现出其深厚的画学素养。

105. 山水图扇页

王翚绘　纸本 设色

纵 16.1 厘米　横 50.1 厘米

款题："丁未夏六月，仿井西道人笔，为兰翁砚兄。同学王翚。"钤"王翚"朱文印。"丁未"是清康熙六年（1667 年），王翚时年 36 岁。

王翚（1632～1717 年），字石谷，号耕烟散人、清晖老人等，常熟（今属江苏）人。山水画创作不仅从学于张珂、王鉴、王时敏等名师，而且悉心临摹历代佳作，画艺日趋精湛。主张"以元人笔墨，运宋人丘壑，而泽以唐人气韵，乃大成"。清康熙三十年（1691）奉诏入京，主持绘制《南巡图》，获得赞誉。其画学弟子众多，形成"虞山派"，影响后世颇深。他与王时敏、王鉴、王原祁、吴历、恽寿平合称"清初六家"。

图绘千岩万壑、草木葱茏、瀑布高悬直泻的江南风光。王翚约 16 岁师从同邑张珂学画时，就以元黄公望（号井西道人）的笔墨为宗，刻苦摹学，始终不怠。此图是他早年学黄氏画法的代表作。图中山石以赭色和绿色交替晕染，学黄氏用披麻皴皴擦石面，笔势潇洒而秀润。其石边缘上的苔点要比黄氏的更为繁密，排列整齐的苔点，给高崖峻壑增添了青绿之美，同时，它与以卧笔横点表现的树叶，形成点与点的呼应，全图在"点"的统一下，具有湿润华滋的艺术效果。

106. 江乡秋晚图扇页

王翚绘　纸本 设色

纵 17.5 厘米　横 53.7 厘米

扇页有自题："吴仲圭江乡秋晚图。临似季英先生，甲寅端阳，王翚。"钤"王"、"石"、"谷"朱文联珠印。"甲寅"是清康熙十三年（1674 年），王翚时年 43 岁。

此扇面在构图上采用平和稳定的布局，在笔墨上讲求干湿笔互用，尤其注重以润笔点苔来表现山石的苍茫沉郁之美。在情韵上追求"淡泊以明志，宁静以致远"的意趣。是王翚仿临元人吴镇（仲圭）的精品之作。

107. 山川浑厚图扇页

王翚绘　纸本 设色

纵 17.5 厘米　横 54 厘米

扇页有自题："山川浑厚，草木华滋。乙亥六月写呈诵翁老先生教正，海虞王翚。"钤"王翚"朱文印。"乙亥"是清康熙三十四年（1695 年），王翚时年 64 岁。

创作此图的康熙三十四年，王翚正在京师主持绘制反映康熙皇帝第二次到南方巡视的《南巡图》卷。此时的他离家已四年之久，对家乡的眷念与日俱增。从图中所绘"山川浑厚，草木华滋"的江南风光、停泊靠岸的帆船、骑驴而归的行者、盘膝闲居的高士等，皆可见王翚溢于笔端的希冀离京返乡的心情。图中山石以牛毛皴兼解索皴细笔皴擦，其明净淡雅的线条表现出一种幽淡、清静的格调。全图笔墨沉着苍润，同时又流露出一种文人书卷气，是作者成熟期的代表作。

山川渾厚
草木華滋

108. 林塘诗思图扇页

吴历绘　金笺 墨笔

纵 16.4 厘米　横 51.6 厘米

扇页有自题：“写刘完菴先生林塘诗思。应岩培大辞宗教正，吴历。”钤“吴历”朱文印。

吴历（1632～1718 年），字渔山，号墨井道人、桃溪居士等，常熟（今属江苏省）人。少年时遭遇明亡，信奉佛教，50 岁后改信天主教，在澳门接受洗礼。早年学画于王鉴、王时敏。在澳门期间，受到西方绘画的潜在影响。其画风具有皴擦点染细腻、注重空间层次的特点。他与王时敏、王鉴、王翚、王原祁、恽寿平合称“四王吴恽”，亦称“清初六家”。

此扇页是依据明代画家兼诗人刘完菴的诗意所作。受画人“岩培”被吴历敬呼为“大辞宗”，“大辞宗”是对文翰大家的尊称，因此，吴历在创作这幅送给岩培的画作上不敢有丝毫的怠慢。全图布局开阔平稳，重在描绘杂木繁茂的近景和洲渚水鸟的中景，远景被似烟似雾又似云的虚空之气所弥漫，其幻景具有“无画处皆成妙境”的艺术效果，扩展了画面的想象空间，同时增添了画面朦胧的诗意。图中树叶以中锋落笔点染，笔墨华润蕴藉，既表现出叶片含烟带露的娇柔美，又通过墨的浓淡变化显现出它们交叠错落的自然风貌。

109. 罂粟花图扇页

恽寿平绘　纸本 设色

纵 16.2 厘米　横 50.5 厘米

扇页有自题："茗华阁戏作，南田客寿平。"钤"叔子"朱文印、"南田草衣"白文印。

恽寿平（1633～1690 年），初名格，字正叔，号南田、白云外史等，武进（今江苏常州）人。早年工绘山水，宗元人王蒙画风，笔墨清灵秀洁，意境萧散幽淡。后改绘花鸟，远师宋徐崇嗣，近学明人，注重写生，更发展了没骨技法。所画花鸟禽鱼，很少用笔勾线，主要以墨、色直接点染，追求天机物趣，其画法对后世花鸟画的影响极大。开创了"写生正派"、"常州派"等。他与王时敏、王鉴、王翚、王原祁、吴历合称"四王吴恽"，亦称"清初六家"。

图绘盛开的罂粟花。虽然，恽氏自题"戏作"，但是，他在创作上一丝不苟，以他出古入新创立的"没骨"法精心绘制。图中的花瓣、叶片不用墨笔勾勒轮廓线，全以色彩点染而成，颇具摇曳多姿的娇娆之美，达到了色、光、态、韵俱佳的艺术境界。恽氏的这种注重形似，但又不以形似为满足的没骨写生法，不仅博得清皇室的喜爱，成为清代院体花鸟的正宗，同时也赢得了市民阶层的喜好。不过，以卖画为生的他，生前其画作并没有受到市场的追捧，58 岁病故时，因家贫无力治丧，是王翚为他料理的殡事。

110. 香林紫雪图扇页

恽寿平绘　纸本 设色

纵 17.7 厘米　横 53 厘米

扇页有自题："香林紫雪，云溪寿平。"引首钤"吹万"朱文印、"园客"白文印。又自题："春暮东皋园池赏藤花，天半紫云飘漾，好风吹香，落英缤纷，真奇观也。戏写一枝，以为娱乐。"钤"寿平"白文印。

此图与现藏南京博物院的紫藤画扇（年款"壬戌"，恽寿平时年 50 岁）同名，并且画风、书风相近，由此推断无创作年款的此画也应是恽氏晚年之作。这是一幅对景写生图，作者通过绘紫藤飘扬的形态，暗示出无形的风和"好风吹香"的诗意。全图明净的色彩、娴熟的运笔，均显现出作者敏锐的观察力和精于细节表现的绘画本领。

111. 剑门图扇页

恽寿平绘　纸本 设色

纵 17 厘米　横 52.9 厘米

扇页有自题："庚戌夏六月同虞山王子石谷、陆子翰如，从西城携筇循山行三、四里憩吾国，乘兴遂登剑门。剑门，虞山最胜处也。未至拂水半岭，忽起大石壁，盘空而上，如积甲阵云腾地出，亦如扶摇之翼下垂也。石壁连延中陡削势下，绝若剑截状，辟一牖若可通他境地者，因号为剑门云，余因石谷命画剑门，且属作记，戏题游时所见，约略如此。"钤"寿"朱文圆印、"正叔"白文方印。"庚戌"是清康熙九年（1670 年），恽寿平时年 38 岁。

由自题而知，此图是恽寿平与同擅绘事的好友王石谷、陆翰如同游虞山剑门，被剑门陡峭险峻的山势所震撼，恽寿平受王石谷之托以绘画的形式记下了此行，因此这是一幅最真实地反映虞山剑门风貌的写景图，也是恽寿平早年交友与交游的纪实图，对研究恽寿平的社交活动具有重要的意义。

此图画幅不大，作者为了展示剑门石壁"盘空而上"的气势，没有从山脚下画起，而是仅绘了石壁的一部分，省略的山顶和山脚给人更多的向上伸展和向下探底的想象空间。同时，作者运用比对的艺术手法，将他与友人在山崖处游览的举止亦画在图中，借此更衬托出山体的高耸峭拔。图中山石连皴带染，设色明媚淡雅，笔法松秀，显现出恽寿平山水画灵秀清逸的特点。

112. 陶渊明归去来辞图扇页

焦秉贞绘　纸本 设色

纵 16.1 厘米　横 47.5 厘米

扇页有自题："戊子夏日写陶渊明《归去来辞》，云：'童仆欢迎，稚子候门。三径就荒，松菊犹存。'呈为老太翁先生博粲，焦秉贞。"钤"尔正氏"朱文印。"戊子"是清康熙四十七年（1708 年）。

焦秉贞（生卒年不详，活动于 18 世纪），字尔正，山东济宁人。是天主教传教士汤若望的门徒，通天文，清康熙时曾任钦天监五品官。善绘山水、人物、楼观，以画"御容"称旨，受到奖赏。他在画学上受到西方传教士的影响，在中国画的基础上参以西法，注重近大远小的透视及物象的明暗画法，其画作在清初别具面目。

此图据陶渊明《归去来辞》文意，描绘陶氏辞官隐居，离船登岸时受到"童仆欢迎"的场景。作者作为曾受到西洋技法影响的画家，在此件的创作上除茅屋结构有些许透视外，受西方画法的影响尚不明显，其笔法基本还属于中国传统的人物山水画范畴。作者在图中注重以形写神，将陶氏下船时小心翼翼的举止和童仆们恭敬的神态均刻画得生动传神。

113. 雪渔图扇页

冷枚绘　金笺 设色

纵 16.3 厘米　横 47.9 厘米

扇页有自题："孤舟簑笠翁，独钓寒江雪。偶写唐人江雪诗意。冷枚。"钤"冷枚"朱文印、"吉臣氏"白文印。

冷枚（约 1670～1742 年），字吉臣，别号金门画史，胶州（今属山东省）人。师从清宫廷画家焦秉贞，在技法上颇受西洋绘画的影响。擅长画人物、仕女、山水、花鸟，笔法工整细致，设色浓艳，是康熙朝和乾隆朝重要的宫廷画家。

图绘严冬时节，一老者在冰雪封冻的江面上怡然垂钓的情景。"独钓寒江雪"是唐柳宗元被贬到永州后所写，借以抒发自己孤独郁闷的心情。后世文人画家常借绘此题材，表达不惧世间炎凉，自得其乐的心境。作者为了表现出雪意，特地在山峦、芦苇，甚至是细长的渔竿上都敷上白粉，它们不仅为画面提高了亮度，增强了"光感"，同时增加了画面的寒意，更好地表现了"千山鸟飞绝，万径人踪灭，孤舟簑笠翁，独钓寒江雪"的诗意。

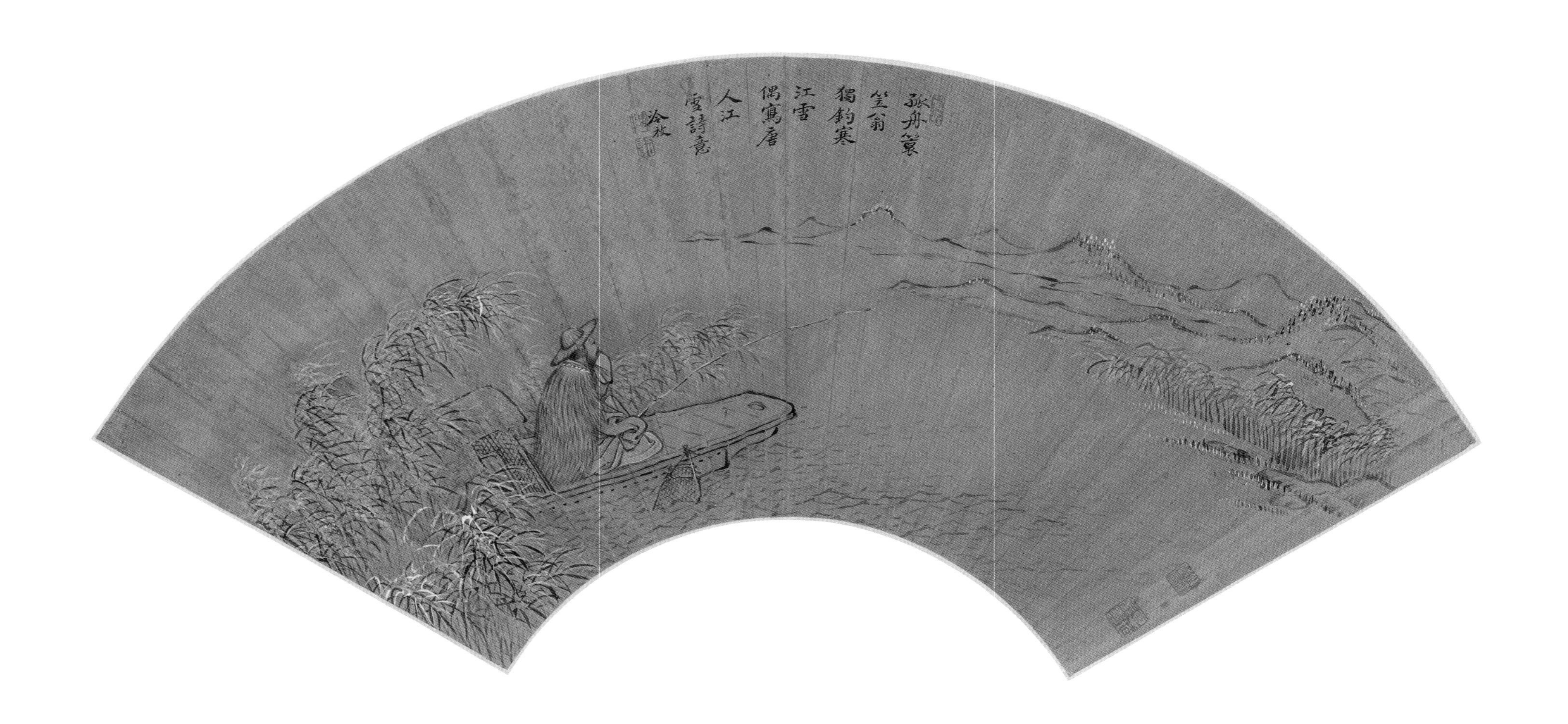

獨釣寒江雪

偶寫唐人江雪詩意

洽枚

114. 山水图扇页

王原祁绘　纸本 设色

纵 16.6 厘米　横 50.4 厘米

扇页有自题："乙卯夏日写大痴设色小景。王原祁。"钤"王原祁印"白文印。"乙卯"是清康熙十四年（1675 年），王原祁时年 30 多岁。

王原祁（1642 年或 1646 年～1715 年），字茂京，号麓台，太仓（今属江苏）人，王时敏孙。清康熙九年（1670 年）进士，官至户部左侍郎，有"王司农"之称。他以精鉴赏、工书画，深得康熙皇帝的青睐，曾奉命鉴定宫中所藏书画，担任《佩文斋书画谱》总裁，并且主持绘制康熙《万寿盛典图》等项活动，是康熙朝重要的词臣画家。他的山水画继承董其昌的绘画理论和实践，以元四家黄公望等人笔墨为宗。用笔沉着，自称笔端有"金刚杵"。清张庚《国朝画征录》评其画"熟不甜，生不湿，淡而厚，实而清，书卷之气盎然纸墨外"。与王时敏、王鉴、王翚合称"清初四王"。追随其笔意的画家众多，被称作"娄东派"。著《雨窗漫笔》、《扫花庵题跋》等。

此图是现存王原祁早年学黄公望画法的罕见之作。王原祁自幼受祖父王时敏的影响，对黄氏画法极为推崇，反复临摹不怠。此图从设色到笔法均取自黄公望。图绘层峦叠嶂，松林山舍，画家心目中理想的仙境。山石以赭色为主调，连皴带染，显现出雨后温润湿滑的质感。树木以横卧点子叶为主，笔法略显稚嫩，缺少空间层次变化，反映其当时画技尚未成熟。

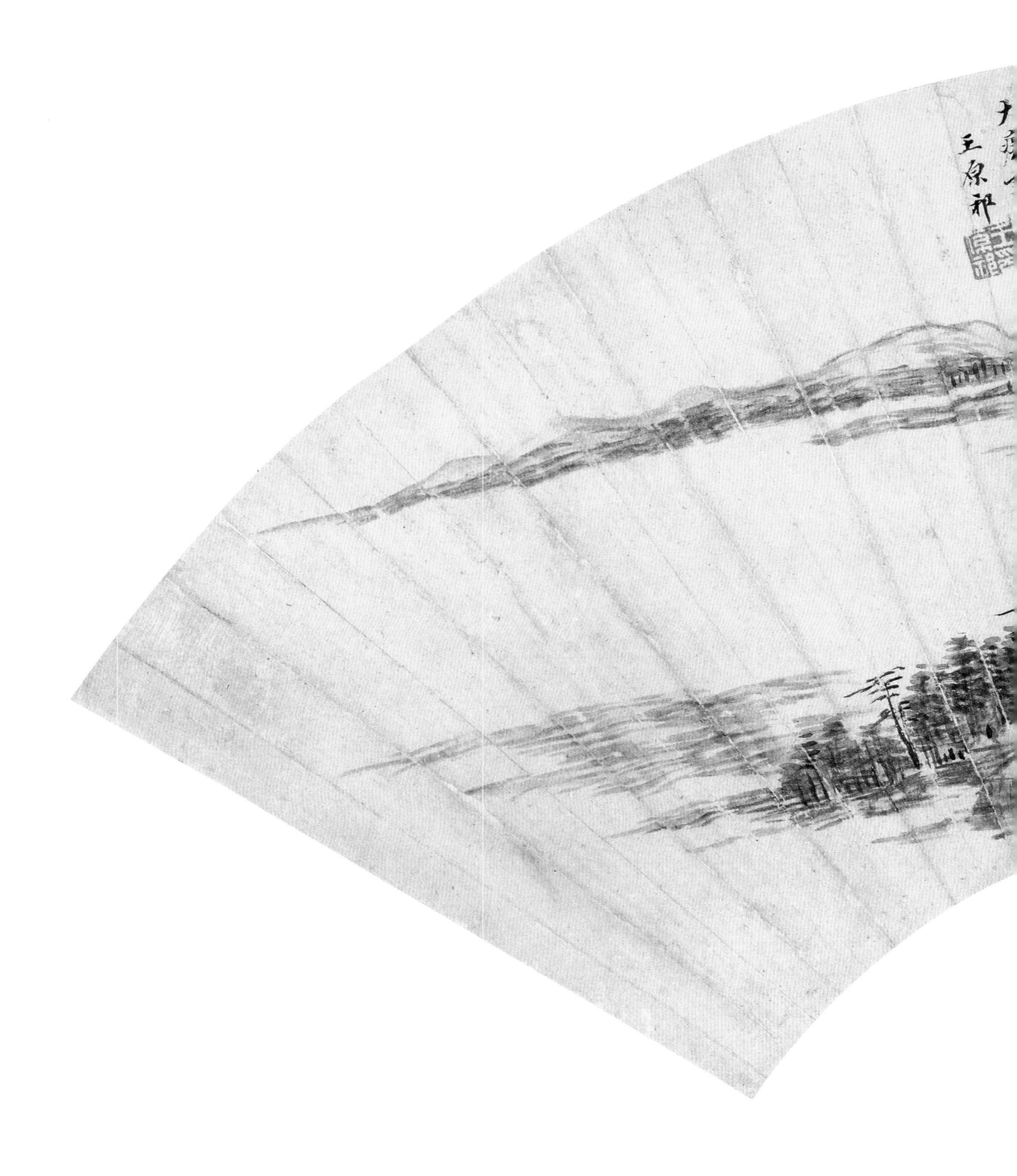

115. 山水图扇页

王原祁绘　纸本 设色

纵 17.2 厘米　横 50.2 厘米

扇页有自题："臣王原祁恭画。"钤"臣原祁"朱、白文印。

图绘茂盛的树木、简约的草舍和由众多小石块叠加的山石，这些都是王原祁惯绘的题材。它们构成典雅清幽的自然环境，是文人画家所追求的理想生存之所。山石的石面以润笔皴擦，并且以墨和绿色点苔，苔点大小间杂，聚散相生，与小笔触点染的树叶相呼应，于细碎中联结成杂而不乱的整体。

此图无年款，由落"臣"字款而知，此图应该是王原祁考上进士后，在宫中任职期间，献给康熙皇帝的画扇。虽然画幅很小，但是，是王氏的用心之作。

116. 仿倪瓒山水图扇页

王原祁绘　纸本 设色

纵 16.5 厘米　横 49 厘米

扇页有自题:“庚寅初秋，为长黄年世兄再写设色云林笔。麓台祁。”钤“王原祁印”白文方印、“麓台”朱文方印，引首钤“三味”朱文葫芦印。“庚寅”是清康熙四十九年(1710 年)，王原祁时年 60 多岁。

此图构图仿自元倪瓒，绘“一河两岸”之景，但是在山石、树木的表现上，比倪瓒的笔墨更加草率、润泽，它实际上是王原祁在仿倪的基础上，又融入了自家秀润笔法的画作。

117. 山水图扇页

原济绘　纸本 墨笔

纵 17.9 厘米　横 55.5 厘米

扇页有自题:“客广陵。十月无山水可寻，出入无路，如坠井底，向次翁、东老二三知己求救，公以扇出示之，曰：‘和尚须自救。’雨中放笔，游不尽的三十年前草鞋根子，亦有放光动地处，有则尽与次翁藏之，使他日见之者云，当时苦瓜和尚是这等习气。丁卯十月清湘石涛济山僧。”钤“老涛”白文印。“丁卯”是清康熙二十六年(1687 年),原济时年 46 岁。

原济 (1642～约 1718 年), 俗姓朱，名若极，广西全州人。明太祖朱元璋后裔靖江王朱守谦的十世孙。明灭亡后削发为僧，法名原济，字石涛，号清湘老人、瞎尊者、苦瓜和尚、大滌子等。擅绘花果兰竹、人物，尤工山水。他师法自然，多次登临庐山、黄山，主张“搜尽奇峰打草稿”，反对摹古不化之风。其运笔纵横奔放，施墨霸气洒脱，构图奇巧险峻，深得元人笔墨意趣。对扬州画派和近现代中国画的影响极大。与朱耷、髡残、弘仁合称“清初四僧”。著有《苦瓜和尚画语录》。

据扇页自题而知，此图是作者闲居广陵 (今扬州) 时，借友人的扇子所绘山水。图中山石延绵叠嶂、奇峰突起，气势撼人。作者为了表现石材坚硬的质感，多以方折的线条勾勒边廓，石面的皴染与勾线相混合，显现出石体的厚重。在原济的山水画创作中以笔法奔放粗犷，施墨酣畅淋漓的作品居多，这种含蓄秀逸的画作颇为少见，此图扇是其细笔清朗画风的代表作。

118. 梅竹双清图扇页

原济绘　纸本 墨笔

纵 17.5 厘米　横 49 厘米

扇页有自题："昨年作别銮江城，□(字残，不辨)来相向邗江明。邗江之水何其清，朝朝暮暮寒潮生。作书作画乘潮起，芒鞋竹杖图身轻。与君父子交三代，骨肉同盟朴素情。欲去不去五湖客，欲眠不眠老大行。放眼高歌一曲短，情真那不说生平。广陵简禹声年世翁博教，石涛济山僧稿又画。"钤朱文一印不辨。

据题而知，这是作者送给友人简禹声的画扇。扇面左图右文。图绘一树劲梅，其背后衬以青竹。有君子之谓的竹与梅相生相伴，犹如同是清高之人，原济与友人间不离不弃的亲密关系。梅竹造型简约，用笔劲健有力，显现出作者白描功底。右侧自题的字体随心所欲，有着大小之分。字迹笔笔方正，具有朴素之美，与不加雕饰的梅竹形成呼应。此图扇虽然用以展示的空间较小，但是，作者通过图文并茂的形式，展示了其能书善画的全面修养。

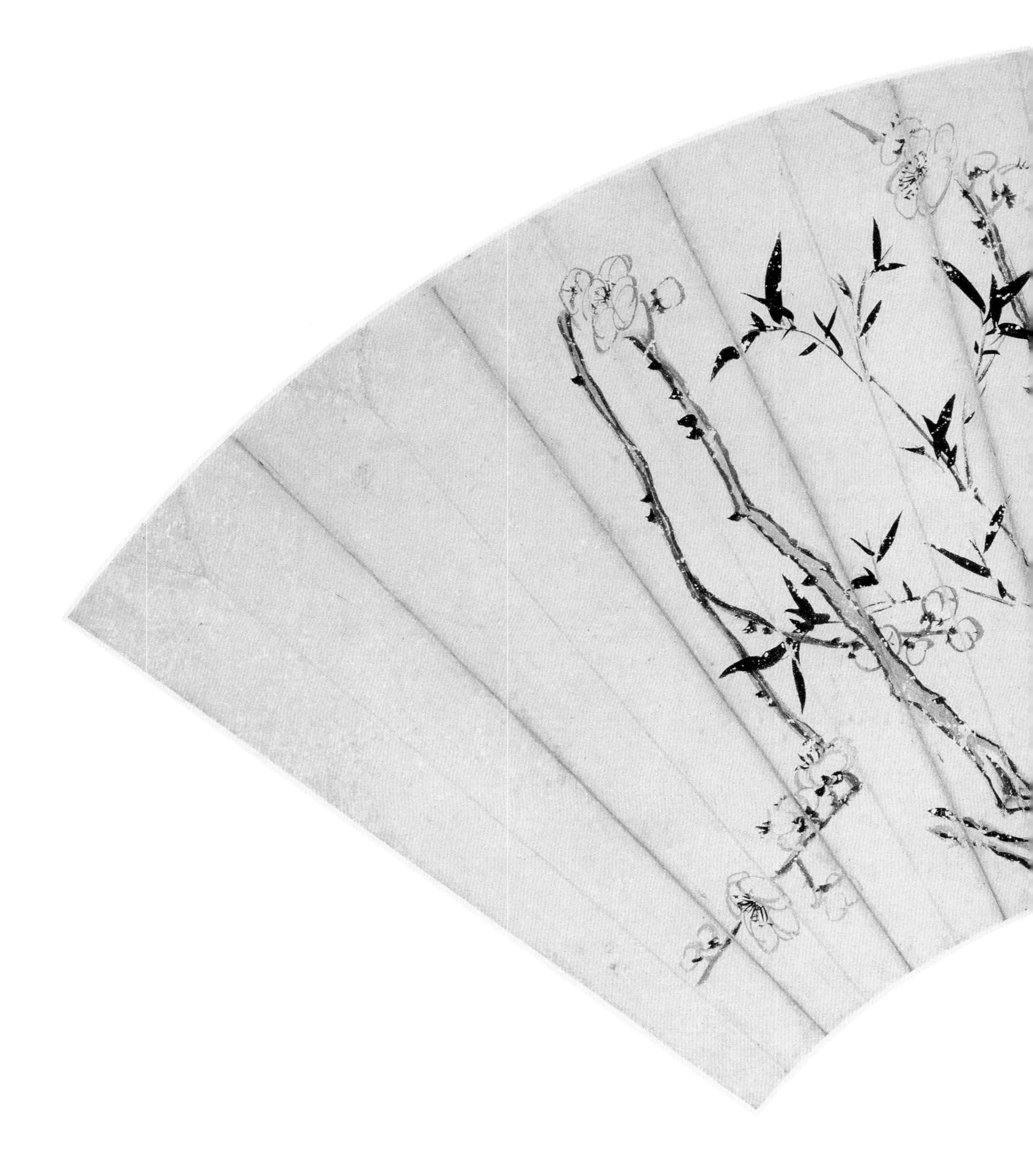

昨年作別蜀江[illegible][illegible]來

相問邛江明邛江之水

何其清朝朝暮暮[illegible][illegible]潮

生作書作畫乘潮起

芒鞋竹杖高舟輕指若

父子交三代骨肉同盟

朴素情欲去不去五湖

客欲眠不眠老大行

放眼高歌一曲短情真

鄰不說生平 廣陵簡

禹穀年世翁博教 石濤濟山僧稿

119. 奇峰图扇页

原济绘　纸本 墨笔

纵 17.5 厘米　横 49 厘米

扇页有自题："夜梦文殊座上，白云涌出青莲。晓向笔头忙写，恍如乙未初年。纪为燕老道翁博教。瞎尊者济。"钤"原济"白文印、"石涛"朱文印。"乙未"是清康熙五十四年（1715 年），原济时年 74 岁。

原济从二十多岁起，一生多次登临黄山。黄山的奇松、怪石、云海、瀑布给他留下了深刻的印象，在所绘《黄山图》中题有"黄山是我师，我是黄山友"之句，黄山也因此成为他创作的源泉，创作了大量以黄山为表现题材的画作。此幅是原济晚年图绘黄山两处重要景观莲花峰和文殊院之作。构图新颖大胆，极尽含蓄隐现之妙。重点刻画的扇页中部的莲花峰以"截取法"表现，着重勾描了它交叠错落的山顶，其山腰以下的部分利用"无中生有"的艺术手法，通过虚无缥缈的白云被隐去，从而反衬出此峰的高深与雄伟，令整个画面也由此成为一个烟云流动、气势壮丽而又深邃空灵的小世界。

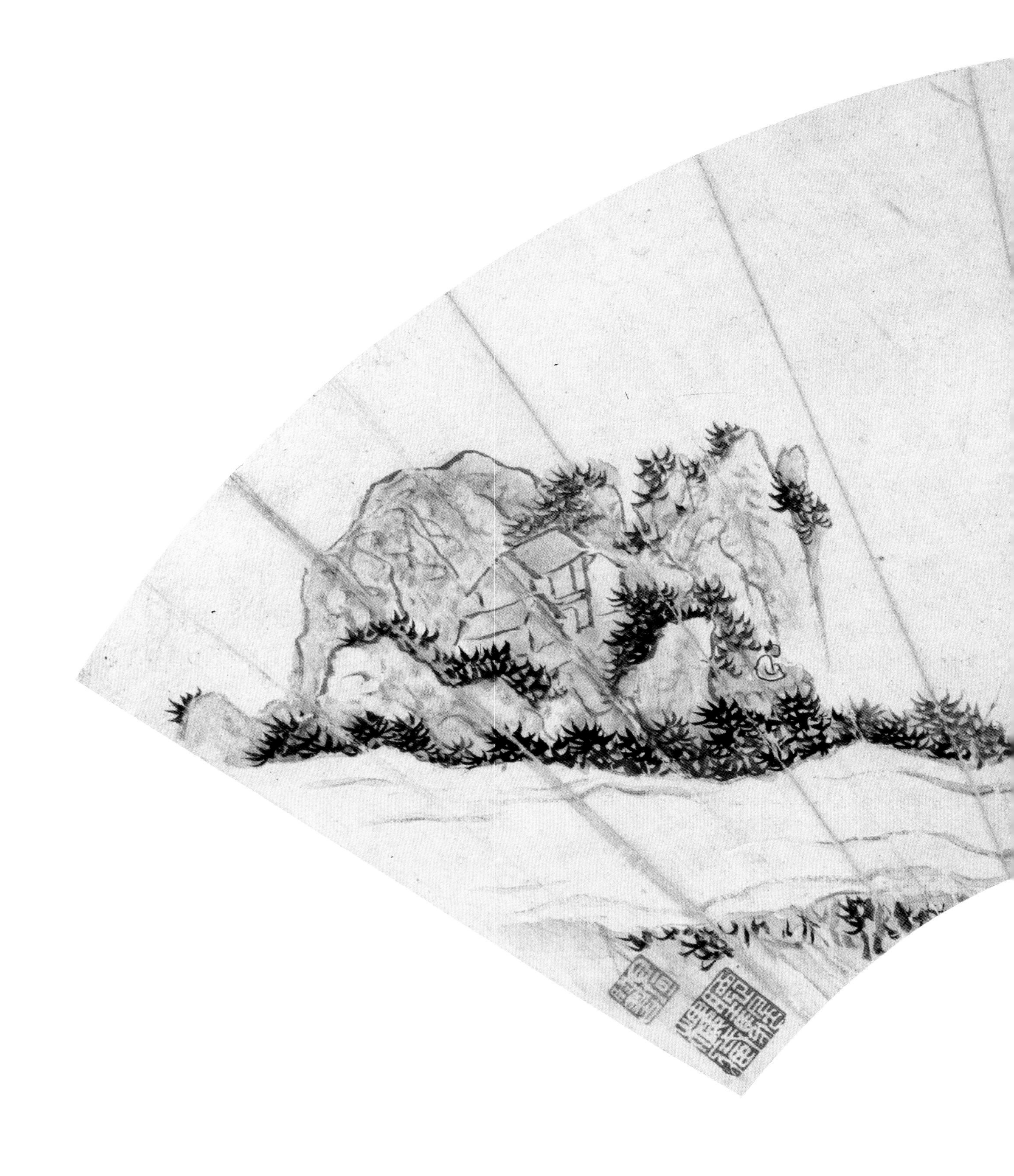

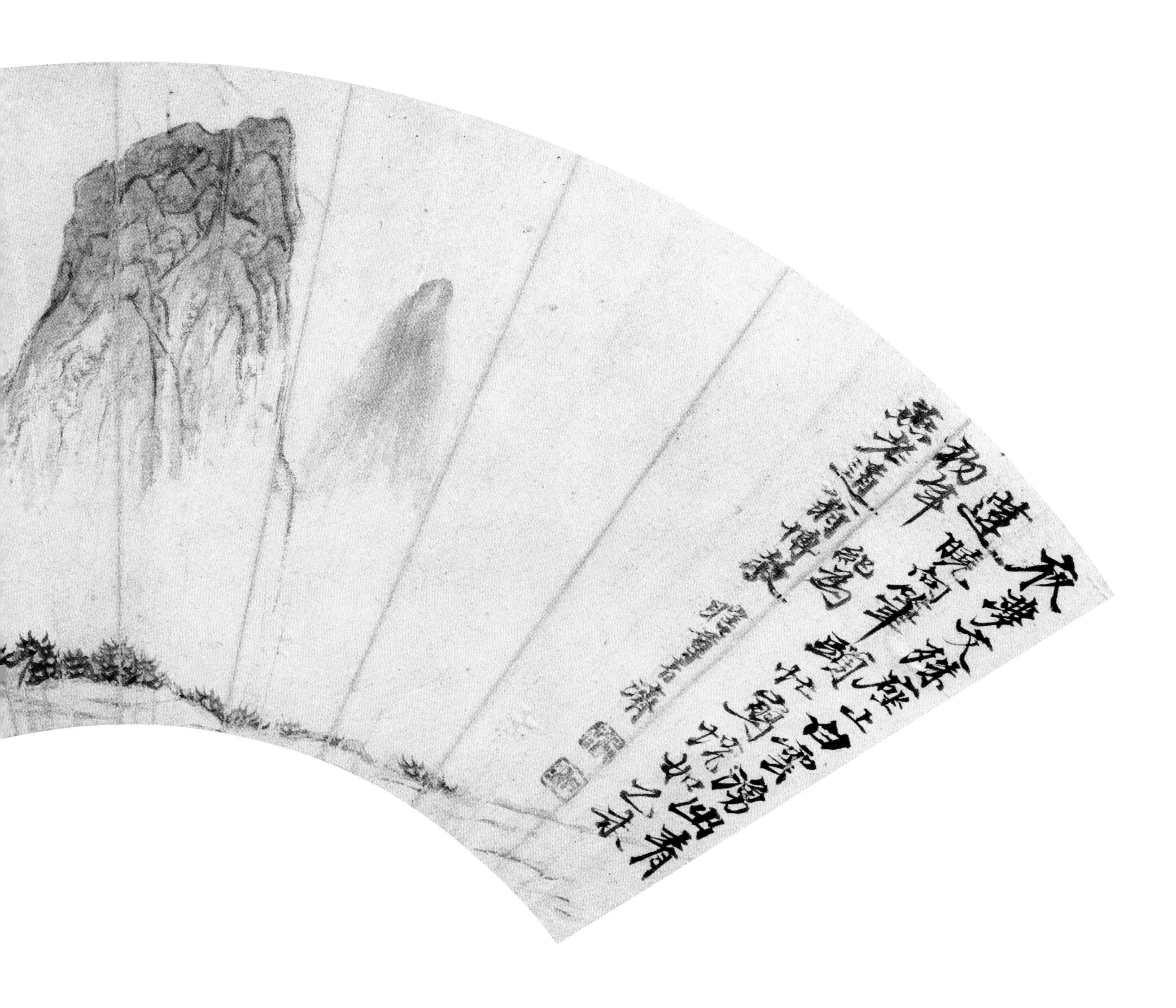

120. 东园万竹图扇页

王概绘　金笺 设色

纵 16.4 厘米　横 51.6 厘米

扇页有自题："园倚杏村花渐发，溪临万竹阁深藏。高台恰对西窗外，负手朝阳即凤凰。己卯春初，仿马遥父东园万竹图，上元翁老先生教。晚学王概。"钤"王概"白文印、"安节"朱文印。"己卯"是清康熙三十八年（1699 年），王概时年 55 岁。

王概（1645～约 1710 年），初名丐，字东郭、安节，祖籍秀水（今浙江嘉兴），久居金陵（今江苏南京）。工书法、绘画，尤擅山水、人物、花卉、翎毛。山水学龚贤，善作大幅及山石等。35 岁时为《芥子园画传》绘制山水、花鸟，成为清代普及绘画技法的著名画谱。

作者为了表现此图中"溪临万竹阁深藏"的"深藏"，绘制了变幻无穷的婆娑竹影做为遮掩。为了显现"万竹"成林的壮观气势，运用了"虚实相生"的表现手法，借助在竹林中穿梭浮动的烟云雾气达到"渭川千亩"之势。其笔墨清爽健硬，境界旷达，是王概匠心独运的扇页画佳作之一。

121. 早朝图扇页

禹之鼎绘　纸本 设色

纵 16.7 厘米　横 50 厘米

扇页有自题："早朝图。都下客窗画，广陵禹之鼎。" 钤 "之鼎慎斋" 朱文印。

禹之鼎（1647～1716 年），字尚吉，号慎斋，江都（今江苏扬州）人。因江都古称广陵，故常自称"广陵"人。清康熙二十年（1681 年）官鸿胪寺序班，以画供奉入畅春园。善画人物、山水，尤精写真。初学蓝瑛笔法，后宗宋元诸家笔墨，打下了深厚的画学基础。肖像画面貌多样，对白描法、墨骨法、江南法都有研究，所绘人物形神兼备，秀媚古雅，被推为"当代第一"，一时名公小像多出其手。

画史记载，禹之鼎因擅画肖像享有盛名，在 34 岁左右被召入京城，任职鸿胪寺序班，主要负责给觐见康熙皇帝的藩属、外邦官员画像，以为留底备查。这段做官的经历，使得禹之鼎对官员赶早朝觐见皇帝之事颇为了解。此图以借古喻今的创作手法，表现的是古时官员在天还未亮时，就在挑灯童子的领引下赶赴宫殿上朝的情景。作者通过寥寥数笔便将官员困乏、疲惫的神态表现得淋漓尽致，显现出其形神兼备的绘画造诣。

122. 桐阴仕女图扇页

王树榖绘　纸本 设色

纵 17 厘米　横 51.1 厘米

扇页有自题：“七十二叟王慈竹甫画于青梧书屋。”钤“王原丰印”白文印、“鹿公”朱文印。

王树榖（1649～1733年后），字原丰，号无我、鹿公、石屋、石屋居士，又号方外布衣、栗园叟、慈竹君、一笑先生等，仁和（今浙江杭州）人。擅绘人物，笔法出自陈洪绶而有所变化，注重以形写神，是清初重要的人物画家。

图绘一女子在梧桐树下，倚石而坐，若有所思的样子。画面大面积的空白给人以充分的想象空间，也增强了对神情落寞女子的关注。图中的仕女形象不同于唐代女性丰腴之美，也不同于宋代女性健壮之美，而是表现出柔弱、病态、顾影自怜之姿。其这种“倚风娇无力”、“病态美人”的仕女形象，与清人的政治环境、世俗环境以及理学思想、女性审美观的改变都有着密切的联系。王树榖之后，改琦、费丹旭又将这种女性柔弱、哀怨的淡雅之美推向极致。

123. 东坡博古图扇页

萧晨绘　纸本 设色

纵 18 厘米　横 51.6 厘米

扇页有自题："东坡博古图，前人有其本，考之书史未见其说，岂好事者为之耶？是篁成于辛亥，时余年已称古稀有四矣，强弩之末，犹有可观，然弄粉涂朱，亦可愧也。兰陵萧晨并识。"钤一印不辨。"辛亥"是清雍正九年（1731 年），萧晨时年 74 岁。

萧晨（1658～？年），字灵曦，号中素，江苏扬州人。工诗，擅画山水人物，尤其是雪景。师法唐、宋传统笔墨，风格工致巧整，有一定的造型能力。

图绘宋代文豪苏东坡与友人聚会鉴赏古物的情景。构图简约，以案头所置青铜、瓷器等古物，渲染出品古的氛围；以人物间相互顾盼的神态，点明鉴古的主题。此图虽是萧晨晚年之作，但是人物、器物等均刻画得一丝不苟，其精细的用笔、淡雅的设色，生动地表现出苏轼等人儒雅的风范和潜心品古的神态。

124. 山水图扇页

王敬铭绘　纸本 设色

纵 16.4 厘米　横 46.7 厘米

扇页有自题："康熙丁亥长夏畅春直庐为逸翁老亲家仿倪黄小景设色。未嵒王敬铭"钤印三方，均模糊不辨。"丁亥"是清康熙四十六年（1707 年），王敬铭时年 41 岁。

王敬铭（1667～1721 年），字丹思，一字未嵒，号味闲，今上海嘉定镇人。工诗擅画，爱砚成癖。康熙皇帝南巡时，他以呈献诗、画受到赏识，遂入京进皇家畅春园，充武英殿纂修。康熙五十二年（1713 年）进士，授翰林院修撰，曾任江西乡试主考官。画学宋元诸家，笔墨苍润，气韵清腴闲远，有"吴门画派"遗风。

据自题而知，此图扇是王敬铭送给亲家的画扇，自言笔墨仿自元人倪瓒和黄公望。其"一河两岸"式构图与倪瓒的相仿。山石树木以中锋行笔，线条粗重，墨色沉郁，与黄氏的画风相近。娴熟的笔法中又流露出作者自身笔墨古拙淳厚的特点。

125. 山水图扇页

袁江绘　纸本 设色

纵 18.2 厘米　横 53.4 厘米

扇页有自题:“法马钦山笔意，时己卯如月。袁江。”钤“袁江”、“文涛”朱文印二方。“己卯”是清康熙三十八年（1699 年）。

袁江（生卒年不详，活动于 18 世纪），字文涛，江都（今江苏扬州）人。擅长绘山水、界画楼阁，工细精致。早年师法仇英，继承青绿山水传统，中年“得无名氏所临古人画稿，技遂大进”。曾偕袁耀至山西省太原作画多年，故其作品在北方流传较多。

图绘江南景色，一边是浩渺的江水，一边是雄奇伟岸的山峦。严整的山石与富有动感的轻舟相呼应，画面形成动与静、繁与简的鲜明对比。此幅作品中，石面略施小斧劈皴，具有宋画风貌，作者尚未使用成熟期的近似“卷云”和“鬼面”的勾斫法，或者状似“弹涡”的点皴法，应属于其早期作品。

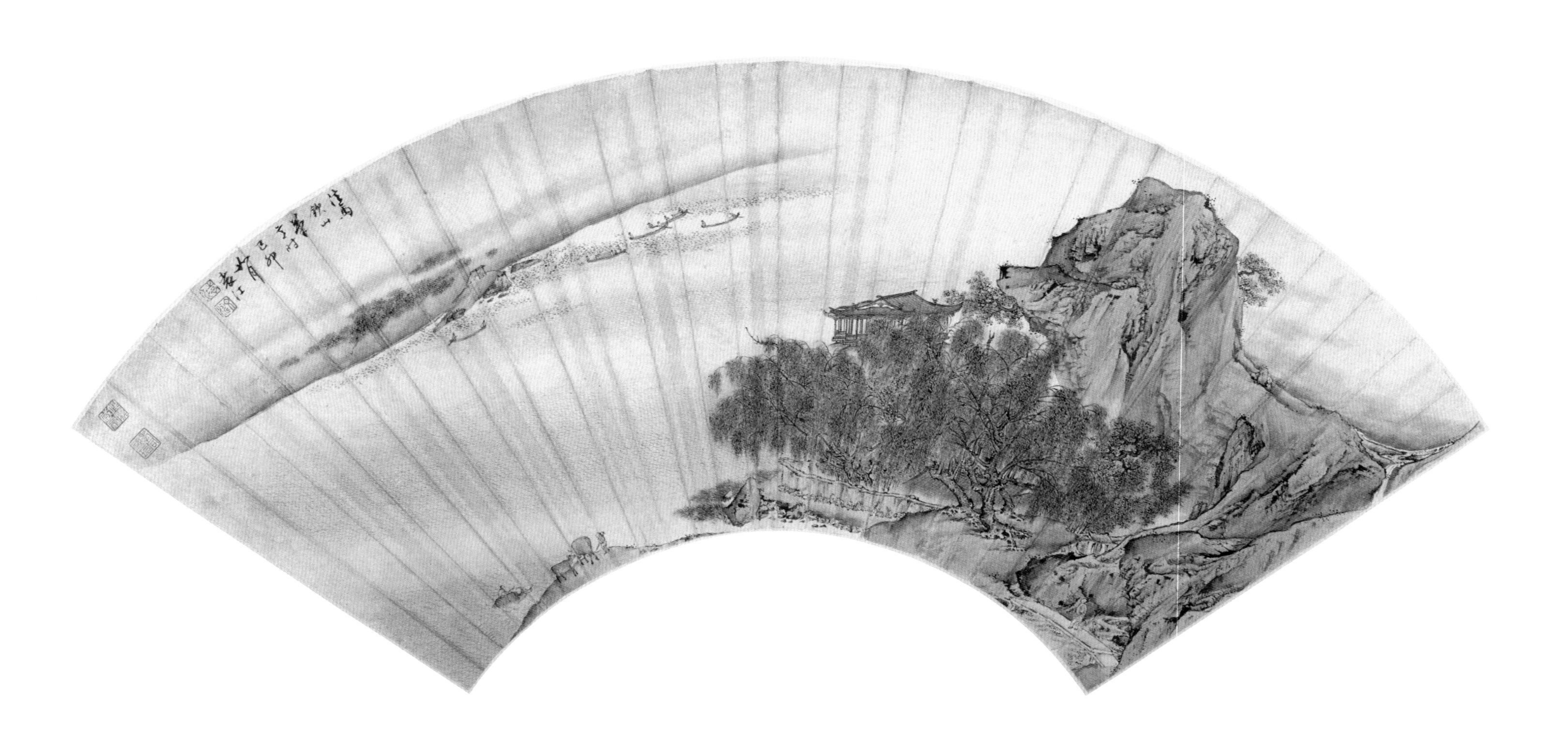

126. 蔬果图扇页

袁江绘　纸本 设色

纵 18.2 厘米　横 54 厘米

扇页有自题："东南风味。戊戌六月邗上袁江写。"钤"袁"、"江"联珠印。"戊戌"是清康熙五十七年（1718 年）。

图绘东南地区日常生活中最常见的萝卜、竹笋、虾和贝壳等食物。扇面本是文人们用以标榜自身儒雅的掌玩之物，因此，在画作的表现内容上，一般选文人用以自我标榜的梅兰竹菊四君子题材，或者是用来言明自己理想隐居之地的高山峻岭、清水小溪，再或者是表明自己学识修养的人物故事画等。虽然民以食为天，但明清画扇中以蔬菜和水产品为表现主题的极少，此图给人耳目一新的感觉。事实上，袁江以食材为表现内容的画作不仅这一件，他还画有《花果卷》（现藏故宫博物院），其中除牡丹、萱草、桂花等花卉外，还有茄子、桃和西瓜等果蔬。此图以设色小写意法绘蔬菜和水产品，用笔灵活，设色晕染层次丰富，不仅准确地表现出萝卜、虾的外形，还表现出它们鲜活的质感，展示了袁氏于山水楼阁界画之外的写生才华。

127. 风雨重阳图扇页

袁江绘　纸本 设色

纵 17.5 厘米　横 52.9 厘米

扇页有自题：“风雨近重阳。己亥冬为公老道翁写，袁江。”钤“袁”、“江”联珠朱文印。“己亥”是清康熙五十八年（1719 年）。

图绘狂风暴雨的景致。此图成功处在于形象生动地表现出风和雨的动感。风本是无形的，作者通过绘树木枝叶一致向右的走势，暗示出强劲的风在自左向右吹。雨，虽然是有形的，但是难以通过笔墨来表现，作者于是通过身披防雨斗笠的行者暗示出雨意，同时又巧妙地将山石的皴法绘成水波状，给人以雨量过大山洪暴发的联想。全图为小写意画，其风格与袁氏所擅长的楼阁画相比大相径庭，别有一番韵味。

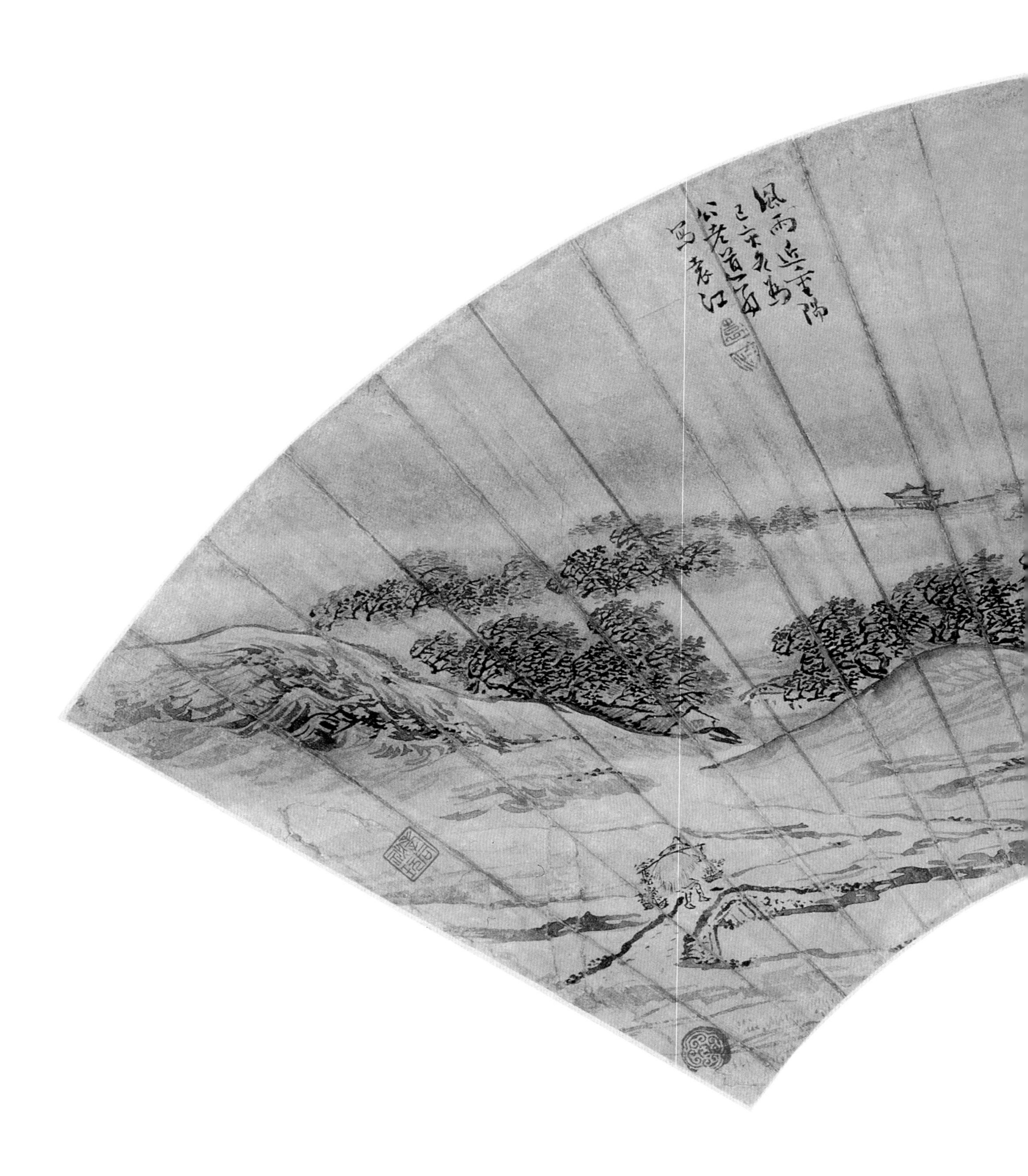

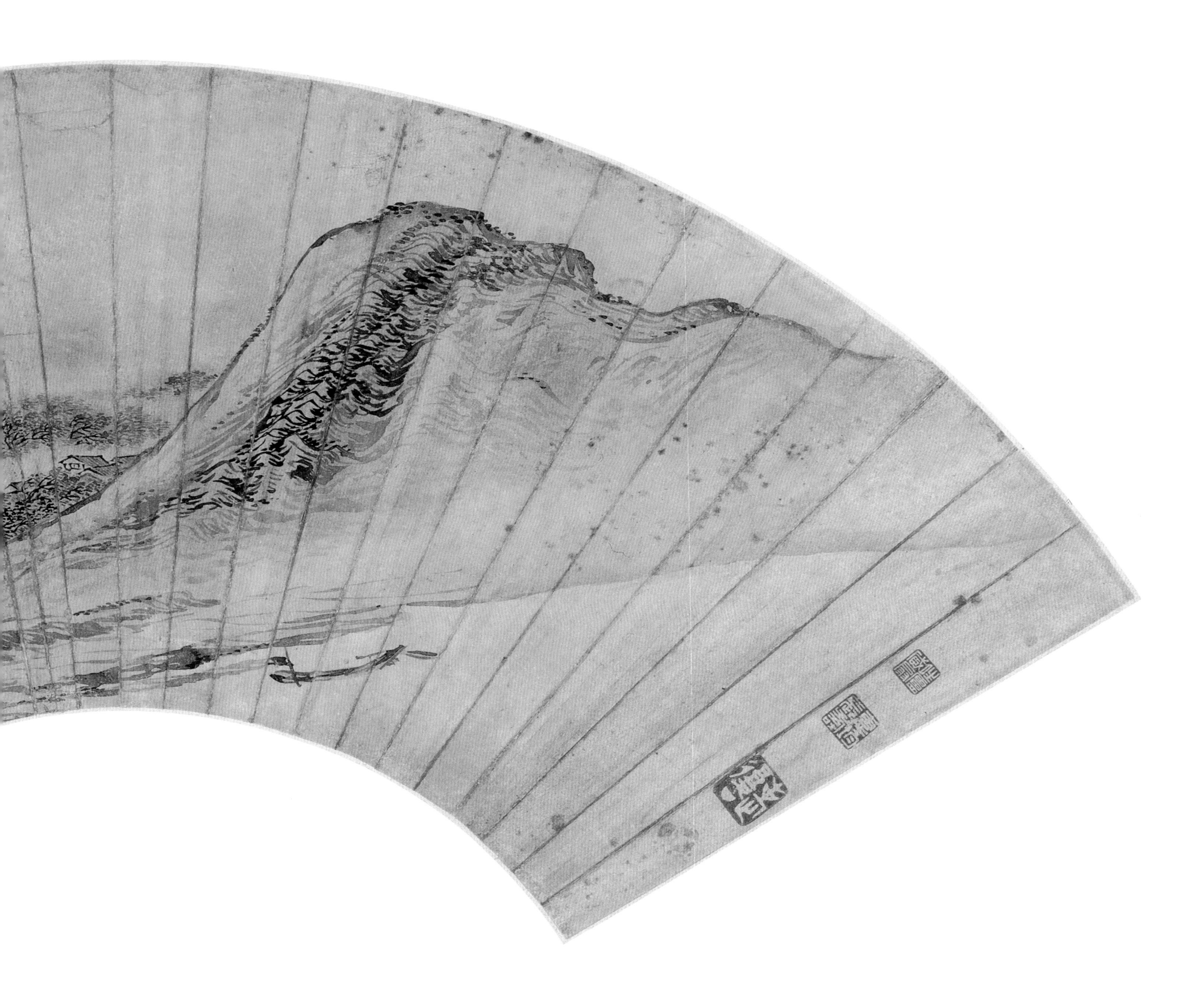

128. 竹溪高隐图扇页

袁耀绘　纸本 设色

纵 17.3 厘米　横 52.4 厘米

扇页有自题，墨迹模糊不辨，款署："邗上袁耀画。"钤白文联珠印，印文不辨。

袁耀（生卒年不详，活动于 18 世纪），字昭道，江都（今江苏扬州）人。擅界画，宗法宋元，所绘水榭楼阁，或以坚实的山岩为依托，或以浩渺的江湖为背景，能够将建筑与山水有机地结合，使二者浑然一体。

此图采取平远式构图，景致开阔平稳。全图设色淡雅，具有诗意般的情趣。山石以色染为主，石面平整少皴擦。树叶以繁复的笔墨点染，叶片细碎多交叠，与石面形成"碎"与"整"的对比，丰富了视觉感受。图中小如豆许的高士和仙鹤既为冷漠的山石增添了色彩和生趣，又为典雅的建筑营造出真实可信的空间。袁耀与袁江一样具有偏于宋人画、笔致工细的画风，这在当时以王时敏、王鉴等"四王"为正宗的清代画坛，不为人所重。

129. 人物山水图扇页

陈枚绘　纸本 设色

纵 18.8 厘米　横 57.9 厘米

扇页有自题："陈枚恭画。"钤朱文印不辨。

陈枚（生卒年不详，活动于 17 世纪末），字载东，号殿抡、枝窝头陀，娄县（今上海松江）人。擅绘山水、花鸟、人物等。画学北宋院体，勾线一丝不苟，敷色晕染生动，所绘物象精细入微，具有较强的造型能力和以形传神的艺术表现功力。雍正初年，经院画家陈善推荐入宫，成为雍正、乾隆朝专职画家，官至员外郎，数次以画作称旨受到皇室的赏赐。

图绘老者策杖，童仆相随漫步林泉的情景。画法工细，人物造型准确，枝繁叶茂的树木，杂而不乱。设色不同于陈枚用色丰富的工笔重彩画，仅以赭色为主，烘染出一种幽淡的氛围，与逍遥优游的主题相契合。

130. 榴花图扇页

陈枚绘　纸本 设色

纵 19.5 厘米　横 57.5 厘米

扇页有自题：“载东陈枚写。”钤“陈枚”朱文印。

图绘一枝欣欣向荣的石榴。作者以细致的观察和写实功底，运用工整细腻的手法，表现了花、叶不同的形貌：花儿有的含苞待放，有的姹紫嫣红，有的则已凋零化作果实；叶儿在刻画和渲染上注重区分老叶、嫩叶以及叶片的受光面和背阴面，令简约的画面充实并具有纯真的气息。此图与追求写实的宋人院体小品花卉画有着异曲同工之妙。

131. 梅竹图扇页

蒋廷锡绘　纸本 墨笔

纵 17 厘米　横 48 厘米

扇页有自题：“壬寅六月仿元人笔意。蒋廷锡。”钤“蒋廷锡印”白文印、“朝朝染翰”朱文印。“壬寅”是清康熙六十一年（1722 年），蒋廷锡时年 54 岁。

蒋廷锡（1669～1732 年），字南沙，号青桐居士，常熟（今属江苏）人。康熙四十二年（1703 年）赐进士，官至大学士。他博学广识、精于典章，擅绘花鸟，受到恽寿平画风的影响，能于工致的法度中显示出意笔的风采，是康、雍朝重要的词臣画家。曾任《古今图书集成》、《圣祖仁皇帝实录》总裁及续纂《大清会典》副总裁。著《青桐集》、《秋风集》、《片云集》等多部诗文集。

梅花以“众芳摇落独暄妍”的品格，竹以“千磨万击还坚劲，任尔东西南北风”的特性，与兰、菊同被历代文人赞美为“四君子”，并且成为重要的绘画创作题材。图绘枝干虬曲的梅向右出枝；叶片肥厚的竹向左取势。作者将本是各自独立、不相连贯的梅与竹有机地结合成一个整体。图中的梅花以墨笔圈线为瓣，线条细劲圆润，显现出“暗香浮动”的诗意；竹叶以润墨阔笔直接晕染，显现出高标清韵的格致。此图不刻意求工、求似，唯求自然天趣的笔墨，显现出蒋氏平淡雅逸的审美意趣。

132. 萱花图扇页

蒋廷锡绘　金笺 设色

纵 16.5 厘米　横 49 厘米

扇页有自题："南沙蒋廷锡。"钤"蒋廷锡印"白文印、"扬孙"朱文印。

此图以折枝法重点刻画了一茎数朵萱花绽放的花头。萱，又名"金针"、"丹棘"、"宜男草"等，是百合科多年生的草本植物，在苏、浙、陕、黑、晋、湘、滇、藏等地普遍种植。一茎多花的现象实属少见，被作者视为祥瑞征兆而加以刻画。其笔墨写实，造型准确，设色为平涂，没有水与色的交融渲染，花、叶略显呆板。此扇面在使用过程中，因频繁的开合，以致颜料有所脱落，对画作的审美效果有一定影响。

133. 兰石图扇页

蒋廷锡绘　纸本 墨笔

纵 16.5 厘米　横 49.1 厘米

扇页有自题："洗研试新墨，香风拂茧纸。莫嫌兰叶稀，叶多伤兰蕊。为石俦二兄，廷锡。"下钤"蒋廷锡印"白文印、"扬孙"朱文印。引首钤"体物"朱文印。

此图用润墨粗笔画出坡石，石面略作皴擦，并且辅以散落的墨点，显得平稳笨拙。石后是用双勾法绘制的一丛幽兰，兰叶向外柔和地伸展，呈随风而动之态。石与兰这种粗放与工整相呼应的笔法，代表了蒋氏工写结合的花鸟画风。蒋氏入内廷任高职期间，以其名署款了一系列笔致正整的花鸟画，如《塞外花卉图》卷等，经徐邦达等鉴定它们多为代笔作，现已知蒋氏代笔人有马元驭、马逸父子等。

扇面上有茶菴题七言一首："谷口松根尽自芳，好风何苦送幽香。教人描画供人看，便似风流初嫁娘。"

134. 仿李营丘山水图扇页

唐岱绘　纸本 设色

纵 18.7 厘米　横 59 厘米

扇页有自题："仿李营丘，唐岱敬画。"钤"唐"、"岱"白朱文联珠印。

唐岱（1673～1752 年后），字毓东，号静岩、知生等，满洲正蓝旗人。承袭祖爵，任骁骑参领。其《绘事发微》自序"幼赋性疏野，读书之暇，有志画学"。工绘山水，拜王原祁为师，推崇黄公望的笔意。其作画喜用干笔积墨法，笔墨生拙，韵味淳厚，色调淡雅。他的这种画风属于当时画坛的主流，因此，深受清康熙、雍正、乾隆三朝皇帝的赏识。康熙皇帝常召他作画并且与之探讨画理，称他为"画状元"。

此扇面的构图层次清晰，以远景的崇山峻岭推出近景的各类杂木，以低矮的房舍树木烘托出山峦的巍然屹立。自题"仿李营丘"，此图在笔墨及气韵上正得李氏画风之旨，即宋郭若虚《图画见闻志》评李氏画作"夫气象萧疏，烟林清旷，笔锋颖脱，墨法精微者，营丘之制也"的特点，由此可见作者对李氏技法的全面掌握与娴熟的运用。

135. 晴霞飞鸟图扇页

华喦绘　纸本 设色

纵 17.3 厘米　横 50.3 厘米

扇页有自题："写得一缕晴霞傍鸟飞。为凤川先生雅鉴，新罗山人。"钤"华喦"白文印。

华喦（1682～1756 年），字秋岳，号新罗山人。上杭（一作莆田，今属福建）人，寓居扬州、苏州。卖画为生。创作题材广泛，人物画仿自宋马和之、明陈洪绶，线条简洁流畅，形象生动富有个性。花鸟画兼工带写，妙趣天然，对清中叶以后的花鸟创作有一定的影响；山水画淡雅设色，有率意空灵之致。著《离垢集》。

图绘老者悠然树下，目送飞鹤的景象。全图构思巧妙，作为画作主角之一的仙鹤，没有占据画幅的主要位置重点表现，而是被画到了扇面的左上侧，几乎出于画幅之外。它被关注完全是通过老者专注的仰视目光，无形的目光穿越空白的画面，将鹤与老者成功地联系在了一起，由此可见作者在人物的体态、眼神的刻画上，已达到了以形传神的地步。

此图没有年款，但是从所绘人物的疏笔画风上推断，应是华喦晚年之作。华喦晚年在宗法陈洪绶、仇英及宋人笔墨的基础上，又吸收了马和之"蚂蟥描"和"兰叶描"的线描法，画风自此一变为疏放的简笔，具有松秀、含蓄之美。

136. 芦雁图扇页

边寿民绘　纸本 设色

纵 17.4 厘米　横 52.5 厘米

扇页有自题：“于陵于陆羽缤纷，岂逐菰蒲野鹜群。昨日秋风看矫翮，一行冲破碧天云。并题为翼翁研长兄清品，苇间居士边寿民。”钤“寿民”白文印、“颐公”朱文印。

边寿民（1684～1752 年），原名维祺，字寿民，后以字行，更字颐公，号渐僧、苇间居士等，山阳（今江苏省淮安县）人。出身贫寒，终生不仕。工诗词书画，善绘花鸟、蔬果和山水，尤以创作芦雁而驰名江淮，有“边芦雁”之称。因常年往来于扬州，被列为“扬州八怪”之一。

此图是作者送给友人的画作。图绘两只大雁在芦塘边欲行又止的情景。边寿民为了画好雁，曾“结茅苇际”与雁为伍，每日细致观察雁的行、卧、翔各种姿态，故其笔下的大雁，符合解剖学原理，具有生动写实的特点。此扇页不打图稿，直接以墨或色加以绘制，显示出边氏对笔墨的熟练运用能力和超强的造型能力。

137. 夏山烟霭图扇页

张庚绘　纸本 墨笔

纵 20 厘米　横 56 厘米

扇页有自题："夏山烟霭。仿元人法似澄之世兄清赏，白苎村桑者张庚。"钤"浦山"白文印。

张庚（1685～1760 年），原名焘，字溥三，后改名庚，号浦山、瓜田逸史、弥伽居士等。秀水（今浙江嘉兴人）人。他聪慧机敏，性情散淡，绘写意花卉传承陈淳、陈书画法，笔墨高迈，一花半叶，淡墨欹毫，自有疏斜历乱之致。其山水画追仿五代董源、巨然及元代黄公望诸大家，同时，注重以自然山水为师，在传统与写生的有机结合中，显现出既有传统又有个性的笔墨特征。著《国朝画征录》《浦山论画》。

扇页绘云横秀岭的林峦烟景。此图在山石的表现上继承了元人的笔法，先以润墨渲染，后用湿笔作皴擦线条，最后以浓墨在石的边缘处作点染。笔势潇洒而秀润，墨色透明而凝重。

夏山烟霭
仿元人法以
瀞之世兄清賞
白苧村桑者
張庚

138. 仿董北苑山水图扇页

张庚绘　纸本 墨笔

纵 16 厘米　横 46.5 厘米

扇页有自题："仿董北苑法似澄之世兄清玩，弥伽居士庚。"下钤朱文印不识。

此图是作者送给友人澄之的另一幅画作。扇面虽然不大，但是作者通过山峦、树木、房舍、河塘等景致的巧妙穿插，以及虚实对比、纵横交错等手法，扩展了远近空间，令扇面小中见大，具有"咫尺千里"的博大气势。山石用湿笔，连皴带擦，树木多以卧笔点叶，灵动秀润。作者自言仿五代董北苑（董源）山水，但是其画风更接近元人黄公望古雅明洁的笔墨。

139. 仿江贯道山水图扇页

蔡嘉绘 纸本 设色

纵 19.7 厘米 横 55.6 厘米

扇页有自题：“乙卯岁九月仿江贯道笔意为云吉先生正，松原野老嘉。”钤印一方，印文模糊不辨。“乙卯”是清雍正十三年（1735年），蔡嘉时年 50 岁。

蔡嘉（1686～1779 年后），字松原，一字岑州，号雪堂、旅亭、朱方老民等，丹阳（今属江苏）人，长期侨居扬州，居“高寒旧馆”。他聪敏好学，幼习银工，后改学诗文书画，工草书，擅绘花鸟、人物及青绿山水，笔墨工细秀润，勾点敷染别有韵致。与高翔、汪士慎、高凤翰、朱冕等交往，时称“五君子”。

据作者自题而知，此图是仿宋山水名家江贯道笔意所绘。江贯道(生卒年不详,名参，字贯道，学仿五代董源、巨然的画法，以工绘江南水乡著称）笔意所绘。本图表现了一江两岸的景致，重点刻画的是近景，随着山势由高向低，绘有飞流直落的瀑布、苍郁茂盛的树木和规整的楼阁。用笔工整细腻，墨色干净清爽，将江南明洁滋润的自然景观表现得亮丽多姿。

140. 秋树茅堂图扇页

张宗苍绘　纸本 墨笔

纵 15.6 厘米　横 52 厘米

扇页有自题："丁巳初夏写读书秋树根句，奉日兄先生一粲。张宗苍。"钤"张"、"宗苍"朱文联珠印。"丁巳"是清乾隆二年（1737年），张宗苍时年 52 岁。

张宗苍（1686～1756 年），字默存、墨岑，号篁村、太湖渔人，吴县（今属江苏苏州）人。师承"娄东画派"传人黄鼎。擅长山水画，用笔沉着，山石多加晕染，具有苍劲秀雅之风，一洗画院甜熟柔媚之习。乾隆十六年（1751年），以绘《吴中十六景图》册敬献南巡的乾隆皇帝，受到赞誉，遂被召入宫成为皇室的重要职业画家之一，清内府编纂《石渠宝笈》著录其画作百余幅。

图绘高士茅堂独坐，临窗远眺的逍遥小景。扇页构图左繁右简，左侧的山石树木及竹叶多以淡墨戳点，庞庞杂杂的墨点，相互交叠错落，令景致融为一体。右侧是空旷的水域，偶露浅滩沙渚，其开阔的画面恰与高士目视的方向相一致，无形的目光充实了画面，同时，在有限的空间内唤起观者无限的想象。全图笔墨技法娴熟，画风清俊，是张宗苍入宫前的代表作之一。

141. 山水图扇页

张宗苍绘　纸本 设色

纵 16.3 厘米　横 48 厘米

扇页有自题："臣张宗苍恭画。"钤朱文方印二"臣"、"宗苍"。

根据自题书"臣"字款而知，此图是张宗苍担任宫廷画师期间献给乾隆皇帝的山水画。图中山石以线条皴染，再以焦墨点苔多遍始成，令繁复的林壑不失明爽，笔情墨韵间不失苍郁，反映了画家成熟期的典型风格。

142. 花鸟图扇页

邹一桂绘　金笺 设色

纵 16.5 厘米　横 51 厘米

扇页有自题：“丙午春日仿宋人意，为静宜同学兄雅鉴。小山邹一桂。”钤印二方，印文模糊不辨。“丙午”是清雍正四年(1726 年)，邹一桂时年 41 岁。

邹一桂 (1686～1772 年)，字原褒，号小山、二知老人等，江苏无锡人。清雍正五年 (1727 年) 进士，官至礼部侍郎加尚书衔。他能诗善画，花卉仿恽寿平没骨法，构图设势巧于分枝布叶。山水设色明净冶艳，运笔柔中寓刚，是清乾隆朝重要的词臣画家。著《小山画谱》。

此图是邹一桂中进士前一年所绘花鸟小景。其中禽鸟仰首高鸣的样子，极为真切生动，不仅给人“此时无声胜有声”的听觉感受，而且给人以画外之音的想象。图中以勾线和没骨绘制的翠竹和花卉，笔法简洁凝练，墨色淡雅湿润，展现出它们披露带水的清丽风貌。作者自题“仿宋人意”，实际上仿的是宋人追求写实生动的意趣，在用笔设色施墨上，要比宋人花鸟画粗放写意。

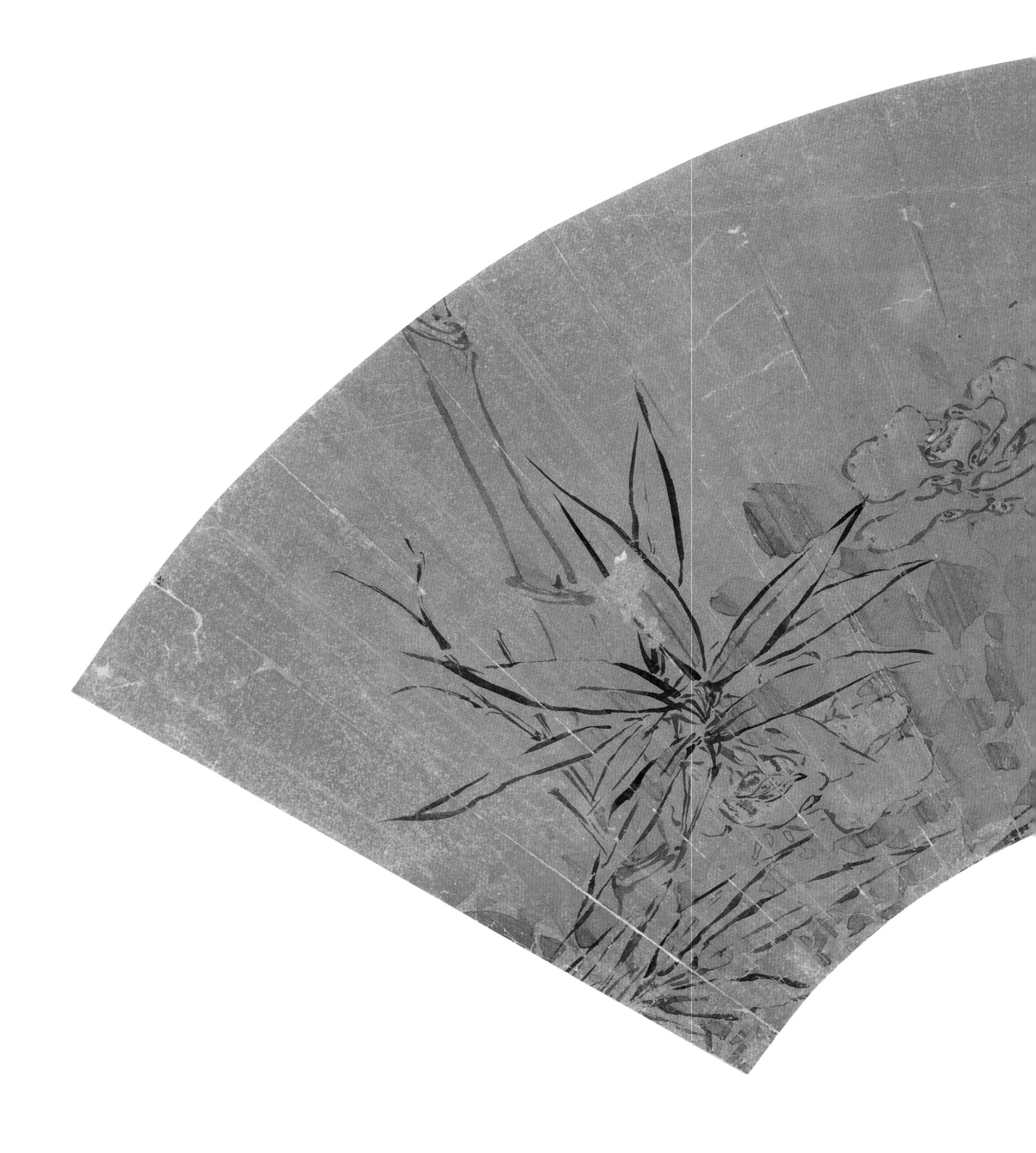

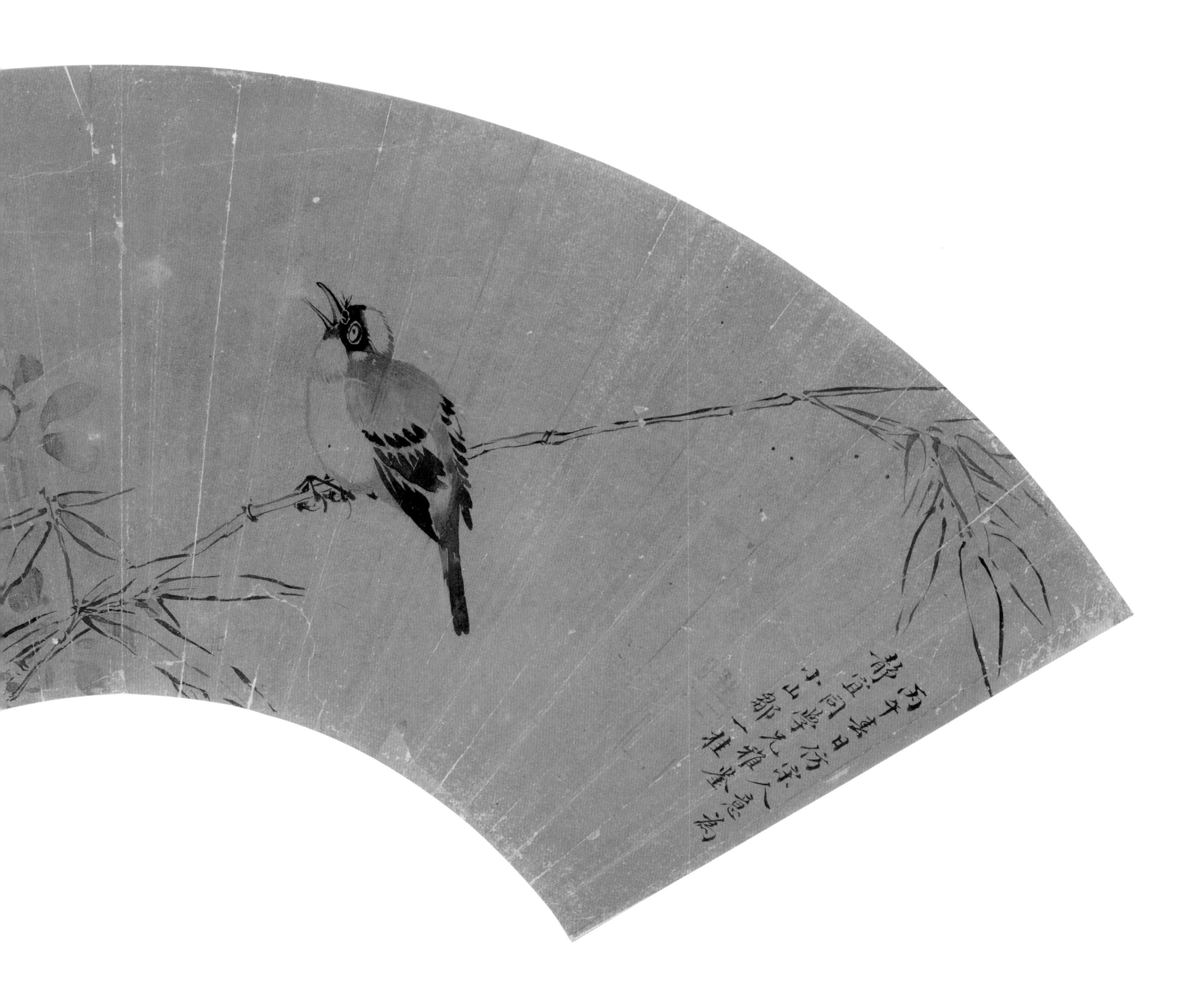
丙午春日仿宋人意為
郡宜同學兄雅屬
小山鄒一桂

143. 霜林云岫图扇页

邹一桂绘 纸本 设色

纵 16 厘米 横 51 厘米

扇页有自题："抚张崔涧霜林云岫，小山桂。"钤"臣一桂"白文印、"恭写"朱文印。

图绘木叶丹黄的秋霜时节，高士闲坐崖石观赏烟云幻灭的山川景色。虽然人物、树木被绘制的简约概括，山峦也没有绘出全貌，但是画面有博大高远的视觉冲击，体现了中国画"笔愈简而气愈壮，景愈少而意愈长"的创作理念。图中以中锋勾勒的云气与以设色晕染的山水树木形成流动与凝重比对，二者相辅相成令简约的画扇表现出"水流心不竞，云与意俱迟"的浪漫情结。

虽然，此图在落款前没有书"臣"字，但是，由钤"臣一桂"和"恭写"印可知，此图有可能是邹一桂为臣期间，献给皇室的画作。

撫張寉澗
霜林雲岫
小山桂

144. 花鸟图扇页

李世倬绘　纸本 设色

纵 16.5 厘米　横 49.2 厘米

扇页有自题：“摹宋人崔子西鸟语花香，岁新时泰伊祁李世倬。”钤“世”、“倬”朱文联珠印。

李世倬（1687～1770 年），字天章，一字汉章，号谷斋、星厓等，三韩（今辽宁铁岭北）人。指头画家高其佩的外甥。历任知州、副都御史、太常寺卿等职，人称“李太常”。工画山水、人物、花卉，各臻其妙。画学远宗唐吴道子、宋李公麟、元倪瓒诸家，近法清王原祁、蒋廷锡等，笔墨秀隽，设色雅淡。曾从高其佩学“指画”，利用手指、掌心、指甲等勾画物象，颇得轻重浅深之功。是乾隆朝词臣画家之一。

此扇面构图呈字母“A”字形，这种纵向分支的构图方式难以安排物象，容易令画面因笔墨分散而失去平和，因此，通常不为画家所用。作者在此通过鸟向右探身的动态和树杈向左伸展的势态，巧妙地连成一条若有若无的横向线条，从而将左右分散的物象归拢，化解了这一难题，并且，通过简洁明快的构图，营造出一派清秋幽旷的氛围。

作者自言该扇页是摹宋人崔子西（名崔白）的画作，其在花鸟形态上得崔氏写生花鸟注重情趣之意，但是在笔墨运用上，较崔氏的更为粗放。

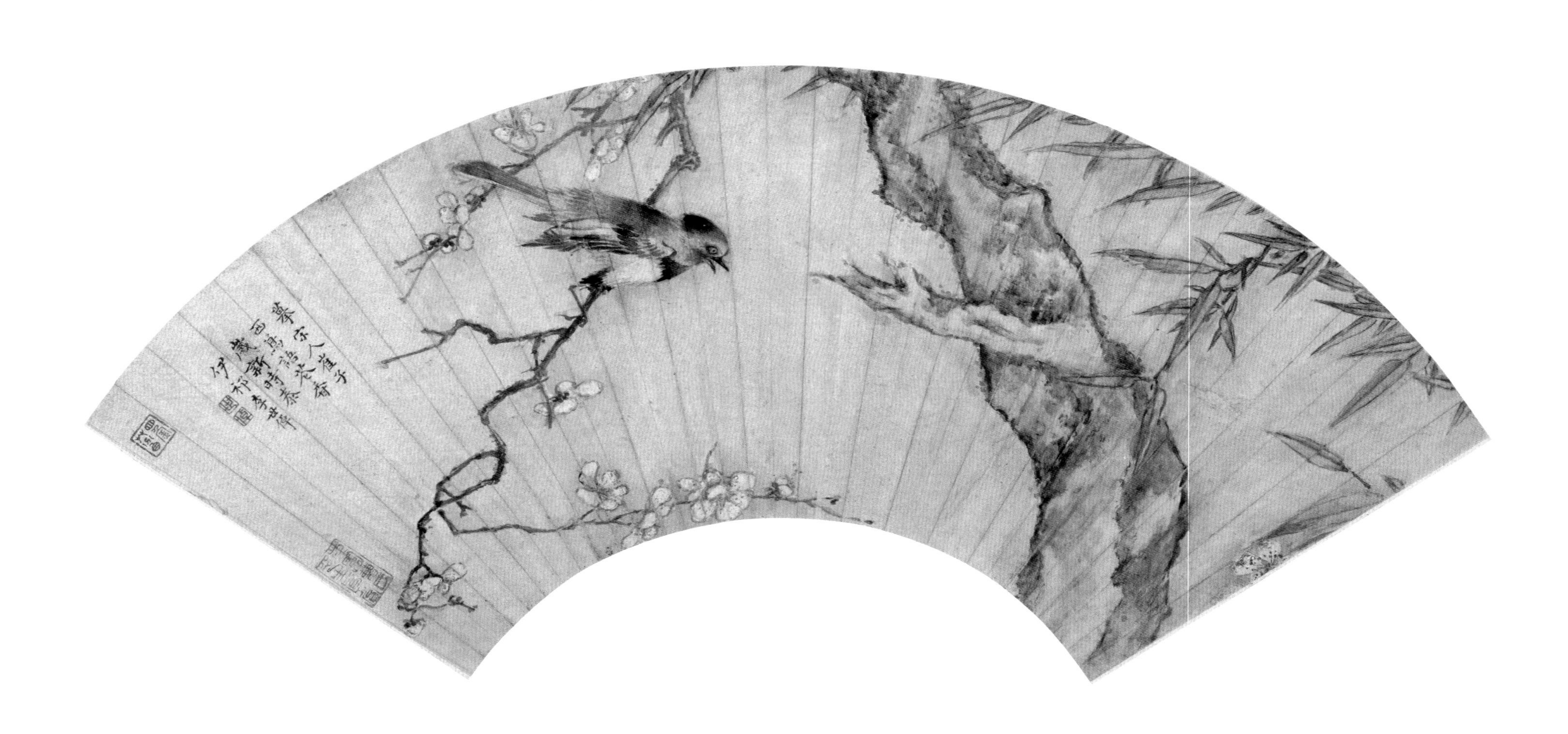

145. 梅花图扇页

金农绘　纸本 墨笔

纵 17.3 厘米　横 51.8 厘米

扇页有自题：“砚水生冰墨半干，画梅须画晚来寒。树无丑态香沾袖，不爱花人莫与看。七十五叟金农画诗书。”钤“金吉金印”白文印。

金农（1687～1763 或 1764 年），字寿门，号冬心，又号稽留山民、曲江外史、昔耶居士等。仁和（今浙江杭州）人，流寓扬州。博学多才，诗书画印无所不通。书法出入楷隶之间，自创富有金石味的“漆书”，颇具特色。年 50 岁始学画，善山水、人物、花卉，画风古朴，造意新颖，极具个性。清秦祖永《桐荫论画》评他“涉笔即古，脱尽画家习气”。与郑燮、高翔、汪士慎等人合称“扬州画派”，亦是“扬州八怪”的代表人物。

图绘一树梅花由左上向右下出枝，其布局走向与扇面底边的弧度相一致。又，金农自题的七言诗及款，其书法墨迹，沿着扇面的上方，做弧形排列。字与画巧妙地随扇形布局，可见作者在构图上颇具匠心。全图笔法健挺洒脱，于写意之中见写实功底，表现出梅花高洁素雅、坚韧不屈的物性和迎风斗雪顽强的生命力。

146. 梅花图扇页

金农绘　纸本 墨笔

纵 17.3 厘米　横 53.3 厘米

扇页有自题："七十六叟金农。"钤印文模糊，不辨。

图绘墨梅随扇形横向出枝，枝干穿插得体，其或大或小的梅花花瓣，有的用白描勾圈，显现出冰清玉洁之姿，有的用墨直接点染，展现出温润华滋之美，它们前后掩映，交杂错落，不失"大弦嘈嘈如急雨，小弦切切如私语。嘈嘈切切错杂弹，大珠小珠落玉盘"的动感。其笔墨已达到随心所欲、涉笔成趣的地步。金农一生以梅花为题的画作最多，其中不乏有弟子罗聘代笔之作。

147. 草虫花卉图扇页

马荃绘　纸本 设色

纵 17 厘米　横 48 厘米

扇页有自题："癸卯春日写，江香荃。"钤"马"、"荃"白文联珠印。"癸卯"是清雍正元年（1723 年）。

马荃（生卒年不详，活动于 18 世纪），字江香，江苏常熟人。来自于绘画世家，父亲马元驭、兄弟马逸都以擅绘花鸟著称。马荃自幼深受家学影响，终日里与家人研习画理，铺纸磨墨作画不倦。她既学习五代黄筌及宋代宫廷花鸟画的笔法，注重以工细精整的线条勾勒，也注重学习同时代恽寿平的没骨法，以不见笔痕的点染表现鲜活的花鸟世界。江南人将她与同擅没骨法的恽冰合称为女性花鸟画上的"双绝"。

图绘花儿在明媚的阳光下含英吐艳，蜜蜂和蛱蝶围之起舞的情景。作者通过细致的观察和坚实的写生功底，将苗圃间的这种朴实自然美表现的意趣盎然。蜂、蝶仿宋院体造型准确，用笔精细入微，不失活泼之态。花草以没骨法晕染笔调清新，设色温润雅致而不媚俗。

148. 花卉图扇页

马荃绘　金笺 设色

纵 17 厘米　横 51.1 厘米

扇页有自题：“戊午秋日，马荃写。”钤“马”、“荃”白文联珠印。“戊午”是清乾隆三年（1738 年）。

秦祖永《桐阴论画》记马荃：“尺幅小品，笔意香艳，更饶幽雅之趣。”此图扇以工笔重彩绘兰、梅等花卉，花朵和叶片分别以颜色掺白粉绘制，增强了花瓣的厚重感和叶片的滋润度，显现出花儿的朝气与活力。此图被绘在泥金的扇面上，富丽典雅的金底，把花儿衬托得愈加纯净和娇美。马荃的这种画风，深受时人喜爱，她为应付各方求画者，不得不招一些女婢，帮她磨制颜料或代为染色。见陈康祺《郎潜纪闻二笔》记她：“晚岁名益高，四方以缣素兼金求画者益众。尝蓄婢数人，悉令调铅杀粉。”

149. 藤花翠鸟图扇页

恽冰绘　纸本 设色

纵 18 厘米　横 53.5 厘米

扇页有自题：“四月藤花香满衣，青於恽冰。”钤“恽冰之印”白文印、“兰陵女史”朱、白文印。

恽冰（生卒年不详，活动于 18 世纪），字青於，武进（今江苏常州）人。《武进县志》记恽冰为“南田族曾孙女，善花草，得其家法。”恽冰自幼敏于诗文，潜心于花鸟画创作，用笔、设色一丝不苟，造型生动传神。花瓣常通过灵动多变的用笔，把墨、色与画中的形象完全融为一体。茎枝、叶筋以娴熟的笔力一笔勾就。花叶注重阴阳向背关系，颇具立体感。人称其作品“用粉精绝，迎日花朵，具有光”。

图绘翠鸟衔虫而来，小鸟迫不及待地嗷嗷待哺的样子。紫藤仿恽寿平（南田）的没骨法，以色彩直接点就，显现出灵秀生动的物性；翠鸟为设色小写意，笔致工细，造型准确写实。全图绿、紫、白、赭色相搭配，色调鲜亮明快，显现出明媚的四月春光下，母子情深的暖暖爱意。

150. 山水图扇页

高翔绘 纸本 设色

纵 17 厘米 横 48 厘米

扇页有自题："奔流下危矶，绀宇临江渚。日暮翠微钟，帆收楚天雨。开翁学长兄先生，弟高翔。"钤印二方模糊不辨。

高翔（1688～1753 年），字凤岗，号西唐、犀堂等，甘泉（江苏扬州）人。性格孤傲，终身布衣。晚年右手残废，常以左手作书画。能诗，擅治印，工绘山水，尤精画梅。山水取法弘仁、原济和程邃，提出天成灵秀、不事泥古的创作方法，追求"挥洒任横斜"，气韵生动的笔墨。与金农、罗聘等人同为"扬州画派"重要的画家，是"扬州八怪"之一。著《西唐诗钞》。

高翔熟悉并且热爱江南平静幽淡的生活，表现家乡的园林、村野、水景是其创作的一大特色。图绘下雨时分，一叶轻舟鼓帆前行的江南实景。图中的山石以淡墨乱柴皴皴擦，树木以松散随意的笔法刻画，二者纵横交错的线条，为水汽弥漫的山川增添了浪漫的情趣。

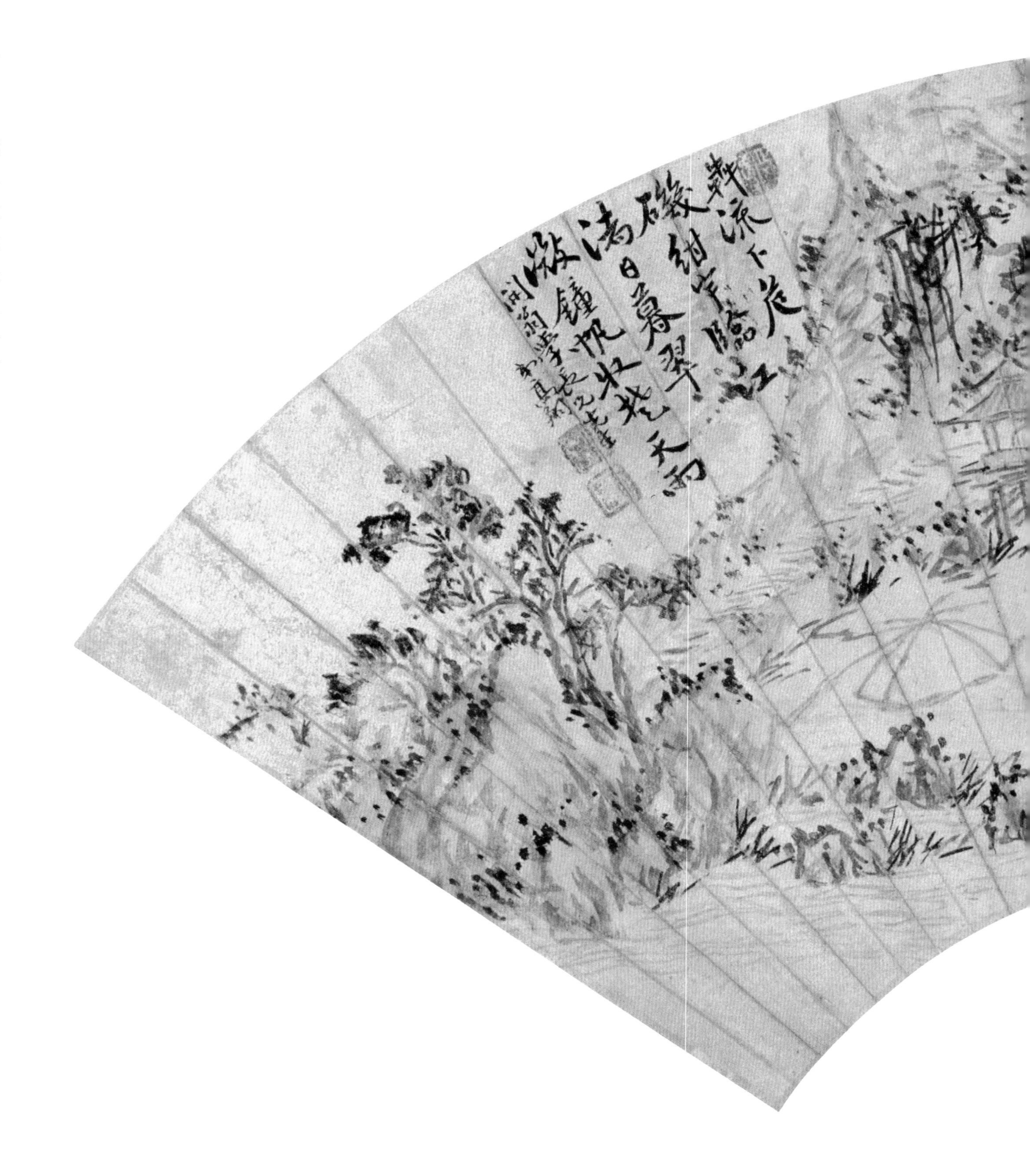

151. 棉花图扇页

余省绘　纸本 设色

纵 16.7 厘米　横 51.4 厘米

扇页有自题：“甲午秋日，鲁亭余省。”钤“曾三氏”朱文印。“甲午”是清康熙五十三年（1714 年），余省时年 23 岁。

余省（1692～1767 年），字曾三，号鲁亭，江苏常熟人。工于花鸟写生，以造型准确生动、笔法工致细腻、设色清丽而享有画名。清乾隆二年（1737），46 岁的余省被内大臣海望力荐入宫，与金廷标、张为邦等人供职如意馆。其画作受到乾隆皇帝的赏识，他被列为一等画家，清内府编纂《石渠宝笈》著录其画作有 37 幅。

本扇页正中绘一枝连花带叶的棉花。棉花作为经济作物，花既不香，色也不艳，一向不被列为花鸟画的创作题材，因此，扇面裱边惠孝同题“此扇写棉花亦奇古。”此图以工细的笔法绘制，设色淡雅清新，可惜花朵中的白色颜料返铅，变成黑黄色，为画作减色不少。左侧有余省的同乡、时年 71 岁的当地著名画家杨晋书录的“白石翁”七言诗补白，它不仅平衡了扇面的左右疏密关系，同时给画作增添了更多的文化气息以及画外的同乡之谊。

152. 墨兰图扇页

郑燮绘 金笺 墨笔

纵 16.8 厘米 横 53 厘米

扇页有自题："古人云：寒花余几□。板桥云：一枝也可入东风。故拈笔作此。'寒'字下落'尽蕙'二字。板桥又记。"钤"克柔"朱文印、"郑燮之印"白文印。

郑燮（1693～1765 年），字克柔，号板桥，江苏兴化人。清乾隆元年（1736 年）进士，官山东县令等职。他以为人耿直、不事权贵而遭贬职，从此在扬州卖画谋生。他于书画上主张学古而不泥古，在承袭传统的基础上追求创新，其绘兰、竹、石取法明徐渭、清原济等人的大写意，运笔秀劲潇洒，横涂竖抹不失章法。其书法创"六分半"体，又称"乱石铺街体"，以隶书体参入行、楷笔法，别有特色。与金农、高翔、汪士慎等人同为"扬州画派"画家。著《板桥全集》。

此图是一幅带有自娱性质的画作，郑燮为了表明"一枝也可入东风"，便单绘一枝鲜花绽放的蕙茎。他为了以简胜繁，同时令简约的画作变得富有情调，在构图上，巧于布置，将蕙茎画成右高左低的倒卧"S"形，不仅打破了左右的平面空间，而且分裂了上下的高低空间，令画面因为分割的面积不同而显得生动富有变化。茎上的花儿也巧于安排，它们处于茎的不同位置，或仰或俯，错落有致。它们通过彼此间的关系，将茎由一根线变成有律动变化的生命体。图中以"乱石铺街体"书写的款题，其正斜疏密的墨迹，成为了画作中重要的一部分，稳定了画面，增强了画作的视觉审美。

153. 丰盈和乐图扇页

蒋淑绘　纸本 墨笔

纵 19.5 厘米　横 58 厘米

扇页有自题:“淑谨画。”钤“淑”白文印、“古香”朱文印。

蒋淑（生卒年不详，活动于 18 世纪初），字又文,江苏常熟人。蒋廷锡女,华亭王敬妻。她自幼秉承家学，擅绘花鸟，极得蒋廷锡工写结合巧妙、色墨相得益彰的神韵。

由扇面上蒋廷锡的墨题“丰盈和乐。雍正三年五月四日赐扇命女淑写此”而知，此图是蒋淑于清雍正三年（1725 年）受命，在雍正皇帝赏赐的白扇上所画。图绘两只麻雀惬意地立于代表丰收的麦穗上，栖息的场景。蒋淑运用象征的手法，绘制有国泰民安之意的吉庆画，颂扬雍正皇帝的朝政清明。该图扇俨然带有鲜明的政治色彩，超脱了一般闺阁画家以花鸟画抒发个人小情调的境界，具有特殊的意义。图中的麻雀生动活泼，一仰一俯富有情趣。麦穗写实，刻画工细，可见作者严谨的创作态度。

154. 山水图扇页

董邦达绘　纸本 墨笔

纵 16.2 厘米　横 47.8 厘米

扇页有自题："臣董邦达恭绘。"钤"臣"朱文印、"邦达"白文印。

董邦达（1699～1769 年），字孚存、非闻，号东山，富阳（今浙江富阳市）人。于清雍正十一年（1733 年）考中进士，乾隆二年（1737 年）授翰林院编修，次年典试陕西。十二年（1747 年），被授予内阁学士兼礼部侍郎衔，十八年（1753 年），主持江西乡试。此后，迁工部尚书，转礼部，复转工部。三十四年（1769 年），以老乞退。谥曰"文恪"。其山水画源于董源、巨然、黄公望及董其昌，所绘峰峦浑厚，云气蒸腾，给人以心旷神怡之感，是乾隆朝重要的词臣画家之一。曾参与编纂《石渠宝笈》、《秘殿珠林》、《西清古鉴》诸书。

此图绘山水小景，构图疏密有致，远近景互衬互映。运笔沉着，墨色层次丰富，得黄公望温润高逸之格，画风在娄东、虞山派之间。董氏画作受到乾隆皇帝的高度赞誉，认为其艺术水平堪与五代大师董源相提并论，已达到所绘物象从笔法到构图、意境均无法挑剔的地步。因此，只要是董氏之作，不论尺幅大小都大量收藏，仅被《石渠宝笈》著录的董氏画作就达 202 件（不含合作）。正如赵尔巽在《清史稿·列传》所记：董氏"久直内廷，进御之作，大幅寻丈，小册寸许，不下数百"。

由自题"臣董邦达恭绘"和钤"臣"朱文印而知，此图是董邦达献给乾隆皇帝的精心之作。

臣董邦達恭繪

155. 花果图扇页

钱载绘　纸本 墨笔

纵 16.2 厘米　横 49.5 厘米

扇页有自题:“八十四老人钱载。”钤“钱载”白文印。

钱载（1708～1793 年），字坤一，号萚石、匏尊、万松居士等，秀水（今浙江嘉兴）人。清乾隆十七年（1752 年）进士，曾参与编纂《四库全书》、《续文献通考》等清内府编修的重要书籍。工诗文，兼绘梅、兰、竹、菊、松等，笔法松秀简淡，追求淳朴稚拙的书卷气，其画风受到时人赞誉，钱泳《履园丛话》评他：“工写生，不甚设色，兰竹尤妙，书卷之气溢于纸墨间，直在前明陈道复之上。”蒋宝龄《墨林今话》记：“萚翁中年花卉雅艳淡逸，绝类瓯香仿元人之作。其后独行己意，纵笔为兰竹杂卉，疏野洒落前无古人。梁山舟学士尤喜之，尝品其所作：兰竹第一，菊次之，枯木又次之。”秦祖永《桐阴论画》言：其画“笔意奔放，兀傲不群，所写兰石，最为超脱，画兰叶纵笔仰，神趣横溢”。

图绘一倒挂枝头的果实，它没有远中近景的烘托，只配有几片疏散的叶子。笔墨概略，属于钱载典型的简约画风。此图果实和果枝的线条粗细不匀，可见作者有严重的用笔发抖现象，这当与钱载晚年患半身不遂、难以把控毛笔有关。

156. 兰花图扇页

钱载绘　纸本 墨笔

纵 15.7 厘米　横 49.6 厘米

扇页有自题："壬子春仲，八十五老人载。"钤"钱"、"载"朱文联珠印。"壬子"是清乾隆五十七年(1792 年)，钱载时年 85 岁。

图中从兰用笔圆润，墨韵高华，全图不施任何色彩，而是注重墨的浓、淡、干、湿变化，给人以洗尽铅华之美，显现出幽兰清高拔俗、自然天成的趣味。

157. 花卉图扇页

张若霭绘　纸本 墨笔

纵 16.5 横 45.5 厘米。

扇页有自题：“去年联袂唱新诗，恰是春光渐丽时。飞絮自萦燕市梦，好风吹动谢庭思。素纨写意凝烟水，芳草连天怅别离。遥想官斋晴昼永，桃花红染几枝枝。小诗寄怀二姊夫人书扇请正。酿花十一弟若霭。”钤“酿花”朱文印。又自题：“乾隆丙辰二月晴岚写。”钤“晴岚”朱文印。“丙辰”是清乾隆元年（1736年），张若霭时年 24 岁。

张若霭（1713～1746 年），字晴岚，安徽桐城人。来自官宦世家，祖父张英、父亲张廷玉均为雍正、乾隆朝大学士。他于雍正十一年（1733）考中进士，官至礼部尚书、翰林院编修、通政司。工绘山水、花鸟，得王毂祥、周之冕遗意。精于鉴赏，品评皇室所藏，颇有见的，与兄弟张若澄同为乾隆朝重要的词臣画家。

此图绘折枝花卉。花以线描为主，表现出鲜花绽放时争妍斗艳的蓬勃朝气。叶片以浓淡墨晕染，淋漓的水墨效果，表现出叶片饱含水分的鲜活。不同的笔墨技法丰富了画面，增强了视觉表现力，也使得画作没有因为造型的简约而显得单薄。全幅刻画写实，不仅叶茎勾描细致，而且将花瓣上的丝丝纹脉也以工整的笔墨一丝不苟地加以表现，可见作者严谨求实的画风。此图作为作者早期的画作，尚缺少笔致生动的气韵。

158. 花卉图扇页

钱维城绘　纸本 设色

纵 20 厘米　横 58.6 厘米

扇页有自题：“臣钱维城恭画。”钤“臣”朱文印、“城”白文印。

钱维城（1720～1772 年），字宗磐，号幼庵、茶山、稼轩，武进（今江苏常州）人。清乾隆十年（1745 年）状元，官至刑部侍郎。擅绘，其花鸟画追仿日臻盛行的恽寿平没骨画法；其山水画，远师以黄公望为代表的“元四家”，近学皇室十分推崇的以王时敏、王鉴为首的“四王”画风。他通过博采众家所长，最终形成自己的笔墨风格。在设景布势的构图上，独具匠心，能够在有限的空间内巧妙地安排和处理人、物间的比例关系和前后左右的位置，通过局部与整体关系的恰当把握而构筑出深远的意境；在用笔上，能够通过笔的轻重徐捷、墨的干湿浓淡等变化，表现出绘画中的书卷气。清内府编纂《石渠宝笈》著录其画 160 多幅，是乾隆朝重要的词臣画家之一。谥号“文敏”。

图中的海棠花等是作者以恽寿平的没骨法表现的，行笔工细轻秀，枝叶穿插有致，通过丰富的色彩，成功地展示出花卉鲜活的美感。

由自题“臣钱维城恭画”和钤“臣”印而知，此图是钱维城献给乾隆皇帝的佳作。

159. 鱼藻图扇页

汪承霈绘 纸本 设色

纵 17.4 厘米 横 54.3 厘米

扇页有自题："轻风不动萍，殊艳满花津。跃波鱼出藻，搅碎一池春。汪承霈。"钤"时"白文印，"斋"朱文印。

汪承霈（？～1805 年），字受时，一字春农，号时斋，别号蕉雪，浙江钱塘人，原籍安徽休宁，吏部尚书汪由敦子。清乾隆十二年（1747 年）举人，累官至兵部尚书。善诗文，工书画，山水学法元人及"四王"，笔墨沉着浑厚。花鸟仿恽寿平，设色清丽。他常奉圣旨作画或以画作献皇室邀宠，是乾隆朝重要的词臣画家之一。

此图是幅以桃花为主题的画作。图绘几瓣桃花飘落池塘，点明时值春暖花开的季节。粉嫩的花瓣与水中的黄绿色浮萍、水草相依相守，共同营造出甜美祥宁的水乡。桃花的入池引得三尾鱼儿欢快地逐食嬉戏，表现出它们逍遥自在的天性。全图以仿恽寿平的没骨法晕染，笔致生动，赋色亮丽，富有浪漫的抒情诗意。此图没有题赠画者的上款，也没有题向皇室进献的"臣"字款，应该是作者自娱自乐的怡情小品。

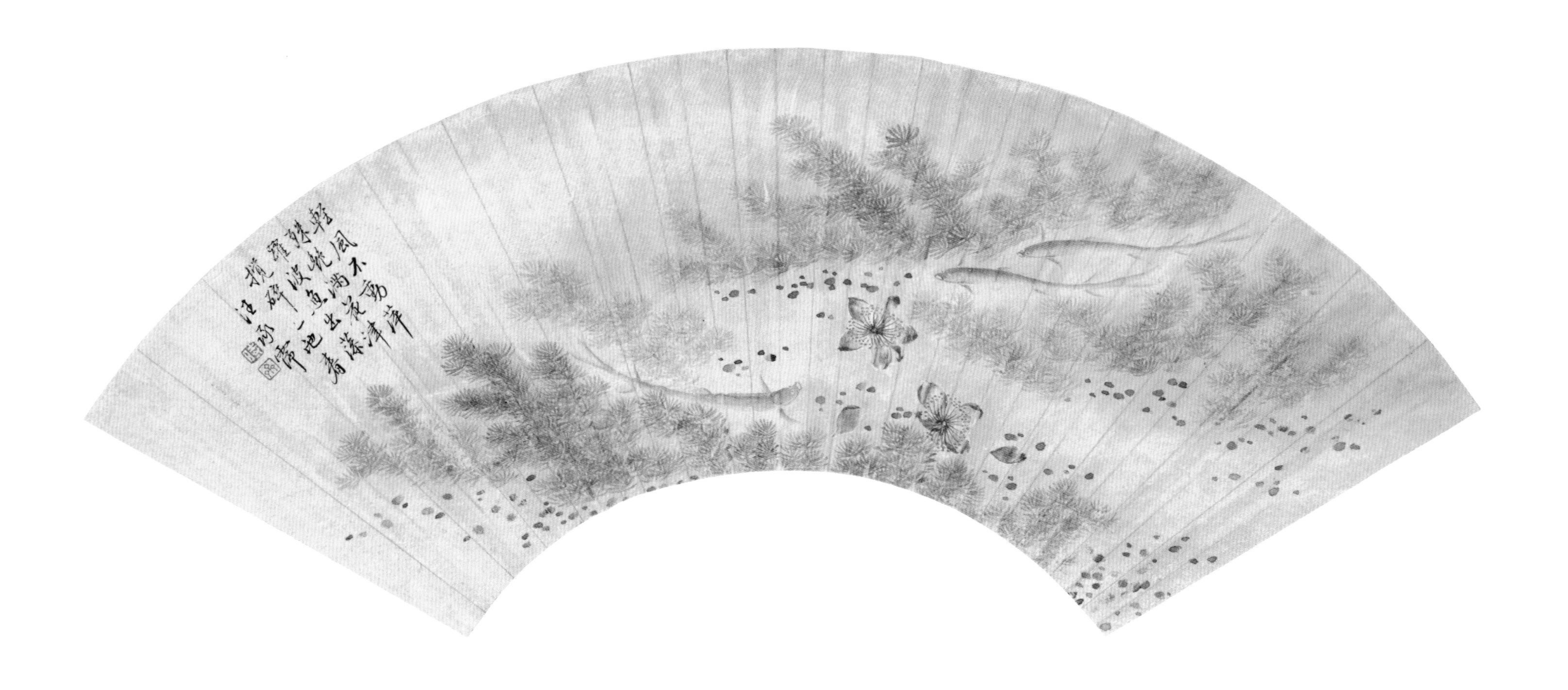

160. 江城春色图扇页

袁瑛绘　金笺 墨笔

纵 15.5 厘米　横 49 厘米

扇页有自题："江城春色。赐扇写为雪老太翁正，时壬辰三月。二峰袁瑛。"钤"袁瑛"白文印。"壬辰"是清乾隆三十七年(1772 年)。

袁瑛(生卒年不详，活动于 18 世纪)，字近华，号二峰，元和(今江苏苏州)人。工绘山水、花鸟，乾隆三十年(1765 年)由户部侍郎李因培推荐入宫，二十年后离宫赴广东任官。其山水在宗法宋、元的基础上，又师仿同代人黄鼎，笔墨浑厚苍润，是乾隆朝中后期重要的宫廷画家。

此图的主题是江城春色。作者将江城推至远景，亭台楼阁在树丛及围城中若隐若现，成为画作中的陪衬。作者重点刻画的是"春色"，通过欣欣向荣的树木、草长莺飞的景象表现万物复苏的春景。全图虽然为水墨画，没有设色，但是，温润的墨与厚实的中锋线条相配合，为画作增"色"不少，具有"最是一年春好处，绝胜烟柳满皇都"的诗意。

由款题而知，作者用的此图扇是皇室所赐。该扇面历经数百年，至今其泥金面不脱色、不变色，可见宫廷制扇工艺的精湛与用料的精良。

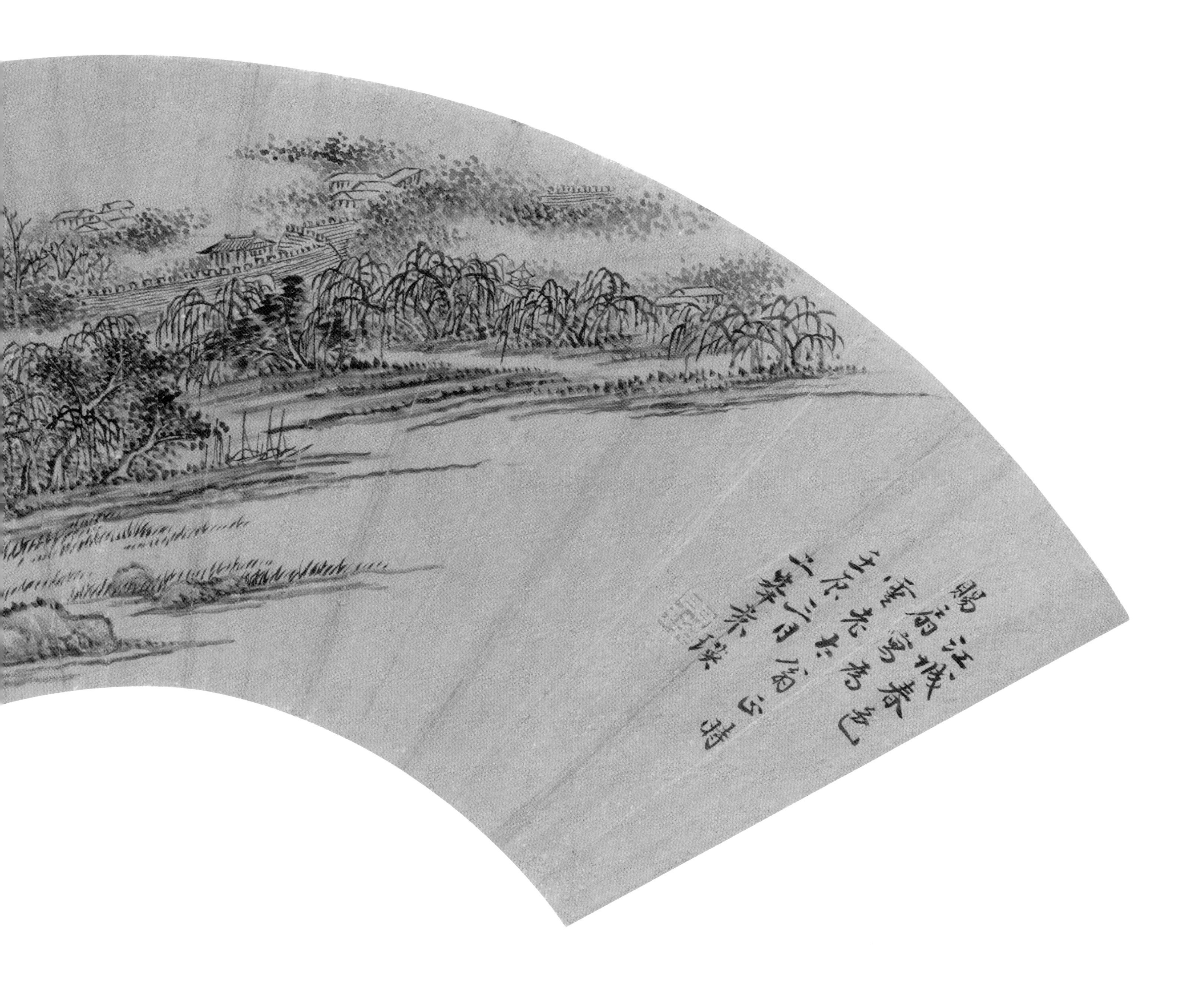

161. 渔乐图扇页

杨大章绘　纸本 设色

纵 18.7 厘米　横 53.2 厘米

扇页有自题："臣杨大章恭画。"钤"恭"、"画"朱文联珠印。

杨大章（生卒年不详，生活于 18 世纪），善画人物、花卉、翎毛，设色明丽工整，造型写实，笔法精细，是乾隆朝后期重要的宫廷画家。

图绘渔民满载而归后卸货、分拣、称重的忙碌劳动场景。全图设色淡雅，以汁绿和赭色为主调，渲染出祥和喜庆的氛围。画作人物众多，造型生动传神，彼此间通过举止的过往或眼神的顾盼，形成一个外散内紧的活动群体，富有生活情趣。据自题"臣"及"恭画"而知，此图是作者献给皇室之作，其所表现出的渔家安居乐业的生活状态，带有歌功颂德的性质，迎合了皇室的审美观和企盼子民皆幸福安康的统治理念。

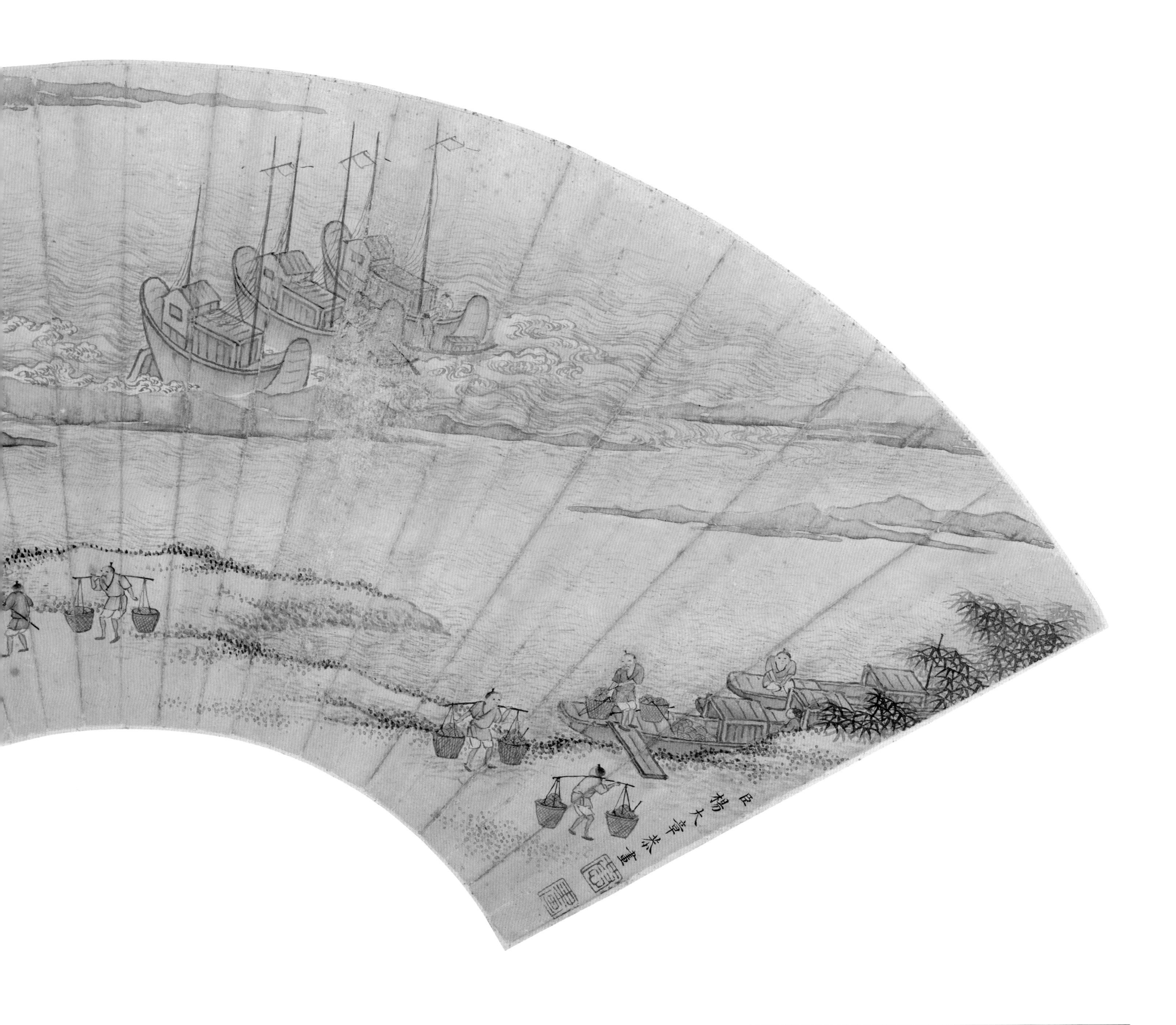
臣楊大章恭畫

162. 西园雅集图扇页

冯宁绘　纸本 设色

纵 19 厘米　横 57.1 厘米

扇页有自题："臣冯宁恭画。" 钤 "臣" 朱文印、"宁" 白文印。

冯宁（生卒年不详，活动于 18 世纪），擅长画人物、楼阁、鸟兽。用笔简劲锐利，轻重顿挫似有节奏，墨法枯润适中，是乾隆朝后期至嘉庆朝的宫廷画家。

此图通过芭蕉、竹石等园林的自然景观，巧妙地将画面分割成六个表现文人雅集活动的场所。文士们有的挥毫写书作画，有的题壁留墨，有的拨阮演乐，有的在与高僧对晤等。每个场景在形式上各自独立，在内容上高度统一，突出了 "雅集" 的主题。历史上最著名的雅集当属晋朝王羲之等人的"兰亭雅集"，文人们希望与志同道合的友人吟诗作画或者讨论学问，作为国朝天子的皇帝对这种文事活动也非常向往，因此谕令冯宁绘此图扇，以示心迹。图中人物形象众多，姿态各异。作者以写实的手法，将人物的身形相貌表现得栩栩如生，展示了其于花卉画之外的人物画功底。

163. 荷花图扇页

冯宁绘　纸本 设色

纵 17.8 厘米　横 52 厘米

扇页有自题：“乱碧风初卷，新红霞半含。拟南田粉本，冯宁。”钤“臣”朱文印、“宁”白文印。

此作以没骨法绘前后景，前景是以绿色横涂斜抹的芦苇，后景是“碧叶喜翻风，红英宜照日”的特写荷花。芦苇为风所动，其纵横离乱的姿态没有干扰荷花端庄大气的整体形象，反而以其天然荒率的恣致，衬托出荷花作为水中仙子高华绝俗、“出淤泥而不染，濯清涟而不妖”的品质。冯宁作为宫廷画家，其这种气韵高雅的画风迎合了清皇室的审美意趣。

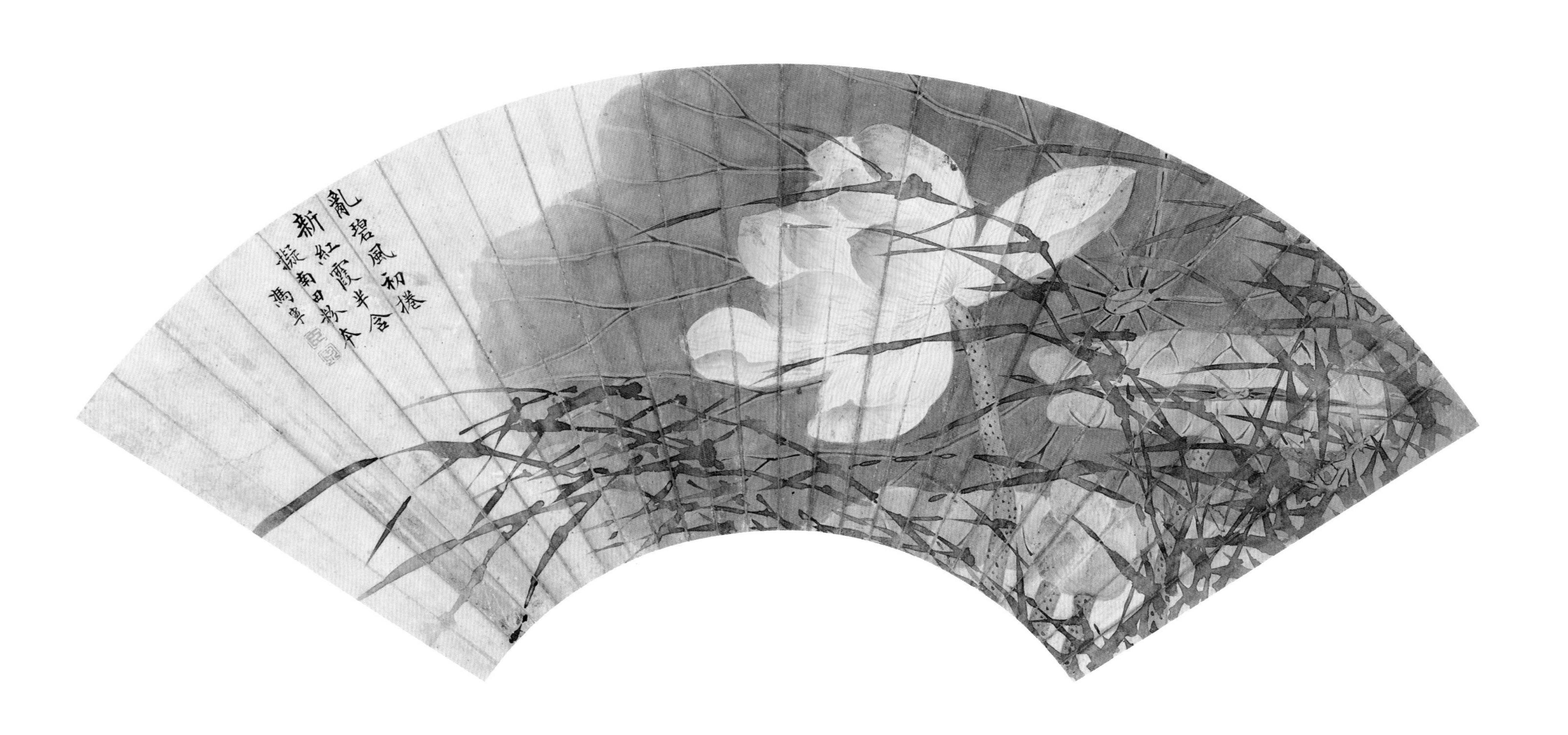

164. 松堂读书图扇页

钱维乔绘　纸本 墨笔

纵 21 厘米　横 59.8 厘米

扇页有自题:“远岫澄云色，平溪澹夕阳。涛声何处起，松下读书堂。兼用子久、仲圭画法。维乔。”钤“乔”朱文印。

钱维乔（1739～1806 年），字树参，号竹初居士等，武进（今江苏常州）人，钱维城弟。工书画，擅戏曲。山水画推崇元黄公望、吴镇、倪瓒、王蒙，以及明沈周、清王翚等诸家的绘画风格，强调笔墨技法，追求蕴藉平和的审美意趣，以笔笔有古意为创作宗旨。其画风与钱维城相近，因此，他们被称为“常州二钱”。钱维乔有给钱维城代笔之嫌。

此图山峦重叠，林木扶疏，平湖静水，一派祥和安宁的江南风光。树叶的画法多样，或墨笔白描勾圈，或以中锋画“介字点”，或仿米芾以卧笔横点取势，不同造型的树木，显现出不同的神态形貌，可见作者细致的观察力和灵活多变的表现力。图中的山石或勾或皴，显现出葱郁深秀的美感，这与作者长期以来追摹黄子久（公望）、吴仲圭（镇）的笔墨技法不可分。

165. 春山烟霭图扇页

钱维乔绘　纸本 设色

纵 21 厘米　横 60 厘米

扇页有自题:“春山烟霭。嘉庆己未新秋拟乌目山人意于小林栖。竹初乔。”钤“维乔印”白文印、“季木”朱文印。“己未”是清嘉庆四年(1799 年),钱维乔时年 61 岁。

图绘树木与山石、水榭相互掩映,烟云与湖水萦绕穿插的江南春景。作者自题仿自王翚(号乌目山人)笔意,然而它又融入了钱氏自身粗笔中不失秀润的风韵,是画家晚年在宗法各家所长的基础上,带有自身笔墨特点的精心之作。

春山煙靄
嘉慶己未新
秋擬烏目山人
意於小林棲

166. 春山晴翠图扇页

董诰绘　纸本 设色

纵 16.5 厘米　横 49.9 厘米

扇页有自题："春山晴翠。抚赵文敏笔意。董诰谨画。"钤"柘"、"林"白文联珠印、"董诰"白文印。

董诰（1740～1818 年），字雅伦，号蔗林、拓林，大学士董邦达之子。清乾隆二十八年（1763 年）进士，历任礼、工、户、吏、刑各部侍郎及户部尚书等职。他以政治上忠诚、机敏、睿智著称，被乾隆、嘉庆两朝皇帝重用；以艺术上能书法，工绘山水、花卉，富有深厚的学识修养，为乾隆、嘉庆两朝皇帝赏识。其山水学法元赵文敏（孟頫）、清王原祁，构图疏密呼应得当，运笔柔中寓刚，是"虞山画派"重要画家；其花卉学仿清恽寿平，以没骨法设色，笔致写实生动。他是清宫重要的词臣画家之一，现有 500 余件套画作藏于故宫博物院。

此图属于文人画家惯用的"一河两岸"式构图，远近景分别向扇页两侧延展。作者着重于近景树木的刻画，以不同的技法表现繁茂的树叶，有的用卧笔大横点，有的是卧笔小横点，有的用笔尖戳点，有的则用双勾填色，可见作者对树叶的表现技法有着深入的研究，并且能够娴熟地加以运用。作者自言"抚赵文敏（元赵孟頫）笔意"，实际上在山石树木的画法上，融入了更多元黄公望及明沈周的笔墨风格。

春山晴翠擬趙文敏筆意
董誥謹畫

167. 山水图扇页

弘旿绘 纸本 设色

纵 16.8 厘米 横 50.4 厘米

扇页有自题："臣弘旿敬绘。"钤"臣"、"旿"白文联珠印。

弘旿（1743～1811 年），字卓亭、仲升，号瑶华道人、杏村农等。清康熙皇帝第二十四子诚恪亲王允祕的次子。能诗，善画，工书法，号称"三绝"。其花木宗法明代陈淳、陆治，笔墨洒脱，富有气韵；山水画远师五代董源、巨然及元人黄公望，近学董邦达，构图繁复，线条细碎而不零乱，于交错叠加中，显现出江南丘壑苍茫之美。

弘旿常将画成之作献给乾隆皇帝，每每博得皇帝的高度赞赏，不仅在其画上题御制诗，而且加以收贮，仅被清内府编纂《石渠宝笈》著录的画作就有 37 件之多。此图是弘旿所献众多画作中的小品。图中景致纷繁，其笔法尖峭，皴法松秀，既有元人遗韵，又得宋人笔墨之工，成功地渲染出世外桃源静谧舒适的雅境，可见作者具有较强的构意造物功力。

168. 云山图扇页

弘旿绘　纸本 墨笔

纵 16.5 厘米　横 49 厘米

扇页有自题:“臣弘旿敬绘。”钤“臣”“旿”朱文联珠印。

此图是作者仿宋人米氏云山法绘制的山水小品，远山、流云、树木没有作具体细致的描绘，只是以苍润的笔墨写其形貌。米氏的这种“信笔作之，多以烟云掩映树石，意似便已”的画风，自形成以来，一直受到各阶层画家的喜爱，弘旿作为清皇室画家亦不例外，由自题“臣”“敬绘”推断，此图当是献给乾隆皇帝的精心之作，由此而知，乾隆皇帝对米氏的这种似草草而成，却天趣横生的画法也是认同的。

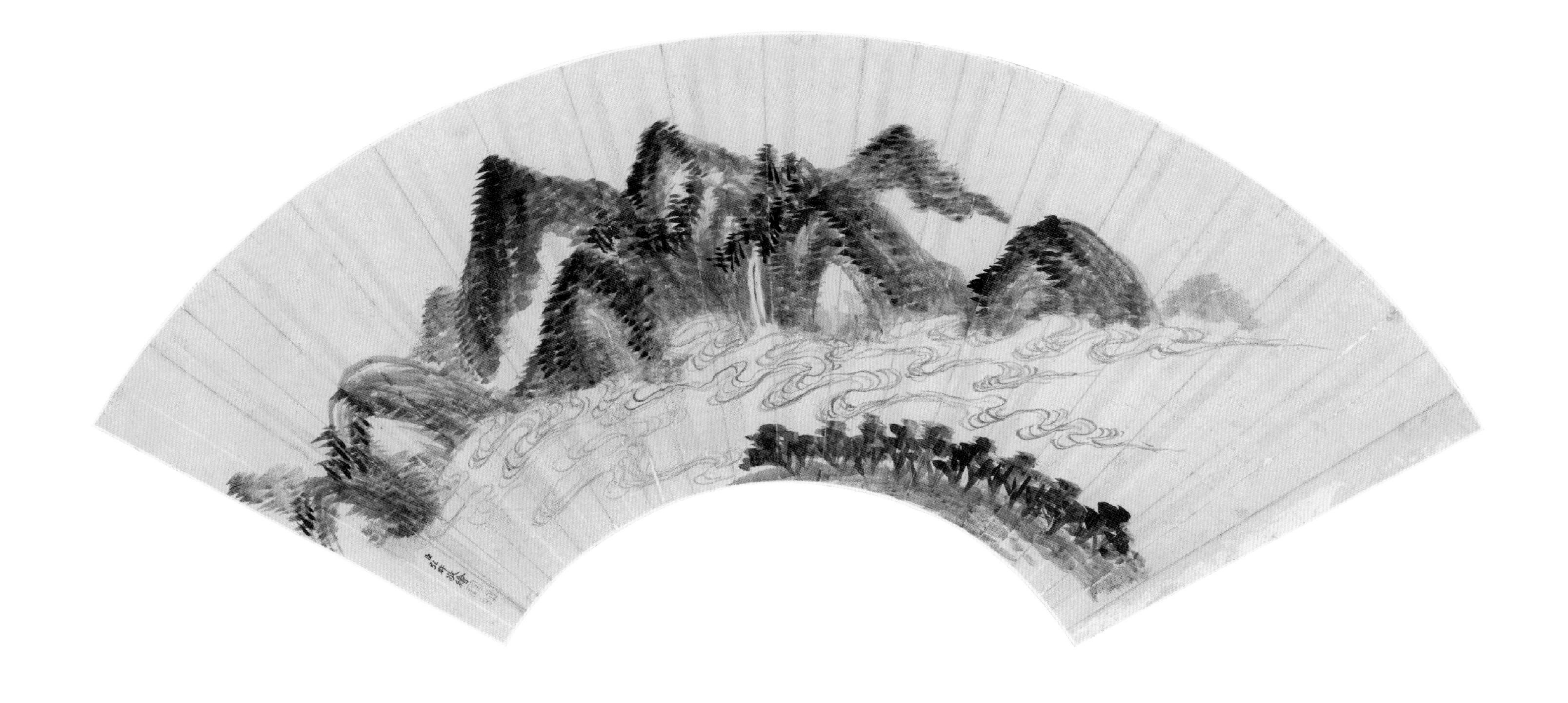

169. 蕉竹图扇页

永瑢绘　纸本 设色

纵 17 厘米　横 49.3 厘米

扇页有自题："无心蕉展叶，有节竹成竿。共绿招凉席，清风入手看。皇六子并题。"钤"皇六子章" 白文印、"师米" 朱文印。时风题："高士幽栖处，萧萧绿荫涵。清风如可接，应近写经菴。时风。"

永瑢（1743～1790 年），号九思主人、西园主人。清乾隆皇帝第六子，其母是纯惠皇贵妃苏佳氏（？～1760 年）。乾隆二十四年（1759 年），乾隆皇帝将他过继给皇叔多罗慎靖郡王允禧为嗣，降袭为贝勒。三十七年（1772 年），晋封为质郡王。五十四年（1789 年），晋封为和硕质庄亲王。他通天算，工绘画，富文采。任《四库全书》总裁。著有《九思堂诗抄》传世。

永瑢擅绘山水、花卉。其山水画法元人黄公望，多绘繁茂的景致，展现山林的葱郁明净之气。花卉宗法明人，笔墨秀润拙中有巧，淳朴自然而又洒脱雅逸，具有文人气。其画作颇得乾隆皇帝的赏识，宫中多有收藏。

此图是作者用以自娱的水墨小写意画，绘"扶疏似树，质则非本，高舒垂荫"的阔叶芭蕉与细竿青竹相佐的夏季景致。竹以浓墨表现，用笔工细，表现出竹柔韧坚挺的风姿。芭蕉以淡墨晕染，温润华滋，表现出芭蕉饱含水分的宽厚特性。作者通过笔法的不同、墨的浓淡变化刻画竹与芭蕉，进而分出远近层次，扩展了画面的空间。

170. 山水扇扇页

宋葆淳绘　纸本 墨笔

纵 16.3 厘米　横 48.9 厘米

扇页有自题:“葆淳为梅村作。”钤“宋葆淳印”白文印。

宋葆淳（1748～？年），字帅初，号芝山，晚号倦陬，安邑（今属山西运城）人。清乾隆五十一年（1786 年）举人。具有多方面的修养与才艺，其书法隶、行、楷等皆入能品。其绘画得宋元人之法，绘山水苍茫嫣润。他还工于篆刻、金石考据及甄别古物等。

图绘江南水乡的秋景。画作的主体是近景的杂木。虽然树木不多，但是富于形态变化，或直干仰叶，或曲本斜柯，或枯荣相间，或高低参差。它们的多样性，既丰富了画面的空间层次，同时，也给幽寂的山湖带来了生趣。全图物象以小写意法勾画，笔墨松散灵动，于简淡中不失冷逸。

171. 菊石图扇页

永瑆绘　纸本 墨笔

纵 16 厘米　横 48 厘米

扇页有自题：“鞠有黄花。为三姪作。”钤“皇十一子”朱文印。

永瑆（1752～1823 年），号镜泉、诒晋斋主人等。清乾隆皇帝第十一子，生母为淑嘉皇贵妃金佳氏。乾隆五十四年（1789 年）封成亲王。工诗文、书画，尤其以深得古人用笔之意的真、行、篆、隶书法，名重当时，与刘墉、翁方纲、铁保并称清中期四大书家。谥曰“哲”。

图绘野外盛开的菊花，花瓣以墨线勾勒，花叶以浓淡墨晕染，虽然笔墨技法尚不成熟，花叶的脉络不够清晰，枝叶的搭配缺乏层次，但是于朴拙中不失一种温雅纯和的风韵。这种风韵在永瑆的书法作品中亦有所体现。

172. 天中景映图扇页

恽怀英绘　纸本 设色

纵 17.8 厘米　横 52.5 厘米

扇页有自题:“天中景映图。法南田笔意,甲辰五日午时喜写。兰陵女史芝仙。”钤“芝仙书画”朱文印。“甲辰”是清乾隆四十九年(1784 年)。

恽怀英(生卒年不详,活动于 18 世纪),字芝仙,号兰陵女史,武进(今江苏常州)人。画家恽源濬(铁箫道人)季女,同乡吕光亨妻。吕光亨于清乾隆十六年(1751 年)登进士,官户部员外郎,为官期间病逝京师。恽怀英因家贫不能归故里,遂鬻画自给。俞蛟《读画闲评》记她:“幼承家学,擅花鸟,落笔雅秀,设色明净,尤长于墨菊。书法亦娟好。”卒年 50 余岁。

图绘枇杷等各色花果,它们以五彩染就,不见笔痕,色调巧妙搭配,浓淡变化自然,于妍丽中见秀雅,粉墨中露清姿,颇得恽寿平(南田)花鸟画灵秀天趣之美,呈现出一派喜庆祥和的景象,与作者自题“喜写”的意愿相契合。

173. 菊花图扇页

钱楷绘　纸本 设色

纵 18 厘米　横 52.5 厘米

扇页有自题："白衣不至酒樽闲，掩卷高吟深闭关。独向篱边把秋色，谁知我意在南山。戊戌秋日仿南田草衣法。亦南楷。"钤"楷"白文印、"亦南"朱文印，吟首钤"游于艺"白文印。"戊戌"是清乾隆四十三年（1778 年），钱楷时年约 19 岁。

钱楷（约 1760～1812 年），字宗范，号亦南、裴山（一作棐山）等，嘉兴（今属浙江）人。乾隆五十四年（1789 年）进士，任翰林院庶吉士、光禄寺卿、广西巡抚等职。能书善画，其山水在师法宋元人及清代王鉴、王原祁笔墨的基础上，注重写生，文献记载，他在典试蜀中时曾遍写所经山水，曰《纪胜图》。其花鸟画，学仿清恽寿平的没骨法，笔致生动，赋色鲜妍，造型秀逸多姿。

图绘紫、红、白诸色菊花争芳斗艳的秋景。冷暖色调相互映衬，画面鲜亮明快。菊花为双勾填色，在极工中求意趣。叶为没骨晕染，不用笔勾线，直接上色点染，具有典型的恽氏没骨画风。此图右侧书录的是恽寿平的七言诗，其字的结体完全学恽氏的笔法，即在宗法唐褚遂良书风的基础上，得纤疏清逸的意趣，从而与其高雅秀迈的画风相得益彰。由此图可见，钱楷早年时学仿恽寿平的书风和画法，已达到惟妙惟肖的地步，正如裱边惠孝同题："此扇字画俱仿南田，是能得瓯香三昧者。"

錢楷字裴山嘉興人善畫乾隆嘉慶時名列九錢之一此扇字畫俱仿南田是能得甌香三昧者款署亦南心折久矣山左宫氏藏扇有名於世此爲其篋笥中尤物無怪頌閣相國之特加激賞也

晴廬

174. 古木寒鸦图扇页

张崟绘　纸本 设色

纵 18.4 厘米　横 56.3 厘米

扇页有自题："古木寒鸦，仿李希古。右甫四兄先生正，张崟。"钤"张崟之印"白文印。

张崟（1761～1829 年），字宝厓（厓一作岩），号夕庵、且翁、城东蛰叟等，丹徒（今江苏镇江）人。一生不求官名，隐于家乡，与潘恭寿、王文治、邓石如诸名流相往来，能诗善画，工于山水、花卉、竹石及佛像。其山水画仿学明文徵明、沈周，并且注重写实，遇山水赏心处，则累月不归，摆脱了画坛以清王时敏为首的"四王"窠臼，形成笔致细密、设色雅致的画风。从学者较多，有"京江派（又作丹徒派）"之称。他因为妙于绘松木，与擅绘柳树的顾鹤庆，享有"张松顾柳"之誉。

在清中期政治的束缚和地域隐逸文化风尚的双重作用下，张崟有一种逃世的心态。他在其山水画中，以刻画远离世俗，到自然界中寻幽探访的题材为主，此扇面便是他寄托着隐逸情怀的画作。图绘在江南青山秀水间，高士乘轻舟举目观鸦，悠闲自在的景象。在创作上，张崟利用了对比的手法，如通过中景大面积的空白水域和远景朦胧的似有似无的山峦呈现出的简，比对出近景细致刻画、具象而写实的山石树木的繁。又如通过群鸦归巢的喧闹噪动，比对出高士观望时的静，这种默默无语的静又恰似"此时无声胜有声"的动，从而令画作在静观的行为中感受到生动的气韵。

175. 藤萝图扇页

廖云锦绘　纸本 设色

纵 16.2 厘米　横 49.5 厘米

扇页有自题："壬子秋仲，为眉洲弟写。织云。"钤"锦云"朱文印。"壬子"是清乾隆五十七年（1792 年），

廖云锦（生卒年不详，活动于 18 世纪），字蕊，号织云、锦香居士，江苏青浦（今属上海）人。自幼从父廖古檀吟诗作画，年长后嫁泗泾马氏为妻。她极富才情，以诗文拜袁枚为师，成为随园女弟子中重要的一员；又以绘画拜贺永鸿为师，成为清代闺阁花鸟画家的代表。姜怡亭《国朝画传编韵》记，廖氏"早寡守节。幼耽书史。喜画花卉翎毛。出阁后师钱唐画史贺永鸿，得其钩染之法且摹古力学，画日益进。其品格亚于马江香，为王述庵司寇所激赏。尤工诗，尝与庄槃山金翠峰张蓝生诸女史相酬唱"。

此图为工写结合的设色花卉。紫藤的藤蔓由右向左延伸，结串的藤花以紫色染就，不见笔痕，具有滋润鲜活的质感；叶片设色轻妆淡写，运笔纤细工整，注重阴阳向背的表现。其画风脱去尘俗，于妍丽中见秀雅，粉墨中露清姿，自出性灵别有格调。

176. 秋花图扇页

张舒绘　纸本 设色

纵 16.4 厘米　横 47.8 厘米

扇页有自题："捡点新容三径旁，疏篱晚艳傲清霜。昨宵记得狂吟后，醉倒花阴梦亦香。庚午春日醉瓯张舒。" 钤朱文印二"张舒"、"惠侯"。"庚午"是清乾隆十五年（1750 年）。

张舒（生卒年不详，活动于 18 世纪），字怀鸥，号醉鸥，元和（今江苏省吴县）人。工绘人物，更擅花卉画，学仿恽寿平，笔墨风致潇洒，追求写生意趣。曾以善绘供职清乾隆朝，有关其资料甚少。现存画作主要藏于故宫博物院，有《秋花图》扇、《绯桃翠柳图》轴、《花篮图》卷等。

图绘秋花烂漫的景致。作者在仿恽寿平笔意的基础上，注重将写意与写形、没骨与勾勒、工谨与遒媚相结合。同时，在刻画主体菊花上还特别注重虚实对比，花瓣用线造型笔笔为实；叶片设色渲染，水融色虚，虚实相生中表现出菊花淡雅冷艳之美。作者不仅画风仿恽氏，书风也与恽氏相近，显现出对恽氏书画的学习已经达到较高的艺术水准。

177. 西溪月棹图扇页

钱杜绘　纸本 设色

纵 18.2 厘米　横 54 厘米

扇页有自题："西溪月棹。临唐子畏本为小眉仁兄观察清赏。丁酉仲秋，钱杜记。"钤"叔美"朱文印。"丁酉"是清道光十七年（1837年），钱杜时年 74 岁。

钱杜（1764～约 1844 年），字叔美，号松壶，钱塘（今浙江杭州）人，嘉庆五年（1800 年）进士，官主事。一生好游走，遍历云南、四川、湖北、河南、河北、山西等地。工诗文、篆刻，善画山水、花卉和人物。其笔墨因过于秀媚而略显雄健不足。著《松壶画诀》《松壶画忆》《松壶画赘》等。

此图是作者晚年送给同僚的画扇。图绘红衣高士独坐舟头，顺流而下的情景，表现了文人理想的幽居生活。图中人物及舟用笔细密工整，于古拙中流露出灵秀之美，带有文徵明"细笔"风范。两岸郁郁葱葱的树木枝叶在运笔上豪放不羁，以线条和黑、白墨点错落交织，具有乱头粗服之美，其洒脱的笔墨与刻画精微的人物、舟船在尺幅之间形成了有机的互补，相得益彰。

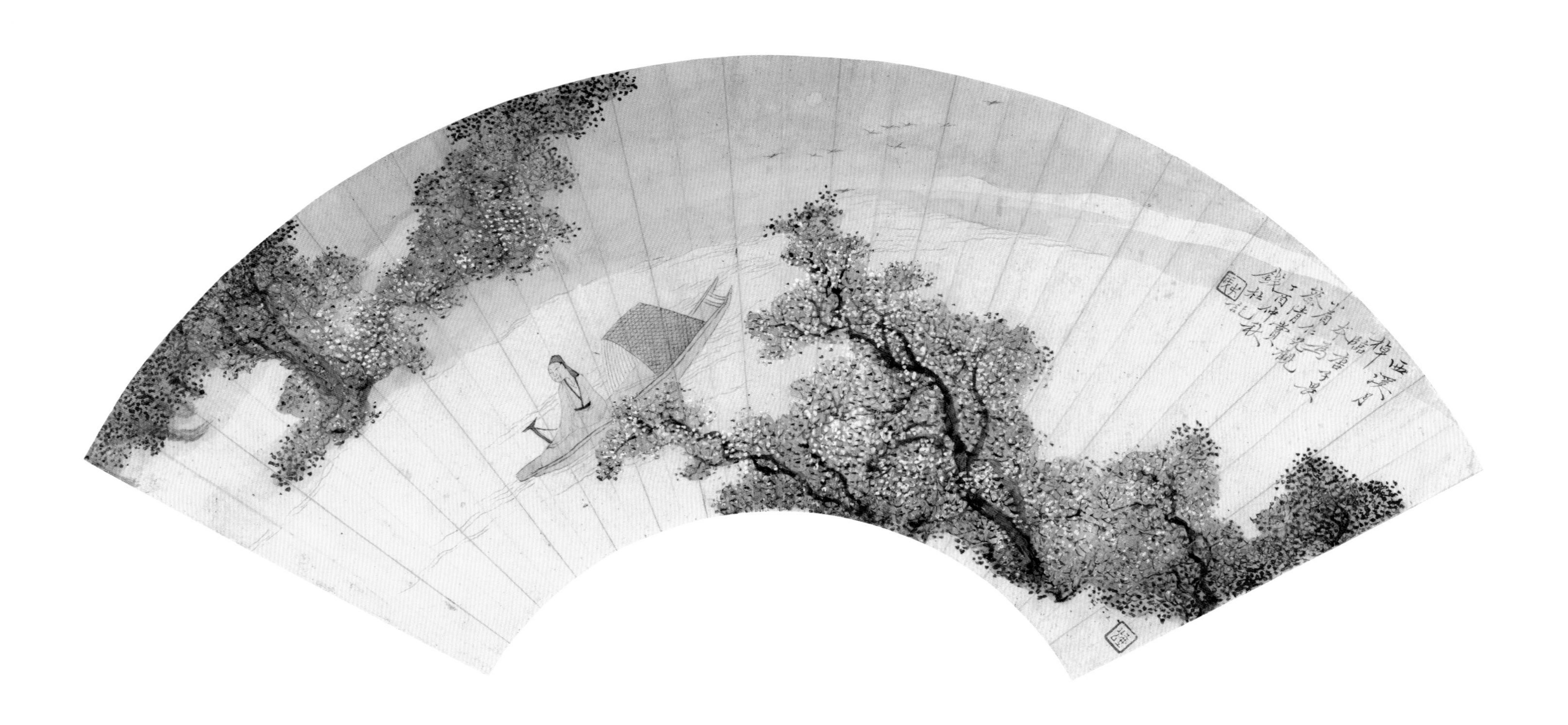

178. 海棠蛱蝶图扇页

恽珠绘　纸本 设色

纵 16 厘米　横 49.2 厘米

扇页有自题："蓉湖女史恽珠写。"钤"星"、"联"白文连珠印。

恽珠（1771～1833 年），字星联，号瑜浦，一作珍浦，晚号蓉湖夫人，自称毗陵女史。阳湖（今江苏常州）人，女画家恽冰之侄女，温州知府完颜廷璐妻，南河河道总督麟庆母。工绘花鸟草虫，并且能诗文，擅织绣。其画风属于恽南田精整工致一派，邓之诚《骨董琐记》记她："受笔法于族姑青於（恽冰），深得瓯香神韵。"李浚之《清画家诗史》亦言她："工花卉，得其家南田老人法。"辑《国朝闺秀正始集》，著《红香馆诗草》。

此幅为花蝶小品画，以对角式构图绘制浪漫的田野风光。图中花蝶点染生动，画面简洁精致，设色鲜活明丽，具有恽南田的写生风貌。

179. 西溪探梅图扇页

改琦绘　纸本 设色

纵 19.2 厘米　横 54.9 厘米

扇页有自题：“一夜东风吹雪霁，前山空翠已模糊。扁舟□到西溪渚，无数沙鸥伴老夫。拟冬心画，以松壶句题之。改琦。”钤“七芗”朱文印。

改琦（1773～1828 年），字伯蕴，号七芗、玉壶外史等，回族，祖先是西域人，移居松江（今属上海市）。工绘山石、人物，运笔松秀，落墨洁净，设色妍雅，于朴拙之中颇具装饰意趣。著《玉壶山房词选》。

图绘高士沿溪行舟，观赏两岸梅花的情景。根据自题而知，此图是作者仿金冬心（农）笔法，表现的钱松壶（杜）诗意。作者在溪水的刻画上独具匠心，通过弥漫的烟云将西溪的边界隐没，从而扩展了水域的有限空间，使之伴随着人们的想象延伸到画扇之外，步入“意到笔不到”的审美境界。此外，作者还成功地运用了“巧借”的艺术手法，如通过借助轻舟，让人感受到水的存在；通过借助岸边整齐的小草，让人感受到一丝丝水纹的涌起；通过借助以白色擢点的梅花，则让人感到浪花飞溅的律动与气势。

一夜東風
吹雪霽
山空

180. 兰花图扇页

王玉燕绘　纸本 设色

纵 15.2 厘米　横 49.3 厘米

扇页有自题："玳梁。"钤"玉"、"燕"朱文联珠印，"空谷兰心"白文印。

王玉燕（生卒年不详，活动于 18 世纪），字玳梁，丹徒（今江苏镇江）人，著名诗人、书法家王文治女孙。她自幼在王文治的引导下，潜心于诗文书画创作，尤工绘兰、梅、水仙等花卉画。冯金伯《墨香居画识》记她："年未笄，能诗善写兰，多渍草绿为之，婉丽可喜。"

图绘一丛香兰在清风的吹拂下摇曳之姿。叶片和花儿均仿恽寿平没骨法，直接以色笔一挥而就，表现出兰娇柔婉约之美。王文治在扇面右侧题七言诗二句，并且感叹道："女孙玳梁写兰近日腕下渐有力矣。"由此可见王文治对王玉燕画学一直都很关注，对她的点滴进步都能够加以洞察。这也促使王玉燕的画艺日臻提高，而成为清中期著名的闺阁画家之一。

181. 柳溪牧马图扇页

沈振麟绘　纸本 设色

纵 17.5 厘米　横 52.4 厘米

扇页有自题："臣沈振麟恭画。"钤"臣"白文印、"麟"朱文印。

沈振麟（生卒年不详，活动于 19 世纪），字凤池，一作凤墀，元和（今江苏省吴县）人。他创作题材广泛，花鸟虫鱼、人物山水各臻其妙，擅以工细写实笔法刻划物象，是晚清重要的宫廷画家，任如意馆首领达数十年。

此作描绘的是在垂柳蓬茸时节，六匹无拘无束的马儿在溪水岸边小憩的情景。沈振麟是清代道光、咸丰、同治、光绪时期重要的宫廷画马名家，只是他的画马技术已无法与乾隆朝擅绘马的宫廷西洋画家郎世宁、艾启蒙及王致诚等相提并论。图中他使用细劲的线条勾画马儿形体和筋骨，动态略显呆板缺少活力。由自题"臣沈振麟恭画"和钤"臣"印而知，此图是沈振麟为清皇室所绘，因此，他对衬景的创作也持一丝不苟的认真态度，图中垂柳的柳叶及浅溪回汀中的芦苇刻画得极为工细，笔笔清晰，富有交叠错落的层次变化，可见其良苦用心。

182. 花卉蜂蝶图扇页

沈振麟绘　纸本 设色

纵 17.5 厘米　横 52.4 厘米

扇页有自题："沈振麟恭画。"钤"振"、"麟"朱文联珠印。

图中的花卉或直接以色彩点染，或先勾勒定形而后填彩，不同的表现技法有着异曲同工之妙，表现出花团锦簇的绽放之美。图中添加的相对而飞的一蜂、一蝶，它们虽然体态小巧，但增强了画作的生活气息与艺术情趣，呈怀抱式构图的花儿成为蜂蝶起舞的观赏者，展现了自然界中最生动的天趣。

由款"恭画"而知，此图当是沈振麟在宫中供职所绘，画作鲜亮的色彩与皇室喜欢喜庆画面的审美相合。

沈振麟恭畫

183. 红线盗盒图扇页

费丹旭绘　纸本 设色

纵 18.7 厘米　横 53 厘米

扇页有自题：“己亥首夏作于依旧草堂。晓楼丹旭。”钤“子茗”朱文印。“己亥”是清道光十九年（1839 年），费丹旭时年 39 岁。

费丹旭（1801～1850 年），字子茗，号晓楼、环溪生、偶翁，乌程（今浙江湖州）人。自幼从父珏（芝原）习画，擅绘仕女，笔致轻灵淡雅，颇得女性娟秀之美，病弱之态。他亦工于肖像，以如镜取影、情神酷肖为人称道。他还兼能山水、花卉，取法恽寿平，笔墨洁净清丽，具闲散意趣。他长年寓居上海、江浙一带，交游于文士间，艺术修养广博而深邃。

此画取材于唐杨巨源《红线传》，描绘的是红线女盗盒救主的故事。红线女是山西潞州节度使薛嵩的侍女，善韵律工剑术。她闻知节度使田承嗣欲吞并其主薛嵩之地，于是，自告奋勇前往田承嗣处打探，并且将田保管严密的金盒盗回。由此，田知薛嵩部中有强手，遂取消了灭薛的想法。

图绘红线女成功盗得金盒，出城而归的场景。费丹旭作为清中晚期的仕女画家代表，其笔下的红线女已失去了个性特征，只是美人画的程式化表现。红线女本是位懂剑术，性情仗义的侠女。但是，在作者笔下，她除被配画一柄剑，表明具有功力外，其纤瘦柔弱的外形和所流露出的闺怨惆怅之情，完全没有侠女的风度。作者这种不考虑女性的出身背景、个人性情、社会境遇，只注重对女性外在形体的追求，是当时对仕女画小描绘的一种风尚，它最终导致无论是皇族贵妇、贫民女子，还是风尘中的青楼女性，均千篇一律的面目，即修颈、削肩、柳腰的体貌，长脸、细目、樱唇的容颜，“倚风娇无力”的仪态风致。

184. 桐阴赏菊扇扇页

秦炳文绘　纸本 设色

纵 14.5 厘米　横 51.3 厘米

扇页有自题："桐阴赏菊图。乙丑小春上浣，炳文写。"钤"炳文"朱文印。"乙丑"是清同治四年（1865 年），秦炳文时年 63 岁。

秦炳文（1803～1873 年），字砚云，号谊亭，江苏无锡人。清道光二十年（1840 年）举人，官吴江教谕，晚年曾在京谋得户部主事之职。擅画山水，初师法王鉴，后宗法黄公望、吴镇，笔墨沉着润泽，设色淡雅清新，具有文人画书卷之风。

图绘高大的梧桐树，枝叶茂密，树荫下草舍横列，一高士坐于室内目视童子搬移盆菊的情景。此图通过对自然景色和人物赏菊行为的描绘，营造出一种宁静闲适、乐天自得的意境，寄托了作者屏绝尘累、不涉世事的生活理想，表现出他所向往的陶渊明"采菊东篱下，悠悠见南山"的生活方式。全图笔法娴熟，点染生动，具有文人画清幽雅静的审美意趣。

185. 凤仙花图扇页

张熊绘　金笺 设色

纵 17.9 厘米　横 51.5 厘米

扇页有自题："肖泉七兄先生属。庚戌夏六月，子祥张熊。"钤"子祥"朱文印。"庚戌"是清道光三十年（1850 年），张熊时年 48 岁。

张熊（1803～1886 年），字子祥，别号鸳湖外史，秀水（今浙江嘉兴）人，流寓上海。工诗词、通音律，喜爱金石书画收藏，擅花鸟、人物、山水，其画设色注重冷暖色调的相互映衬，具有艳而不俗的平和之美。从其学画者甚众，时称"鸳湖派"。与任熊、朱熊合称"沪上三熊"。著《题画集》《银藤花馆诗钞》。

此图绘凤仙花、菊花等盛开的鲜花。它们鲜艳的色彩配合没骨小写意的笔法，表现出花儿的美艳和其旺盛的生命力。扇页左下侧的山石，其坚硬的质感烘托出花儿的娇媚；其平整的大块面，将细碎的花瓣、叶片收拢，令构图不至于过度零散，起到了稳定画面的作用。由此可见，此图虽是小幅应酬之作，却也反映出作者严谨认真的创作态度。

186. 梅花仕女图扇页

汤禄名绘　金笺 设色

纵 17.8 厘米　横 52.5 厘米

扇页有自题："伯符大兄大人雅正，汤禄名。"钤"乐民"半白半朱印。

汤禄名（1804～1874 年），字乐民，武进（今江苏常州）人，寓居金陵（今南京）。画家汤贻汾之子。官两淮盐运使。工白描和银钩铁线画，善以线塑型绘人物、仕女，风格在仿宋代李公麟的基础上自成简约面貌。

图绘闺阁女子倚窗赏梅的小景。画家笔墨娴熟，线条婉转流畅，施墨有浓淡变化，设色以雅淡为宗，较好地表现出女子明媚秀雅的神态。女子细眉小眼、瓜子脸以及瘦体溜肩的体态，具有鲜明的时代特征，正是晚清时期仕女画的典型风貌。

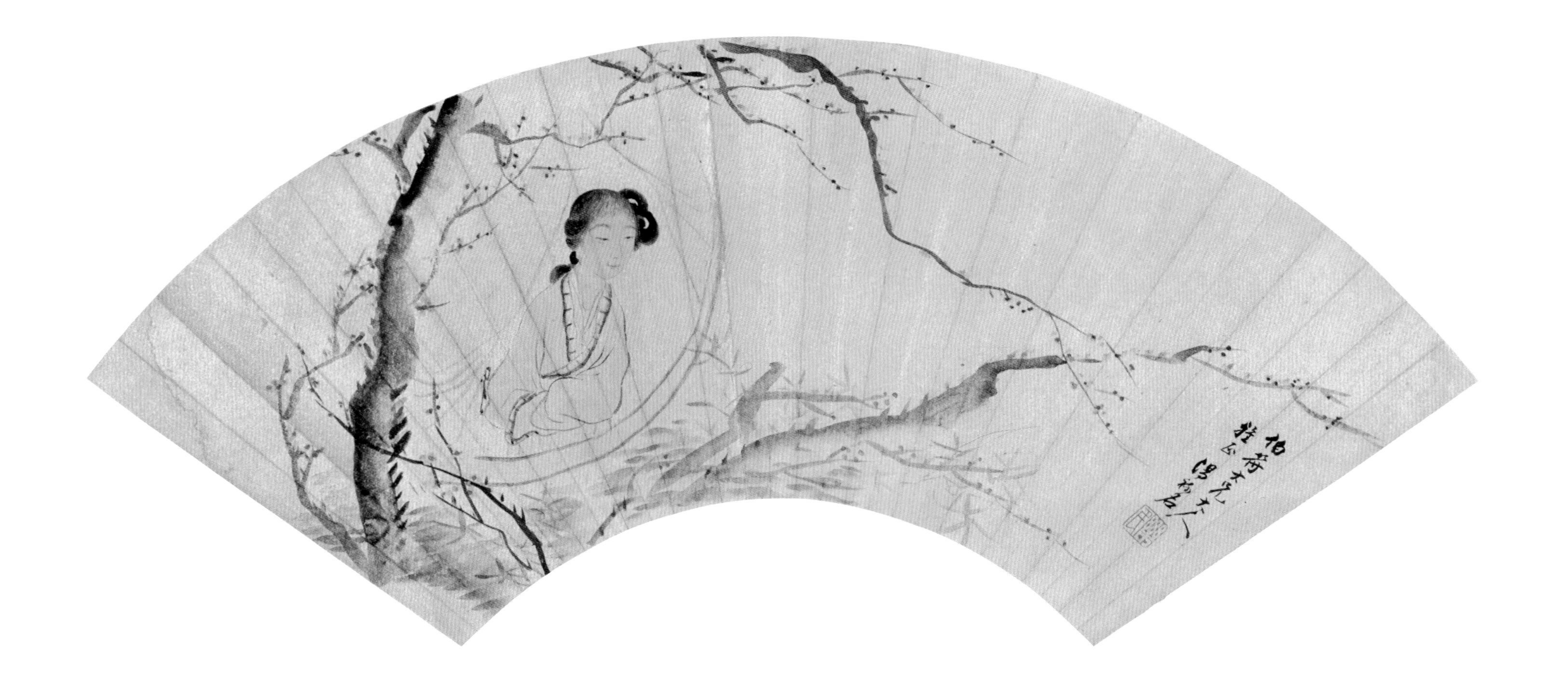

187. 菊花图扇页

虚谷绘　金笺 设色

纵 19.6 厘米　横 52.3 厘米

扇页有自题:“博山尊兄先生清玩。虚谷。”钤“虚谷”白文印。

虚谷（1823～1896 年），姓朱，名怀仁，出家为僧后以虚谷名，号紫阳山民等，祖籍新安（今安徽歙县），寓居扬州、苏州、上海等地。卖画为生。能诗擅画，工于书法，尤以善绘花卉、鱼蔬、禽鸟、山水等为人称道。多以侧锋、逆锋行笔，在侧逆中求方正。喜用枯笔淡墨，具有拙于外秀于内的笔墨特点。与任颐、胡公寿等交往密切，是晚清著名的海上名家。

图绘数朵秋菊于矮篱前绽放争艳。作者在章法布局上巧于构思，图中与菊花相佐的不是人们常用的块面状的土丘、山石，而是线条形的篱笆，篱笆的线条断续而有节奏，增强了画面的灵透性，也使得画作更贴近生活，富有园林情调。菊花的花瓣用双勾填彩法，先以笔勾出轮廓线，再以白粉和曙红填色。花儿在线条的束缚下显得含蓄凝重，具有冰肌玉骨之美。叶片用没骨法，饱含水分的笔醮绿色颜料直接落纸晕染，水与色充分地交融，有“润含春泽”之味。

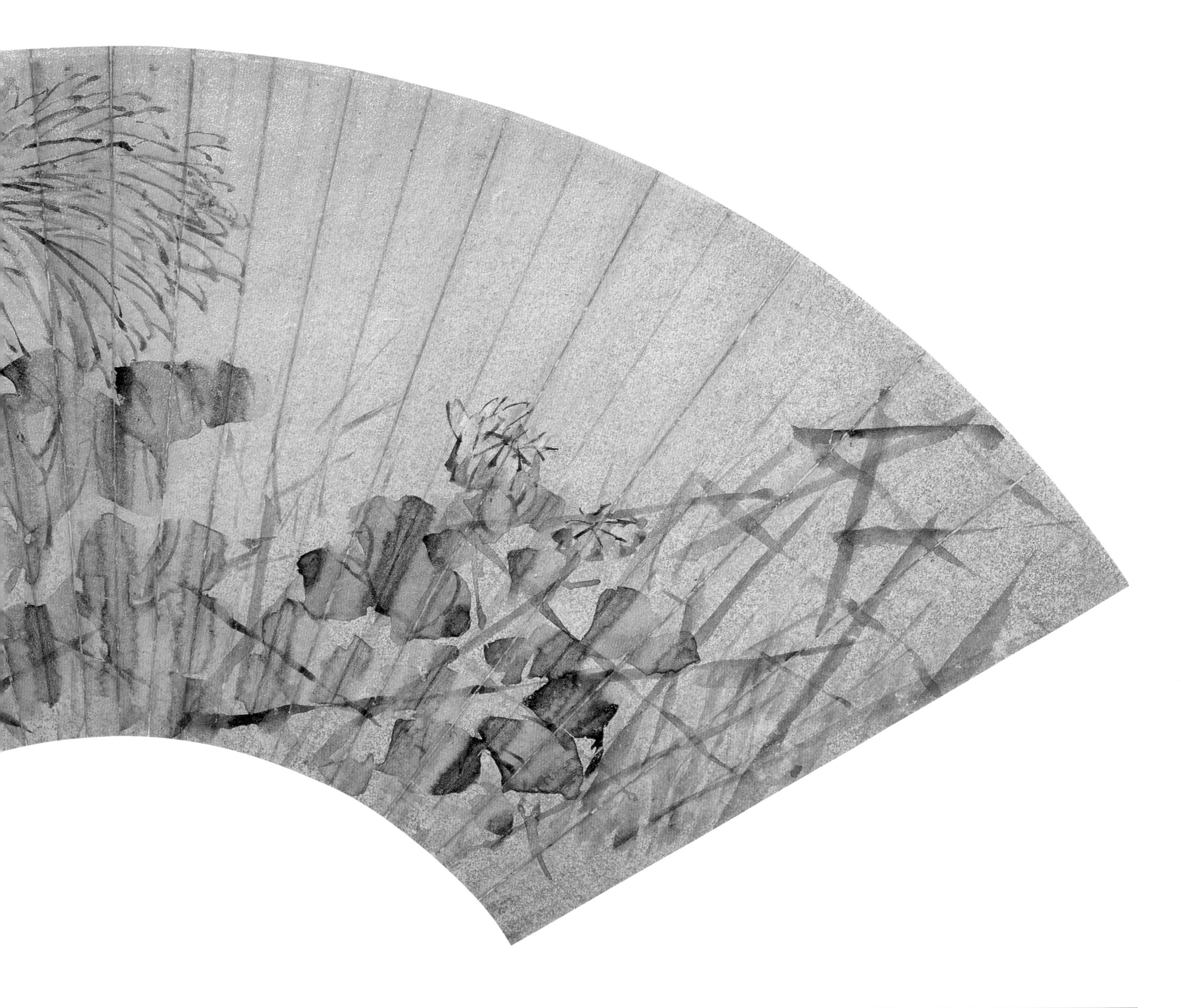

188. 牡丹图扇页

任熊绘　金笺 设色

纵 17.6 厘米　横 50 厘米

扇页有自题："立斋大兄属正，任熊渭长。"钤"渭长"白文印。

任熊（1823～1857 年），字渭长，号湘浦，萧山（今属浙江）人。自幼喜爱绘画，创作题材广泛，山水、花鸟、虫鱼无所不能，师法古人，尤推崇明陈洪绶、清恽寿平笔墨，在写意、工笔画创作上均有极高的艺术造诣。他以鬻画为生，曾得到姚燮器重，以依据姚燮诗句创作的《姚大梅诗意图》册著称。与任薰、任颐、任预并称"海上四任"，与张熊、朱熊合称"沪上三熊"。

任熊的花鸟画，既学宋人的双勾重彩法，又学徐渭、陈淳、恽寿平的写意法。此图是其写意法的代表作，所绘牡丹以没骨积染法刻画，行笔迅疾洒脱，水与色有机地交融，形成了过渡自然的干湿、浓淡变化。作品表现出牡丹外在的生命力和它内在贵而不骄的神韵。

189. 饮酒图扇页

沙馥绘　纸本 设色

纵 18.5 厘米　横 53 厘米

扇页有自题：“唐学士饮酒图。写于粟隐庵，懋庵仁兄大人正之。戊戌春三月，沙馥。”钤“山春”朱文印。“戊戌”是清光绪二十四年（1898 年）。沙馥时年 68 岁。

沙馥（1831～1906 年），字山春，江苏苏州人。出身于绘画世家，善画人物、仕女、花卉，先后拜马仙根、任熊为师，后转学改琦、费丹旭的人物画，作品风格淡雅，笔姿秀逸灵动，是“海派”晚期的重要人物画家。

“唐学士”指唐代著名诗人李白，图绘李白举杯畅饮的画面。作者构思巧妙，以李白醉酒后倚坐在坡石上，仍然在向童子要酒的举动，表现出他拥有酒仙之名，名不虚传，同时也突出了“饮酒”的主题。人物以墨线勾勒，线条转折方硬，通过人物的衣纹表现出人物的动态。图中点景的山石、树木皆用淡彩直接点染，令画面素雅清幽，增添了文人画的高逸之气。

190. 听鹂图扇页

钱慧安绘　纸本 设色

纵 19 厘米　横 53.3 厘米

扇页有自题：“双柑斗酒听鹂声。壬午秋日仿新罗本，沂青仁兄大人雅属。清溪樵子钱慧安。”钤“吉生”朱文印。“壬午”是清光绪八年（1882 年），钱慧安时年 50 岁。

钱慧安（1833～1911 年），初名贵昌，字吉生，号双管楼等，宝山（今属上海市）人。卖画为生。善人物、仕女，间作花卉、山水，笔意闲雅清爽。曾一度在天津杨柳青创作画样，名重一时。

作者描绘的是“双柑斗酒听鹂声”诗意。图绘一文士侧耳静听，但是有着悦耳鸣声的鹂鸟（亦称“黄莺”、“仓庚”、“黄鸟”）并没有在图中出现。鹂鸟的“存在”，完全是通过童子举手轻指的动态，以及文士全神贯注的“听”表现出来的，由此可见，作者对人物形态有着细致的观察力和准确的造型能力。

191. 停琴待月图扇页

任薰绘　纸本 设色

纵 18.7 厘米　横 52.8 厘米

扇页有自题："达夫仁兄大人雅属，阜长任薰写于吴门。"钤"任薰"白文印。

任薰（1835～1893 年），字阜长，萧山（今属浙江）人。任熊之弟。擅长人物、花鸟，与其兄同宗法明陈洪绶。笔墨秀劲，具有装饰味。与任熊、任颐、任预合称"四任"。

此幅构图简约，前景绘泛黄的树叶和凋零的枝干，表明时为红衰翠减的深秋季节；后景绘一老者独坐船头手抚琴弦的情景。萧瑟的秋风佐以琴音，给人以寂寞的情怀。任薰的人物画受任熊和陈洪绶的影响较大，造型夸张，不失高古之态。

192. 梅竹幽禽图扇页

任薰绘　金笺 设色

纵 19 厘米　横 53.6 厘米

扇页有自题：“湘屏仁兄大人雅属，阜长任薰写于吴门。”钤“任薰”白文印。

设色画坡石梅竹，一鸟引颈昂头栖于石上，神态安逸悠闲。坡石以方折之笔勾勒轮廓，显现出石质的坚实硬朗。鸟的羽毛以饱含水分的浓淡墨直接点染，显现出羽片柔软的质感，不同的物象以不同的笔墨加以勾描晕染，显现出作者全面的艺术造诣。

193. 寒江独钓图扇页

胡锡珪绘　金笺 设色

纵 17.8 厘米　横 50.3 厘米

扇页有自题："子英五兄大人属，胡三桥写寒江独钓图。"钤"三桥"朱文印。

胡锡珪（1839～1883 年），原名文，字三桥，号盘溪外史、红茵生等，江苏苏州人。幼习丹青，花鸟画仿学恽寿平、李复堂，水晕墨章，栩栩如生。人物画摹学华喦、改琦，笔法工细，注重以形写神。

此扇图绘的是唐柳宗元《江雪》诗意："千山鸟飞绝，万径人踪灭。孤舟蓑笠翁，独钓寒江雪。"作者为了表现下雪的情景，特地在江面、蓑衣、斗笠及竹叶上敷以白粉，白色不仅暗示出雪意，也增强了画面清凉的意境，与垂钓者自得清娱的高逸品格相应。全图用笔一丝不苟，正如吴俊卿所评：其画"精细如发，而笔锋劲厉"。

194. 荷花鸳鸯纨扇页

任颐绘　绢本 设色

纵 27.5 厘米　横 27.9 厘米

自题："光绪己卯春杪写应公蓼仁兄大人属正，任伯年。" 钤 "颐印" 朱文印。"己卯" 是清光绪五年（1879 年），任颐时年 40 岁。

任颐（1840～1896 年），初名润，字小楼、伯年，绍兴（今属浙江）人，寓居上海卖画。擅长人物、肖像、花鸟、山水。其绘画虽受父亲任鹤声的启蒙源自民间，但又受任薰、萧云从、陈洪绶等文人画家的影响，加之能兼取西画速写、设色诸法，遂形成重视写生、造型生动传神、格调清新的独特画风，成为 "海派" 代表画家。与任熊、任薰、任预合称 "海上四任"。

此幅构图奇巧，作者没有将主要描绘对象鸳鸯和荷花画出全貌，而是在圆形的画面中，绘二只鸳鸯若即若离，并且它们被垂俯的荷叶及白色的荷花所遮掩，如此布局营造出的荷塘充满想象空间，从而达到以小见大、以偏见全的艺术效果。全图用笔工写结合，于精纯秀润的笔墨之外，不失疏散通脱的审美逸趣，是任颐中年时期的佳作。

光緒己卯春杪寫應
公壽仁兄大人屬正任柏年

195. 花鸟图扇页

任颐绘　纸本 设色

纵 18.2 厘米　横 53.3 厘米

扇页有自题："秋馥仁兄大人雅正。辛巳八月望后，伯年任颐写于春申浦上寓次。"钤"任伯年"白文印。"辛巳"是清光绪七年(1881年),任颐时年 42 岁。

作者在构图上匠心独运，花枝组成一个"口"字，枝上添加鸟儿一只，鸟儿不仅打破了画面原本四平八稳的纵横关系，使之由"口"字变成"中"字，而且安然惬意的神态为画面增添了情趣和"春去花还在，人来鸟不惊"的诗意。花鸟造型不以线条为主，而是以色、墨直接晕染其形，表现出花鸟的自然生态之美。

196. 花鸟图扇页

任颐绘　纸本 设色

纵 17.8 厘米　横 50.8 厘米

扇页有自题："瑞华仁兄大人雅属即正。光绪癸未十月上浣，山阴任颐伯年甫写于沪。"钤"任伯年"白文印。"癸未"是清光绪九年（1883 年），任颐时年 44 岁。

图中的花鸟，以没骨写意法绘，笔墨精熟而洒脱，设色以中间色调为主，得平易近人之趣。图中白色的牡丹花，由于白色颜料品质欠佳，以致氧化变黑并且大部分已脱落，仅剩下印迹，它的退色成为该扇面的遗憾。

197. 荔枝图扇页

吴俊卿绘　纸本 设色

纵 18.7 厘米　横 51.1 厘米

扇页有自题："公之来先生属写妃子笑，为放（仿）戴石屏设色，而顾茶老以为极似张孟皋。丙午闰四月病臂草草。俊卿记。"钤"缶"朱文印。"丙午"是清光绪三十二年(1906年)，吴昌硕时年63岁。

吴俊卿（1844～1927年），名俊、俊卿，字昌硕，号缶庐、苦铁等，安吉（今浙江湖州）人。他先工诗文，继而习书法及金石篆刻等，于石鼓文用功最多。其画始于五十岁左右，近师赵之谦、任颐，远法沈周、朱耷诸家。工绘花鸟，色酣墨饱，行笔雄健，以金石篆籀之笔法入画是其主要画风。著《缶庐诗存》。

图绘没有任何背景陪衬的妃子笑荔枝斜向出枝。饱含汁液的荔枝果，先用粉红色铺底，再以深红色在其上添画，丰富了果实的层次，增加了立体效果。枝与叶使用了朴茂雄健的草篆笔法，显现出书法中气贯神通的审美意趣。作者这种画气不画形，"以作书之法作画"的艺术手法，对中国近现代绘画及日本绘画均有较大的影响。

198. 柳湖归棹图扇页

任预绘　纸本 设色

纵 18 厘米　横 52 厘米

扇页有自题："柳湖归棹。拟南田翁本，立凡任预。"钤"立凡"朱文印。

任预（1853～1901 年），字立凡，浙江萧山人，任熊子。善绘人物、山水及禽兽，受任熊、任薰影响，后得赵之谦指教，笔墨工整细腻，设色艳丽雅致。与任熊、任薰、任颐并称"海上四任"。

图绘草木葱茏、翠竹依依、湖塘曲水、轻舟归岸的夕阳小景。该画略有南田（恽寿平）清雅纯美的遗意而又稍有变化。图中近景的翠竹以浓墨挥写，其清晰圆润的笔墨与笔致模糊的山峦、草木形成实与虚的对比，其浓重的墨色不仅丰富了全图的色调，也起到点醒浑浊画面的作用，令扇页具有清新的朴素美。

图版目录

后记

《故宫经典》是精选故宫博物院数十年来行世的重要图录，由时下俊彦、雅士修订再版的图录丛书。

故宫博物院建院八十余年，梓印书刊遍行天下，其中多有声名佼佼人皆瞩目之作，越数十年，目遇犹叹为观止，珍爱有加者大有人在；进而愿典藏于厅室，插架于书斋，观赏于案头者争先解囊，志在中鹄。

有鉴于此，为延伸博物馆典藏与展示珍贵文物的社会功能，本社选择已刊图录，如朱家溍主编《国宝》、于倬云主编《紫禁城宫殿》、王树卿等主编《清代宫廷生活》、杨新等主编《清代宫廷包装艺术》、古建部编《紫禁城宫殿建筑装饰——内檐装修图典》等，增删内容，调整篇幅，更换图片，统一开本，再次出版。唯形态已经全非，故不再蹈袭旧目，而另拟书名，既免于与前书混淆，以示尊重；亦便于赓续精华，以广传布。

故宫，泛指封建帝制时期旧日皇宫，特指为法自然、示皇威、体经载史、受天下养的明清北京宫城。经典，多属传统而备受尊崇的著作。

故宫经典，即集观赏与讲述为一身的故宫博物院宫殿建筑、典藏文物和各种经典图录，以俾化博物馆一时一地之展室陈列为广布民间之千万身纸本陈列。

一代人有一代人的认识。此番修订，选择故宫博物院重要图录出版，以延伸博物馆的社会功能，回报关爱故宫、关爱故宫博物院的天下有识之士。

2007 年 8 月